Why don't you
write something
I might read?

Why don't you write something I might read?

Reading, Writing & Arrhythmia

SURESH MENON

cntxt

First published by Context, an imprint of Westland Publications Private Limited, in 2021

1st Floor, A Block, East Wing, Plot No. 40, SP Infocity, Dr MGR Salai, Perungudi, Kandanchavadi, Chennai 600096

Westland, the Westland logo, Context and the Context logo are trademarks of Westland Publications Private Limited, or its affiliates.

ISBN: 9789391234591

10 9 8 7 6 5 4 3 2 1

Typeset in Candara Regular by SÜRYA, New Delhi
Printed at Thomson Press (India) Ltd.

To Anil Kuruvilla,

memory brushes the same years ...

Contents

Preface

The birth of the reader, wrote Roland Barthes, must be ransomed by the death of the writer. That is the only time you will see that name in this book. Or the names of Adorno or Spivak or Derrida. Nothing personal; in fact, literary theorists can be fascinating even when you understand what they are trying to say.

What they often do, however, is make us long for what Terry Eagleton has called a 'pre-theoretical innocence'.

There is no bridge across the literary theorist and the average reader that can be crossed without something giving way. The reader who picks up a book because he hopes to enjoy it is not fussed about structure and style, theory or counter-theory.

Literary writers occasionally write on their passion for sport. Hence, Joyce Carol Oates on boxing, Nabokov on chess, Stephen Jay Gould on baseball, John Updike on golf, Ramachandra Guha on cricket. The traffic is seldom in the other direction. This book is a small attempt to redress that—a sportswriter writing on a passion for literature.

The American writer Guy Davenport, in introducing a collection of his essays, said he was not writing 'for scholars or critics, but for people who like to read, to look at pictures, and to know things'. That works for me too, except I might add another category: for people who don't like to read and might realise what fun it is!

Reading doesn't make me better than anybody else, although I do sometimes come across as a bookish snob, a trait that has destroyed the odd book club where I have been a member.

I was a weird child. I began collecting photographs of writers long before I had read them or even seen their books. Alongside pictures of cricketers (cut out from magazines), the Nawab of Pataudi, Garry Sobers, Gundappa Viswanath and Bishan Bedi, I had those of Hemingway and Eliot, Narayan and Dickens. There was a third album too—for Einstein, Edison, Ramanujan, Fermi and so on.

At twenty-one, I became a journalist. A sports journalist, because a sports editor invited me to be one during a rain break in a cricket league match both of us were playing in. Soon, I realised the great Indian novel would have to be written by someone else. I was enjoying my job as a sports reporter too much to break away. If you have literary ambitions, avoid journalism.

Years later, I met V.S. Naipaul and made a joke about 'hack writing'. It upset him. 'Don't look down on journalism,' he said. 'It is a very special skill. Some great novelists would make terrible journalists.'

Then I read an essay by Márquez where he called journalism 'the best job in the world' and said, 'I am basically a journalist.'

If it's good enough for Naipaul and Márquez ...

Much of this collection was written during the COVID-19 pandemic and may be read in any order you wish. Perhaps not too many on the same day, as we don't know yet what the normal dose might be.

A word about the dedicatee. Anil Kuruvilla is that rare

person—someone who has read as deeply as he has read widely. A philosopher by temperament (and academic qualification), his unwritten books are on a par with, if not superior to, many of those actually written.

In *My Unwritten Books*, George Steiner says, ‘A book unwritten is more than a void. Philosophy teaches that negation can be determinant. It is the unwritten book which might have made the difference.’

Anil’s unwritten books have been an inspiration over the years.

On reading

Every author I have read is a character in my life story, every book a milestone. V.S. Naipaul said he was the sum of his books; I am the sum of other people's books.

Just what set of circumstances makes one pick up this book rather than that one, leaves authors unread or makes one focus on a few writers to the exclusion of others is a matter of taste, circumstance, influence (parents, teachers, friends, critics, media), curiosity and state of mind. Sometimes it is pure luck. I discovered Borges among an acquaintance's collection of crime novels and began a lifelong relationship.

Taste is developed through these same routes. The keyword here is 'developed'. Taste is not something one is born with, it is acquired, like a taste for good wine or for a specific type of art or music. It is politically correct to say of someone who is reading a book you look down upon that 'everyone is entitled to his taste'. What you really mean is, 'Gosh! I wouldn't be seen dead with that book.'

But tastes can change. The book you dismissed as a no-hoper in your twenties can turn out to be a masterpiece in your fifties. And vice versa.

We 'know' that *The Da Vinci Code* is not a great book and that

Dan Brown is not a great writer. We 'know' that Chetan Bhagat will not be spoken of in the same breath as Vikram Seth. How do we know this? How can we recognise the negative easily but often struggle to define what is great? Neither Brown nor Bhagat is likely to be offended by our judgement; they can't be bothered to take a detour while laughing all the way to the bank. Consensus, however, cannot be the basis of approval.

One way of alighting upon the quality of a book is to draw up a list of the ones you consider masterpieces and see what these have in common. But that can only get you so far. Such exercises tend to leave out pleasure, an important element. Pleasure is not always dependable as a guide, though, but then, neither are books about the 100 novels you must read before you die or the list of classics every intelligent woman should read before the world ends.

Taste is a complex issue. Any discussion of taste will have to bring in the philosophers Immanuel Kant and David Hume, who have written extensively and often confusingly on this. Kant's concept of 'subjective universality' says in effect that taste is subjective, but suggests that beautiful objects tend to have universal appeal. By reducing it to a single line, I know I am distorting a lifetime's work!

A taste-decider, if we believe Hume, would possess a 'strong sense, united to delicate sentiment, improved by practice, perfected by comparison, and cleared of all prejudice,' and the combined opinions of such rare individuals decide the standards of taste.

There are two problems here. It doesn't explain why anyone likes anything (Amazon algorithms tell us what we like, but not why), and it brings in the concept of what one *ought* to like. This is the worst recommendation in music, art or literature, this idea of what one ought to like.

When the artist Duchamp exhibited a urinal at an art show, he was saying, 'Art is whatever I say it is.' Writers cannot (or, at least, do not) say, 'Literature is what I say it is.' Critics who tell us what is good in art use words to do so; likewise in music. Only books are examined using the tools they work in. Words.

The interests of a writer and the interests of his readers are never the same, wrote the poet Auden. If they happen to coincide, that is a lucky accident.

When we read, we sieve the writer's experiences through our own, and the chances of two people having the exact same experiences and responses are virtually zero. The two probably share the big picture, understand the abstract—love, disappointment, rage, goodwill, sorrow—but individual reactions are unique. Perhaps this is what Kant meant by subjective universality. Maybe it is universal subjectivity.

Why read at all when you can get all your experience from life itself?

Actually, any reason to read is a good one. Some endorse the poet Paul Valery's somewhat utilitarian if harsh motive: 'One only reads well that which one reads with some quite personal purpose. It may be to acquire some power. It can be out of hatred for the author.'

To start reading at an early age, some conditions appear necessary: a childhood that is lonely and bereft of entertainment, a house filled with siblings where the youngest is too young or the oldest too old, an absent parent or two, an encouraging parent or two (*My father made me read Mexican history: Carlos Fuentes*), early illness leading to hours alone in bed (*I was greatly blessed by asthma: A.S. Byatt*), a love for lively fictional characters rather than towards the living, a view of books as an escape route (*Burrowing in mystery novels for the secret passageway out, the path of avoidance and vindication: John Updike*).

But these are conditions usually imposed in later life. It is easier to print the dots once the picture is complete.

Books are a way of marking milestones in life. Most obsessives can recall when and where and, indeed, how they read a book. 'My history is all books,' as Ray Bradbury wrote.

It was said of Cervantes that he was such a compulsive reader he read bits of torn paper he found in the streets. As a boy I did much the same, without actually touching the torn papers but contorting myself instead. I read everywhere, in bed, in moving vehicles, in the toilet, to pass time between reading, along with my breakfast, lunch or dinner. Reading while eating was initially discouraged by my parents, but when they saw I was obsessed and would gladly read the writing on a box of Bournvita, they gave in.

I grew up in a household that didn't have too many novels—my father read Perry Mason for entertainment but mostly stuck to his technical books as a senior executive. The only books outside of these that I can remember are the German novelist Erich Maria Remarque's *All Quiet on the Western Front*, and, by the same author, *A Time to Love and a Time to Die*. Later, I discovered Remarque was married to Paulette Goddard, Charlie Chaplin's leading lady in *Modern Times* and *The Great Dictator*. Even as a boy, I had a fascination for such trivia.

Two other books I remember on Dad's shelves are *Good English: How to Write It* by G.H. Vallins, with a delightful red cover, which stood alongside another one of similar mien, *Read Well and Remember* by Owen Webster. These books I had with me for a number of years before they fell martyrs to moves from house, city and country.

My father read the daily newspaper virtually from the masthead to the final dot on the sports page (which was then the last one), a habit I picked up early. He instilled in me a love for words, often calling out interesting words from the newspaper which I then had to spell and look up the meanings of.

He also gave me money to buy books I wanted to read, which I bought after building up a 'bank' of regular contributions. I had no interest in shoes or clothes or Meccano toys (an engineering and metal version of Lego).

My mother read Malayalam novels, and taught me to read and write the language. But I didn't follow her example. That's one of the things I feel embarrassed about, the fact that I can't read a book in any language other than English. I did soldier through a Malayalam novel once, and in college, as part of the syllabus, something in French which I don't recall now. I keep telling myself it isn't too late; Tolstoy learnt to ride a bicycle at sixty-seven.

The first 'adult' authors I read were H.G. Wells (*The Time Machine*), Arthur Conan Doyle (*Sherlock Holmes*) and Charles Dickens (*Nicholas Nickleby,* many times over). Mark Twain, too. *Huckleberry Finn* was my friend at an age when I thought the imaginary was more reliable than the real. I enjoyed entering a book; it was almost physical. I read everything. Indiscriminate reading was an important step towards more discriminating reading.

Surely there can be no more fundamental reason for reading than enjoyment?

The choice between Dostoevsky and Dan Brown is not a difficult one for readers exclusively of either type of book. One is for the literary scuba diver, the other for the ice skater. One lets you dive deep, the other is all surface. I read somewhere that reading a page-turner teaches you nothing other than to turn pages. Still, if enjoyment is the key, then we cannot cavil at personal choices. For reading calls for imagination just as writing does.

Novels with ambiguities are often attractive for they give the imagination free reign. Ambiguity often comes from what critics later called the unreliable narrator. I could accept *Lolita* as an important novel only if I thought Humbert Humbert was an unreliable narrator. 'The greater the ambiguity, the greater the pleasure,' wrote Milan Kundera. I am not so sure, but there is something to be said for uncertainty, which is a close relative.

When life, love, relationships, history and the future are all uncertain, it takes a particularly confident writer to reflect all that in his writings. Sometimes neatly tied up issues don't work as well on the page as this reflection of uncertainty. What Keats valued most in Shakespeare was a capacity for 'being in uncertainties, mysteries, doubts, without any irritable reaching after fact and reason.' He called it 'negative capability'.

Do books explain life, give it a sense of order, or do they anticipate it? Art has no responsibility to uplift or inspire, but it often does both, although only incidentally. Reading, like listening to music or getting absorbed in a great work of art, is a sensual activity. A terminally ill Clive James wrote: 'If you don't know the exact moment when the lights will go out, you might as well read until they do.' Exactly.

A child of the library

Some weeks into the coronavirus pandemic, my wife stumbled upon this quote by Cicero: *If you have a garden and a library, you have everything you need*. That's us, we told each other; Cicero would approve. Our small garden is rich and lush and seems to be outgrowing its space. Our library likewise. You can give away a sapling or a cutting without affecting the garden. You can't, however, give away the essays of George Orwell and hope another set will grow in its place.

I was a library addict, and walking between the shelves of one was a treat when I was a schoolboy. The gentleman who once suggested that governments should close down libraries and buy its citizens Kindles clearly sees the library as simply a place of books and nothing else. He fails to see its import as a social, cultural and intellectual hub, and the role of the librarian as that of a facilitator. If the bartender is someone who listens to your emotional problems, then the librarian resolves your intellectual issues.

Before the public library came the private one: my grandfather's in Kerala. It was an impressive one for a six- or seven-year-old, which was my age when I was allowed to run my fingers across the spines of his books. There were Penguins of various colours, two volumes of the collected works of Shakespeare, a number of books on science and history, and fiction. There were too many volumes of books on what was called 'general knowledge', which I found fascinating. They were full of lists of various kinds.

Here was one on Nobel winners, there another on the French Open and Wimbledon champions in tennis, and a third on Oscar successes. US presidents, kings and queens of England, UN Secretary-Generals, all had their appointed places. I have remained a list-lover and list-maker ever since.

After annual vacations at his place, my grandfather would let me come back home with a book or two. The sight of these neatly arranged on a shelf in my bedroom always reconnected me with the holidays.

In one of grandfather's shelves was a collection of diaries written in Malayalam in a small hand by my small grandmother. Nothing of what happened in the course of a day was missed for close to fifty years. It was a great settler of arguments—who came home on which day, what colour saree was worn, which movie was seen on what occasion—these and more were all there in rigorous detail. Over the years, the exercise had become a bit of a family joke, and the sight of my grandmother sitting at her table pouring out the day's events into a diary became one of the least commented on sights since it had both the regularity of a clock and its reliability.

Years later, by the time I realised how valuable the diaries might be as a source of not just family history but as a record of the times, they had all disappeared. I would have paid a fortune for the lot; it would have been interesting to read the entry for the day I was born, for instance, and many others, like the dawn of India's independence.

As I entered adolescence, I gloried in a library of my own. I made a list of books I had, and counted them regularly. The obsession with lists and with numbers came together nicely. With thirty or forty books in my 'library', I began to divide them by subject matter. Fiction was mainly Perry Mason, Erle Stanley Gardener's lawyer whose most famous line of objection was: 'It is incompetent, irrelevant and immaterial.' Dad loved to use it on me (and I on him) when we got into a debate.

There were always books from libraries lying around the house. From the school library were books on science that I borrowed both because I enjoyed them and because it impressed the lady librarian who spoke about it to some of the teachers. Then there was the City Central Library in Shantinagar. You could borrow two books at a time. It was usually one fiction and one non-fiction. The library was a couple of kilometres from home, and meant a half-hour walk, sometimes in the company of a friend.

Nearer home, and off a shorter walk, was the library of the All India Institute of Mental Health and Neuro Sciences. The institute allowed schoolboys in the area to use the library as well as its table tennis room. I read virtually every book written by P.G. Wodehouse from this collection. The library was an important community centre.

The largest and most satisfying library was the British Council Library. Four books per visit from a wider range and the possibility of reserving books for the future brought in a mixture of potluck and certitude. The cricket section was well stocked, as were biography, history, science and literature.

I was fascinated by the card index at these libraries, and marvelled at the system of organising books. It is all digitalised now around the world, and I have no issue with that. However, when I read *Double Fold*, Nicholson Baker's idiosyncratic and intensely personal rant against the disappearance of the card catalogue (and more seriously, the manner in which libraries destroyed books in order to preserve them), I could sympathise with the author.

Gradually, as one moved into university and beyond, some of these libraries dropped out of one's life. But the British Council remained. You could pick your books, walk downstairs to Koshy's—the city's legendary coffee shop—meet friends or sit quietly and start reading while waiting for friends. The added advantage was the Premier Bookstore a couple of minutes away, so it was always a pilgrimage. Whether weekly, fortnightly or monthly, it was a most enjoyable aspect of library-visiting.

Libraries like the British Council and the American Center in Chennai were especially popular in summer when the air conditioning in these places attracted a whole different set of readers. They were also good places to meet girlfriends and boyfriends, and many romances either bloomed or collapsed around their shelves.

Every residential area also had what were called 'circulating' libraries. 'Circulating' referred to the books which moved from member to member at a fairly rapid pace. Mostly stocked with fiction and the latest bestsellers, these libraries turned over the bestsellers quickly, sometimes twice or thrice in the same day. The librarian opened a ledger with the names of the customers on the different pages and methodically wrote everything down. Fines were charged and paid. Books beyond repair were taken out of circulation. James Hadley Chase and Oliver Strange (who wrote westerns full of gunslingers and shootouts at sunrise) were the most popular authors then.

Nearly everybody I knew had a favourite author and

considered it their mission to read everything written by this author. There was a deep satisfaction (besides bragging rights) in reading through a list, and for a short while becoming a relative authority on the subject.

It all seems so quaint and unreal now. Whenever there is a cry over the amazingly small number of libraries in India and these too gradually disappearing, I add my voice to it. The last census showed that in rural India, serving 830 million people, there were 70,187 libraries. In urban India, for 370 million people, there are just 4,580 libraries. Thus, one library for 11,500 rural Indians while 80,000 urbanites have to manage with one. But the fact remains that I have not visited any of the libraries in my city for years now. I prefer to buy the books I want, while some of the best libraries for research are outside my city, and outside the country too.

When I look back, however, I realise I am a child of the library system. Every child deserves to be initiated into the world of books through a public library he feels ownership for.

Showing off

I once had a brief Tom Wolfe moment. This was at the Hay-on-Wye Literary Festival where he spoke while I attempted to photograph him. I can't remember what he talked about, but he wore his patented three-piece white suit, a white handkerchief with a black border sticking out of his pocket.

Looking back, it seems appropriate that I remember the form and not the content of that session; I had the same relationship with his books.

Wolfe is the kind of writer you admire when young but who turns increasingly annoying as you grow older. *The Kandy-Kolored Tangerine-Flake Streamline Baby* was programmed to fire the imagination of the twenty-somethings; it fired mine. That was probably the demographic Wolfe excited the most, with his outrageous punctuation, repetitions, strange words and sounds.

He was a maverick, he broke the rules, and that was attractive. He once began an essay with the word 'hernia' repeated fifty-seven times. Was this the prophet of the 1960s or an undergraduate having fun?

Wolfe's so-called new journalism (it was neither new nor, strictly speaking, journalism) had its attractions too. You wrote around the subject, you looked for the telling gesture, the unexpected quote that revealed everything in a sudden cascade of light.

It was fun, this immersive style, but the temptation to make things up was strong. You were a part of the story, and often the story was about your reaction rather than what was out there. 'Tom may be the hardest-working show-off the literary world has ever owned,' wrote Norman Mailer, no mean show-off himself.

Yet, when Wolfe divested himself of his mannerisms, he could be both funny and perceptive. *The Painted Word*, his take on modern art, is delightful. For not only was he a satirist, he was, to coin a word, a sarcasticist, simultaneously distorting and dismissive.

Wolfe decided in an essay, 'Stalking the Billion-Footed Beast', that the American novel had deteriorated into something 'weak, pale, tabescent' and that its future lay in the documentary novel of the Emile Zola school. His debut novel *Bonfire of the Vanities,* written after he turned fifty, was, in his words, an exemplar of such a work.

Both Wolfe and the American novel survived, the former despite attacks from the likes of Mailer, Updike and Irving. Mailer compared reading a Wolfe novel (he was speaking of *A Man in Full*) to making love to a 300-pound woman: 'Once she gets on top, it's all over. Fall in love or be asphyxiated.' No welcome into the pantheon for Mr Wolfe, then.

It may be Wolfe's fate to remain a cult figure rather than the father of a school of writing that he wished to be, his once cutting-edge style reduced to a mere curiosity.

Did Updike really sign this?

This is how it turned out. To adapt something parents of about-to-be-married children sometimes say—I lost a bathroom, but gained a library. The plan, to rip out the fittings in the toilet attached to my study, put up shelves, remove the door, convert the frame into a more pleasing arch and clear up floor space, table space, chair space and overcrowded shelf space around the house, went without a hitch.

It meant even more questions along the lines of 'Gosh! Have you read all your books?'

My normal reaction to the question is a pitying look accompanied by an expression which says, 'How illiterate of you to ask such a question,' and a gentle grunt which could mean anything from 'Ha ha!' to 'What makes you think I buy books to read them?' Or I borrow from Anatole France and respond to the philistine thus: 'I haven't read one-tenth of them. I don't suppose you use your Sevres china every day?'

In a seventy-year period of reading a book a day, we would complete just over 25,000 books, which, according to the philosopher and writer Umberto Eco is 'a trifle'. Eco had between thirty and forty thousand books in his collection. He recoiled when anyone asked him that 'have you read everything ...' question, and many potential friendships were nipped in the bud thus.

'Unread books are much more valuable than read ones,' explained Nassim Taleb, using Eco's library as an example in *The Black Swan*. He called the unread books the 'antilibrary'. Eco reacted because he thought his visitor was somehow castigating him for showing off the floor-to-ceiling collection. But, in fact, it was a sign of both a greater acquisition of knowledge as well as a greater thirst for it. As Taleb says, 'The more you know, the larger the rows of unread books.'

All of which is wonderful. I possess neither Eco's range of books nor his vast spread of knowledge and original thinking, but I love the concept of the antilibrary, and will pretend that Taleb's explanation applies to me as well. It is some consolation for the panicky feeling all of us get occasionally: 'So much to do [in this case, read], and so little time.'

But how do I introduce it into the conversation when someone asks, 'Have you read etc.' without sounding pretentious? Perhaps I should say, 'These books aren't for reading. They are merely decoration.' The visitor will take it as confirmation that I buy books merely to show off (which is not a bad thing by the way—it is better than buying French perfumes to show off). And go away satisfied.

I once had an idea for a book: I would go through my shelves, pick out books I hadn't read yet and write about finally catching up on my reading and reconnecting with my books, and thus pay a tribute to books and what they have meant in my life. Perhaps I wouldn't buy another book till I had read every one of those I already owned. I quickly dropped that last idea, however. Suppose I had 520 unread books, and read them at the rate of two every week, it would take me five years to go through the lot. Neither practical nor desirable. Perhaps I would write about just a small portion of unread books.

While I was making these calculations, I came across British writer Susan Hill's *Howards End is on the Landing,* a book identical to the one I had been planning to write, except that she had written it four years earlier. 'I wanted to repossess my books,' she writes, 'to explore what I had accumulated over a lifetime of reading, and to map this house of many volumes.' Couldn't have put it better myself.

Books are seldom about themselves. They are about dates and circumstances, travels and relationships, gateways and possibilities. My copy of *The Stolen Light* by Ved Mehta is different from every other copy in existence. For not only does it tell the story of Mehta going to college in California and the challenges he faced, it is equally a book that tells the story of my meeting with Mehta on a hot afternoon in New York, and the start of a friendship. We met on 1 June—I know because Ved's signature in the book carries that date.

No book belongs to the author alone. We preserve books for what they tell us about our lives. And not just in the sense Jean Baudrillard meant when he said, 'Here lies the whole miracle of collecting: It is invariably oneself that one collects.'

Somewhere at home is a slim children's book. I can't remember the name, but there is a mark on page thirty-eight, which is a reminder of my then infant son's oral reaction to food. It is as evocative as any of the photographs taken of him at that stage, a gateway to a flood of memories.

Yet, I am no book collector. First editions don't interest me. Others can bid for the first edition of Emily Bronte's *Wuthering Heights* and pay a fortune for it (someone actually did so, forking out £114,000) or Dashiell Hammett's *Maltese Falcon* (£50,000 with original dust jacket, £500 without it), but I'd rather curl up with my copy of John Carter's *ABC for Book Collectors,* the classic on the subject.

Author inscriptions—now that's another matter. In that charming little book, *Ex Libris*, Anne Fadiman tells the story of W.B. Yeats asking Thomas Hardy about how he dealt with requests for inscriptions. Hardy took Yeats to a room filled with books from floor to ceiling and said, 'Yeats, these are the books sent to me for signature.' Today, thanks to literary festivals, book tours, bookstore signings, it is easier to get an author to sign your copy of their book. Some write a message (V.S. Naipaul, Stephen Fry, Augusten Burroughs), some go with 'Best Wishes' (Ian McEwan, Karen Armstrong) and others just sign their names (Richard Dawkins, Tom Stoppard). Here too, different people will have different experiences. If you know someone well, he is unlikely to fob you off with just a signature. Lord Byron, for example, once wrote a 226-word note before he affixed his autograph.

In my 'signed books' shelf is a copy of *Couples*, signed by the author John Updike. It is inscribed with best wishes to 'Patrick K'. I'd like to believe the signature is authentic, and not a version of the pranks we played in school, signing 'With best wishes, William Shakespeare' in our copies of *Hamlet* or *Merchant of Venice.*

The Updike book rests beside *East West,* a collection of Salman Rushdie's short stories. This book too is signed by the author, although I am not sure where, or indeed if that actually happened. Sure, Rushdie has been to India a few times and might easily have had a book signing somewhere, security threat or no security threat. One year he was at the Hay on Wye Festival which I attended as a journalist. But we didn't meet. In any case, I bought the book in India. Perhaps it was inscribed for someone else who then sold it.

Why do people get rid of books inscribed by the author to them? It can't be because—as I was told by a dealer in antiquarian books—a book with such inscriptions is less valuable than one with just the signature. After all, this is emotional value versus the merely monetary.

Why would Mike and Jane, for example, dispose of the biography of Descartes, inscribed to them 'with warm good wishes' by the author, the philosopher A.C. Grayling? There might be a whole novel waiting to be unearthed behind that act. I love buying books in second-hand stores inscribed to other people and creating stories in my mind about such gestures.

Susan Hill's book ends with her settling down to read *Howards End*. In the climactic scene of Forster's book, a character is crushed to death by a collapsing bookcase. Each generation has interpreted this in its own way (the book was written in 1910). Perhaps, as E.M. Forster himself suggests, the 'gulf that stretches between the natural and the philosophical man' could not be bridged by the working-class character. A later critic saw this as the danger of education when pursued by the wrong people.

Today we might interpret it as symbolic of the death of not just books but those who ignore progress and the easy availability of e-book readers. But sometimes a collapsing bookcase killing someone is just that and nothing more.

No plan B

The voice on the phone was distinctive. 'Naipaul here,' it said, as if it were the most natural thing in the world for a famous author to call up a young sports journalist. 'Can we meet?' It remains the most startling call I have received.

The word most often associated with Naipaul, then and now, has been 'fastidious'. He was described as a 'cold, sneering prophet'.

I was prepared to meet such a man. The man who came out of the lift at his hotel, and walked with bird-like but precise steps, seemed to have an invisible wall around him; you sensed that. There was a look in his eyes that suggested he was constantly assessing the people around him and redefining his own self in relation to them.

'Madras is a city of pristine beauty. There is much charm in conservatism. The idli is a piece of art,' he said—not in that particular sequence, and not without context. 'I see so much change around me. India is investing in change (this was in 1989). Still, Indian newspapers are so boring. The emphasis on second- and third-rate politicians is all wrong.'

He signed my paperback copy of *A House for Mr Biswas*, checked the price and pronounced it was 'too expensive'. I agreed with him, but didn't say anything.

Over the next few days we met on and off, spending time

with former Naxalites, some of whom had been jailed for murder. In the evening he would read from his red notebook and ask, 'Have I got that right?' It was all there—the descriptions, the conversations, the opinions that would later appear in *A Million Mutinies Now*. The fastidiousness was only in the use of language. The prophet was neither cold nor sneering.

That is the Naipaul I would like to remember. The man who said, 'I want to capture the moment when the theoretician takes up arms.' He was talking of the anti-Brahmin movement in Tamil Nadu, but there was something universal and exciting about the motivation.

He came home for dinner. We had a tiny apartment in Chennai, made tinier by the front room being filled with my wife Dimpy's half-finished sculptures and material.

Naipaul arrived with his companion whom he introduced as 'Margaret'. He wore a three-piece suit and a red tie. The night was hot and sultry as only Chennai nights can be, yet he kept his suit on, and wanted to have the ceiling fan switched off. In the other room, our son, not yet a year old, was expressing himself loudly, perhaps complaining about the heat. Naipaul affected not to notice.

He was a man of infinite curiosity. He knew the lost wax process for bronze casting, but wanted to clarify something; he knew about the food we were having, his favourite fish and idlis among the fare. He wanted to know about Robin Singh, the cricketer from Trinidad who had moved to Chennai and would play for India. Margaret was cheerful—the stories of Naipaul's cruelty to her would emerge later—and involved.

What did Naipaul think of the fatwa against Salman Rushdie? It seemed almost rude to ask. Naipaul's reply: 'Assassination is an extreme form of literary criticism.' Sadly, we didn't have a camera. But Naipaul signed a photograph, with the date and the occasion ('dinner at their flat') on it.

When a friend from work, an aspiring writer, showed some of his work—this was something I was hoping to avoid—Naipaul didn't seem to mind. 'All your characters speak in the same voice,' he told him. 'When you write fiction you should split yourself into many people, and ensure they sound different from one another.'

Which of his books were personal favourites? Naipaul ticked them off in my copy of *Mr Stone and the Knights Companion.* It was quite straightforward: *Miguel Street, A House for Mr Biswas, An Area of Darkness, In a Free* State.

Naipaul later called up to say he had enjoyed a piece I had written in the newspaper then. 'Ah! Hack work,' I said dismissively, thrilled but attempting to play it cool. And he said, 'Just because it comes easily to you, don't think it is not important.' It is a lesson I never forgot.

His third book on India, *A Million Mutinies Now*, is remarkable for anticipating the new India with one foot on the world stage and the other still in the wings. It is his most compassionate book on India, written before the economic liberalisation, but with a sense of impending boom.

'The first book (*An Area of Darkness*) was about feeling. The second (*A Wounded Civilization*) about thinking. The first book was about what I felt, the second about what I thought. The third will be about what you think,' he told me. 'My views are not exhaustive. I throw hooks into a subject and write about whatever comes up with them.'

We could write to him, he said, he lived in England. His comment on travelling to the West Indies—I was preparing to report the Indian cricket team's tour then—was startling. 'It's a terrible place. You won't enjoy it.' In the event, I never wrote to him and the West Indies trip was called off. But we did meet again some fifteen years later.

This time, it was at a reading in a bookstore in Bengaluru. 'I don't expect you to remember me,' I said diffidently. But Naipaul—despite his wife Lady Nadira's efforts to tear him away—was forthcoming. 'We met in Chennai,' he recalled. 'You are the sportswriter, your wife is a sculptor. We had fish for dinner and spoke of Robin Singh among other things.' It was astonishing. Years later, his biographer Patrick French told me Naipaul had a remarkable memory for people and events. I am not sure if he used the word 'eidetic'.

Most writers form their opinions through the sieve of their experiences. With Naipaul it was different. He connected dots in a manner unique to himself. In the end, however, only the writing mattered.

With fame came notoriety. When he recognised a chance to provoke, he usually took it. 'Anyone not an Arab who is a Muslim is a convert,' he said. Similar things can be said about most faiths, but Naipaul somehow made it seem sinister.

There are essentially two Naipauls—the great novelist of *A House for Mr Biswas* and the extraordinary journalist of *Among the Believers* and the travel books. The novelist's strength—to generalise from the particular—is also the travel writer's weakness.

Yet, when he brought his novelist's eye to the job of the journalist, he elevated both forms of writing. The imagination required for the former allowed him to see patterns denied to others; the discipline needed for the latter acted as a check on the imagination taking over.

In *India: A Wounded Civilisation*, Naipaul quotes Balzac writing towards the end of his creative life: 'Constant labour is the law of art as well as the law of life, for art is the creative activity of the mind. And so great artists, true poets do not wait for either commissions or clients; they create today, tomorrow, ceaselessly. And there results a habit of toil, a perpetual consciousness of the difficulties that keeps them in a state of marriage with the Muse, and her creative forces.' It is of dharma he is writing, Naipaul tells us.

In his Nobel speech, Naipaul said something similar. 'Each book, intuitively sensed and, in the case of fiction, intuitively worked out, stands on what has gone before, and grows out of it. I feel that at any stage of my literary career it could have been said that the last book contained all the others.'

In *Sir Vidia's Shadow,* Naipaul's protégé Paul Theroux has a story about the blind India-born writer Ved Mehta. At a New York party, someone who doubted the writer was blind decides to take him on. He joins the group Mehta is speaking to, and makes faces at him. He leans forward and waves his hands in front of Mehta's face. He thumbs his nose at him. Mehta continues speaking. Now the man makes one final attempt: he puts his face a foot away from Mehta's and sticks his tongue out at him. Mehta carries on as if he doesn't exist.

Thoroughly beaten and realising how wrong he had been, the man decides to leave the party and says to the hostess on the way out: 'I had always thought Ved Mehta was faking his blindness. I am now convinced he is blind.'

'That's not Ved Mehta,' says the hostess. 'That's V.S. Naipaul.'

For me, that captures the essence of Naipaul. I can picture him observing, making mental notes, listening (Naipaul was a great listener), wondering, but refusing to ask 'Why?' Confident that if he were to write about the incident, the reasons would emerge in the writing.

It is this belief in the writer's craft that was particularly Naipaulean. When he won the Nobel, which he knew must come to him one day, there might have been a sliver of disappointment too. The obvious always disappointed him, unless he was the one to point it out or do the reverse, making the obvious unfamiliar by the power of his writing.

In the earlier Penguin editions of Naipaul's books, the note on the author said, 'V.S. Naipaul was born in Trinidad in 1932. He came to England in 1950 to do a university course, and began to write, in London, in 1954. He has followed no other profession.'

That last sentence has haunted me. Was it just a throwaway line suggesting that the author had a wide range of options to choose from at every stage, but decided to stick to writing? Or were we being told that to reach the top in any profession, it is best not to have a plan B? Choose a path, as the existentialists were saying, and then throw all your energies into it? Or was it a suggestion that the best writers were generalists with a wide canvas and a foray into any other profession would contaminate their real work? Perhaps it was a tribute to the nobility of literary pursuit.

The later Picador editions altered the note to read: 'After four years at the University College, Oxford, he began to write, and since then has followed no other profession.' The publishers were obviously aware of the power of that haunting line, but by joining the sentences had reduced its impact. There is a remarkable self-confidence behind it, a sense of literary entitlement that might even suggest authors who spread themselves in other professions diluted their talent. And their output.

In an interview to *The Paris Review*, Naipaul delineated his early ambitions and how they fed into his one great ambition thus: 'I wanted to be very famous. I also wanted to be a writer—

to be famous for writing. The absurdity about the ambition was that at the time I had no idea what I was going to write about. The ambition came long before the material. I wanted to be a writer by the age of ten.'

He has followed no other profession. It is a statement that both challenges and acknowledges arrogance. I may not be good enough for anything else, it says, but I am the best at what I do.

'Vidia's self—his very being—was his writing: a great gift, but all he had,' wrote his first editor Diana Athill. And even later, when he had established himself, wrote Athill, 'he was still tormented by anxiety about finding the matter for his next book, and for the one after that ... an anxiety not merely about earning his living, but about existing as the person he wanted to be.'

Are all writers play-actors of their own ideals? Did Naipaul behave like a great writer from an early age, knowing that was what he would ultimately grow into? Or are we distributing the dots to be joined after the picture is complete? 'His achievement was an act of will, in which every situation and relationship would be subordinated to his ambition,' wrote his biographer Patrick French.

This is not unusual in driven men, but Naipaul had attributes that sustained that drive: immense talent, and a self-belief nurtured through years of self-doubt. Writing was all that mattered.

While paying him a left-handed compliment, the obituarist at *The Guardian* wrote: 'The greatest literary virtue of the Trinidad-born writer V.S. Naipaul, who has died aged eighty-five, was instant readability. He constructed clear, irreducible sentences, and marshalled them into single-minded paragraphs. His control of language and the rhetoric of his novels were such that he could persuade you into belief even when his truths were only partly true.'

In his Nobel lecture, Naipaul said, 'Everything of value about me is in my books ... I am the sum of my books.'

And what books they were! *A House for Mr Biswas* must count among the great novels of the twentieth century. Naipaul was in his mid-twenties when he wrote the book full of wisdom and compassion and comic sensibilities. In later years, as he wrote more provocatively, indicating especially in his interviews a tendency towards the right wing of the political spectrum, it became increasingly difficult to recall the young writer of sensitivity and humour, the champion of the little man.

Sometimes I think Naipaul should be read, not heard. He was the finest writer of his generation; equally, he was the most annoying of interviewees, challenging us to take him seriously. He told an interviewer that his books helped educate Indians who, before that, lacked the intellectual ability to appreciate them. His rantings about Islam endeared him to the right wing in India.

Perhaps he deserves what George Orwell called the benefit of the clergy, and ought to be allowed a certain amount of irresponsibility. Rather like pregnant women or, as in Orwell's essay, the painter Salvador Dali. We ought to be able to say, 'His politics stinks, but his writing is sublime.' One does not invalidate the other, nor particularly authenticate it.

The Mimic Men (1967), *In a Free State* (1971), *A Bend in the River* (1979) among the early novels were written alongside the non-fiction, the India books, *The Loss of El Dorado* (1969) and collections of essays. 'To arrive at a place without knowing anyone there, to learn how to move among strangers for the short time one could afford to be among them; to hold oneself in constant readiness for adventure or revelation; to allow oneself to be carried along, up to a point, by accidents; and consciously to follow up other impulses—that could be as creative and imaginative a procedure as the writing that came after,' he set out his credo in *Finding the Centre*.

The simplicity of the writer had been gradually taken over by the complexity of the man. 'Creating tensions, insulting his friends, family or whole communities left him in excellent spirits,' wrote Patrick French in his brilliant biography, *The World Is What It Is*.

Naipaul turned out to be a stunningly honest subject, not shying from speaking the truth about rotten behaviour towards his women, or anything else. 'The lives of writers,' he said in a speech quoted in the biography, 'are a legitimate subject of inquiry; and the truth should not be skimped. It may well be that a full account of a writer's life might in the end be more a work of literature and more illuminating—of a cultural or historic moment—than the writer's books.'

The last time I met Naipaul was in an aircraft. We were among a bunch of invitees to the Jaipur Literature Festival returning to Delhi after the year's literary Kumbh Mela. He sat in a wheelchair in front, acknowledging the greetings of those who walked past. He looked tired; his session at the festival had been upsetting. He was eighty-two, and seemed to come and go, struggling for coherence, and clearly in the wrong place at the wrong time. A younger Naipaul would have revelled in being in the wrong place at the wrong time, converting his discomfort into literature. Now he looked wretched.

As I walked past him in the aircraft, greeting him one last time, he reminded me of Edward Said's description of Jean-Paul Sartre when he met the French writer: 'He seemed to me like a haunted version of his earlier self.' I wish I hadn't seen him thus.

Master of the falsely profound

'If I go into someone's house and see the works of Paulo Coelho I have great trouble regarding him as a friend,' said Alberto Manguel, writer, critic, and possibly the world's best-known bibliophile. He was speaking at the Jaipur Literature Festival. I didn't actually stand up and cheer, but there was an aspect of stand-up-and-cheer about the way I sat from then on.

Coelho, already the 'world's most successful writer', once told us about the process of writing. It is impossible to parody it. He said, 'The first stage is ploughing the field: as soon as the soil is turned over, oxygen penetrates into places it could not previously reach. We will thus be prepared for the miracle of inspiration. Next comes the sowing: every work is the fruit of contact with life. The creative person cannot shut himself away; he needs to be in touch with his fellow human beings. He must allow life to sow the fertile ground of his unconscious.

'Then there comes the time of ripeness, when the work writes itself freely, in the depths of the author's soul. Last comes harvest: the moment when a creator brings to a conscious level everything that he sowed and allowed to ripen. If picked too early, the fruit is green; if picked too late, the fruit is rotten. And what should one do with the fruits of the harvest? Again, look to Mother Nature: she shares everything with everyone. When the work is complete, one must share one's soul, without fear and without shame.'

Coelho is the master of the falsely profound, of the apparently insightful, of the speciously perceptive. He writes like a series of get-well cards, his philosophy packed into such nuggets as: 'It is the simple things in life that are the most extraordinary; only wise men are able to understand them.' He is a bestseller in 155 countries—maybe more since I wrote that. Astronomers wonder if all the talk about Mars getting closer to earth isn't merely the tangerine covers of such Coelho books as *The Alchemist* and *Eleven Minutes* being shifted into outer space for readers there. Anything is possible with Coelho.

Maria, the heroine of one of his books (*Eleven Minutes*, which is about 'sacred sex') was inspired by the Andalusian shepherd in a book by a Brazilian writer. Read: *The Alchemist* by Paulo Coelho. That book has sold over twenty godzillion copies or something. Or was it thirty gazillion? It doesn't matter, for wisdom is the province of the aged but the heart of a golden child is pure. That isn't Coelho, but Peter Sellers in *The Party*. Sometimes it is difficult to tell the difference.

It is easy to like Coelho. There is an innocence about a man who believes he can put together short, transparent sentences and pass them off as the spiritual outpourings of a soul in torment or in search of itself. Coelho is a multimillionaire who is seen as a personal guru. His book-signings turn into spiritual experiences for some. He met the lady who became Maria in his novel at a signing of one of his books which had 'inspired her to become a prostitute.'

This is New Age writing at its most challenging—is he saying something profound or merely teasing us? Is he merely Chetan Bhagat in a different accent? Is an orgasm (in *Eleven Minutes*) really like 'floating up to heaven and then parachuting slowly down to earth again'? Even those nudge-nudge, wink-wink books your cheap second-hand bookseller pulls out from behind a row of *National Geographic* magazines describe it better.

Coelho himself is far more interesting than his books. At seventeen, he told his parents he wanted to be a writer. Horrified, they put him in an asylum. He underwent electroconvulsive therapy. By the time he was twenty, he had been sent back to the asylum twice more. He escaped both times. He travelled around the country with a guitar, returning home when he ran out of money. He didn't hold the asylum experiences against his parents. He felt it was a way of protecting him as an artist when the military dictatorship in Brazil was kidnapping, torturing and imprisoning left-wing artists and intellectuals in the country.

He used these experiences thirty years later in *Veronika Decides to Die*, a book which helped change Brazilian law. It is not so easy to put someone in an asylum now. He wrote songs for Brazil's top stars, but some comic strips he made landed him in jail where he was tortured.

Such experiences obviously do something to you. In Coelho's case, it turned him into a pseudo-spiritual figure whose books fall somewhere between the Chicken Soup series and DIY manuals.

It wasn't until he was forty, however, that he found the confidence to return to writing. He turned to his trip the previous year to Santiago de Compostella for inspiration. He began a ritual that continues. Only when he finds a white feather does he start writing. As he prints out the first draft of his books, he touches the plume to each page. It is personal, and symbolic.

But his writing isn't all fable and parable and omen and the banal disguised as wisdom. *Veronika Decides to Die*, for example, is a fine book about a Slovenian girl who takes an overdose of sleeping pills but doesn't die. She wakes up in a mental hospital and is told she has damaged her heart and has only a few days to live. Faced with death, she wants only one thing: to live. Despite the lapses into Coelhoese ('Today death brushed my face with its wing and will probably be knocking at my door tomorrow'), the novel has a feel of authenticity about it.

What happens when the spiritualist turns to sex? *Eleven Minutes* happens. Much humour here. Of the unintended variety. A favourite: 'We got up and I saw that he hadn't even taken off his trousers, he was dressed just as I had found him, only with his penis exposed. I put my jacket over my bare shoulders. We went into the kitchen. He made some coffee, he smoked two cigarettes, I smoked one.'

Fine. But what became of the penis?

Magic and realism

When I was starting out as a journalist, I was told by a colleague: 'This is just marking time. Journalists worth their salt have a novel tucked away in the bottom drawer which they hope to publish soon and become famous.' I didn't, then or ever, but I had been told my place: novelists first, hacks somewhere at the back.

Gabriel García Márquez, however, called journalism 'the best job in the world'.

'I am basically a journalist,' Márquez wrote. 'My books are the books of a journalist.' He founded six publications in his lifetime, and said, 'I do not want to be remembered for *One Hundred Years of Solitude*, nor for the Nobel Prize, but for the newspapers.'

The Scandal of the Century and Other Writings brings together Márquez's journalism; some profound, some brilliant reportage, and some on searching for a subject for a topical piece. In this latter category is 'The Postman Rings a Thousand Times' about where letters that never reach their destination end up. Márquez tells us imagination can enhance reality without distorting it.

Here he is on writing a weekly column: 'I write [this column] every Friday from nine in the morning, until three in the afternoon, with the same will, the same conscience, the same joy, and often the same inspiration with which I should have written a masterpiece. When I don't have a well-defined topic I go to bed grumpy on Thursday night, but experience has taught me that the drama will resolve itself while I sleep and will begin to flow again in the morning, as soon as I sit in front of the typewriter.'

Here, on seeing Hemingway from across a street in Paris. Márquez 'cupped my hands to my mouth, like Tarzan in the jungle, and shouted from one sidewalk to the other, "Maeeeestro!".'

Hemingway, confident there could be no other maestro about, shouted back, 'Adioooos, amigo.' Lovely. There is a wonderful description of Hemingway earlier, a few light touches: 'He was enormous and too visible ... his hips were a bit narrow and his legs didn't have much flesh on the bones ...'

'Writing books,' Márquez says in 'Misadventures of a Writer of Books', 'is a suicidal job.' Themes on writing, writers, Latin America, friends, translation, journalism and more go through the Márquez mill and reappear original, witty, and with great power on the page. There's both magic and realism.

Elegant, lean, immaculate

Ved Mehta hated to be called the blind Indian writer. It described him, but didn't define him. He knew too many adjectives diminished 'writer'. That single word was enough.

He was the finest of prose stylists, writing with a care for words and a felicity which appeared natural but was, in fact, finely honed. No word (or experience) was wasted. His autobiography in twelve volumes, *Continents of Exile*, where each book stands independently, was more than just that. It was his history told against the background of the history of his world—in India, UK and the US where he was a *New Yorker* staffer for thirty-four years.

'Call me Ved,' he says when we first meet at his New York apartment where he is working on a novel (later, when he is finished with it, he doesn't like it and decides not to publish).

We sit in his apartment on Lexington Avenue, high above the traffic noises of New York City. It is a cosy study, twelve paces from the room where we had met a few minutes earlier and where he had been working with his amanuensis. In his brilliant white shirt and dark trousers, he brings to mind Maureen Dowd's description in *The New York Times*: 'He bears a strong resemblance to his prose—elegant, lean and immaculate.'

There is a happy informality about the household. During our conversation, Natasha, the younger daughter, pops in to check something with her father; later, wife Linn welcomes me warmly and apologises for not having returned earlier. In the kitchen, the Brazilian housekeeper is excited that someone has come from India.

His analyst has told him that he both undervalues and overvalues sight. He undervalues it because he keeps thinking that its absence can be ignored, that he 'can do everything that anyone else can do'. He overvalues it because he thinks he is an outcast without it, 'like a beggar asking for the hand of a princess'.

It is possible, as Mehta writes in *Daddyji*, the first book of the series, that an incorrect diagnosis led to a delay in treatment when he had an attack of meningitis at the age of three. The illness made him blind. An obscure doctor in Punjab may thus be responsible for creating one of the finest prose stylists in the English language.

Mehta is both creative storyteller and roving reporter, recording impressions with a precision and feel for the language that is unforced, almost casual, but is in fact the result of many rewrites and rigorous self-editing. He is known to redo a piece 150 times till he gets it right.

With lots to say, Mehta quite early hit upon the form in which to say it—using the autobiography like other writers use the sonnet or the iambic pentameter. The architecture of the series is fascinating. Each book is complete in itself, as well as part of a bigger whole. Sometimes within the books there is a main theme and a subtler motif just below the surface. *The Ledge Between the Streams*, for example, is the story of Partition told by the boy Ved Mehta from the perspective of the man. This gives the book a unique voice as events are both described and interpreted. It is equally the story of apparently dissimilar parents who are in reality more alike than the boy thinks. But that insight is the later Mehta's. *Continents of Exile*, the story of one man, becomes the history of a people and of a period.

Long before Indian writers began getting their due in the West, Ved Mehta was already a fixture on New York's literary scene; his *Portrait of India*, was, according to Salman Rushdie, 'important just as I was starting to think of *Midnight's Children*'. Mehta is the link between the R.K. Narayan–Mulk Raj Anand generation and the Rushdie–Vikram Seth one.

He has written a wider range of English essays than any Indian, bringing to each one a rare sensitivity and humour. He showed, too, a healthy eagerness to jump into a good fight, as in his 'encounters with English intellectuals', *Fly and the Fly Bottle*. For this book he interviewed Bertrand Russell, A.J. Ayer, Iris Murdoch, Ludwig Wittgenstein, A.J.P. Taylor among others, catching many of them in indiscretions and contradictions that kept the community in ferment for a long time. He did the same with theologians for another book. 'Then I stopped,' he says. 'Some people wanted me to continue with economists, scientists and so on. But I hate repeating myself.'

He introduced India in the pages of the *New Yorker*, where he was a staff writer from 1961 to 1994. 'Ved Mehta has educated Americans about India,' wrote William Shawn, the legendary editor of the magazine and a father figure in Mehta's life, 'illuminating that country with an insider's sensibility and an outsider's objectivity.'

Indian readers, unused to such objectivity, took offence at Mehta's interviews with the women in Gandhi's life in his biography of the Mahatma. The uproar pushed up sales and established Mehta's reputation as an uncompromising teller of his truth, a reputation he strengthened in his other India books. India has not forgiven Ved Mehta the way it has forgiven V.S.

Naipaul for the same crime. That of telling the truth about the country. Mehta's area of darkness is both symbolic and literal.

Amartya Sen, friend and one-time rival in love, has called Mehta 'a very systematic contemporary historian'. The more particular a story, the more universal it is, says Mehta, whose personal history is one of the most remarkable literary enterprises ever. 'Personal history' is the rubric *The New Yorker* created for his autobiographical writings; many of his books were first published there. That rubric was his exclusive domain for years till John Updike's memoirs also appeared under it.

Ved Mehta has not been given credit as one of the pioneers of 'New Journalism'. The techniques borrowed from fiction—scene-by-scene construction, use of dialogue, attention to details, use of the flashback—were second nature to him. He knew no other. He had to rely on intensive questioning, impressions and greater alertness to 'get inside his subject's head' and tell us his thoughts and motivations. He had to work at getting right the colours, expressions, gestures and all those visual clues that other writers take for granted.

In the 1960s, as writers like Gay Talese, Tom Wolfe, Joan Didion, Norman Mailer extended the meaning and range of New Journalism, Ved Mehta was polishing his style at the *New Yorker*, ensuring that the essence of all journalism, old and new—the sacredness of facts, the integrity of ideas—remained unchanged. By the end of the decade, when he set out on his 'Proustian' voyage, it was all in place—the technique, the integrity, the choice of the telling detail.

This last involved a mastery over the unsaid, and interestingly for a man who has written so much about himself, an elusiveness that is at the heart of the best poetry.

In *Sound-Shadows of the New World*, the story of Mehta's stint at the Arkansas School for the Blind, he tells us how he developed his hearing and memory and formed mental images. Later, he imposed colours on his childhood and growing years, writing with confidence of 'the yellow of mustard flowers outlined by the feathery green of sugarcane,' for example.

So well did Mehta succeed in his aim—to write as if he could see—that he was sometimes accused of faking his blindness. Norman Mailer once challenged him to a boxing match to settle the issue.

How much could he know about colour? I ask. 'Actually, quite a lot,' he says. 'During therapy in later years, I was able to remember colours and much more.' And then he adds, a little mischievously, 'Of course, my yellow may not be the same as your yellow.'

With today's knowledge and yesterday's energy, would he have written anything differently?

'No. I wouldn't change a word,' he says, adding that everything is as it ought to be. 'In retrospect everything looks inevitable.'

In the foreword to his first collection of essays in 1971, Mehta wrote, 'My whole life is an unprecedented—and so, for the time being, incomprehensible—experiment, conducted by me in the guise of a mad scientist.'

As we speak, I imagine that at seventy-three, the mad scientist, crazy student (known for speeding on bicycles and even driving a car in the US), sometime Lothario, path-breaking writer, family man and inspiration to generations may be forgiven if he thinks he has no more worlds to conquer. He continues to write, however, 'because that is what I do.'

As I bid goodbye, he sees me to the door, calls up the lift and shakes hands warmly. The combination of confidence and vulnerability is captivating. I recall a line from Borges about god, who, 'with magnificent irony, granted me both the gift of books and the night.'

The last time we met was years later at New York's Metropolitan Opera for Mozart's *Clemenza di Tito.* We—my wife and son too—were his guests. We had met for dinner the previous week and admitted to enjoying a modern, fascist-themed version of *Macbeth* with Patrick Stewart in the lead.

'I hate these modern interpretations,' Ved said. 'We should leave Shakespeare alone. There is enough richness, enough unexplored in the plays as he wrote them.' He was a classicist, and the Mozart opera might have been his way of showing us what great works ought to look like.

Ved plunged headlong into life, determined to experience everything it had to offer. After he lost his sight, he worked on developing his insight. He wrote of colours and textures and gestures people made, dipping into his bank of memories of the colours, and trained powers of Holmesian deduction. In *Up at Oxford*, he paid a tribute to his amanuenses who helped him 'as much as Milton's daughters' helped the poet.

When I wrote that the New Journalists owed him for developing their techniques through close questioning and intelligent deduction, he wrote to say, 'I loathe the so-called New Journalists. They imagine what is in people's heads without any documentary evidence, e.g. Tom Wolfe's piece "Radical Chic", where he ascribes all kinds of thoughts to Bernstein, which were never in his head but sprang straight from Wolfe's head as surmises.

'I feel I have much more in common as a reporter with Boswell than I do with the likes of Wolfe, who is an anathema to me.'

Shawn wrote of Ved, 'He writes about serious matters without solemnity, about scholarly matters without pedantry, about abstruse matters without obscurity.'

That works as Ved's epitaph. He died at eighty-six in January 2021.

The ghost in the machine

Ghostwriting may be the oldest profession in the world, or at least one of the two oldest, which might explain the similarity of reactions they evoke. Jennie Erdal, who wrote *Ghosting: A Double Life*, speaks of the time a professor from her university said she was 'no better than a common whore'.

Erdal's charming book—on ghosting for her employer, the flamboyant London publisher Naim Atallah (whom she calls 'Tiger')—caused a flutter when it first appeared. For ghostwriters, like spies, work in the shadows, and watch as other people take the credit for their work. Erdal's was a warm portrait of Atallah, who however, broke off all relations once the book appeared. 'The plumage is a wonder to behold,' Erdal wrote of Tiger's exuberant attire, 'a large sapphire in the lapel of a bold striped suit, a vivid silk tie so bright that it dazzles, and when he flaps his wings the lining of his jacket glints and glistens like a prism.'

The judgement of critics: this lady can write. So why was she satisfied with ghosting for her boss—writing everything from his letters, poems, love notes to his wife, novels—when it seemed like a wilful limiting of her potential? For two decades, Erdal hid her light under a bushel, content that Atallah claim all the glory. At the launch of one of 'his' books, someone asked Erdal if she had read it. She varied her answer from 'Yes, it's a classic,' to 'No, but I hope to,' without ever sinking to 'Read it? I wrote the bloody thing!'

'As a ghostwriter, you have to leave your ego at the door,' said the Sydney journalist Michael Robotham (who wrote the autobiography of Spice Girl Geri Halliwell), whose first novel became a bestseller in twenty-six countries. 'Ghostwriters tend not to make the best novelists,' he said. 'You are in a comfort zone as a ghostwriter. You earn very good money. And you don't have your name on the book. So if it fails, you don't fail publicly.'

Sports stars, movie actors, politicians, businessmen, all use ghosts to write their stuff. There is a certain logic to this. The great inside forward or the method actor need not simultaneously be the literary giant of his generation too. After all, a Hillary Clinton is not expected to fix her own car or build her own house, so why should she be expected to write her own book? Turn to the professional, therefore. And that's what they do.

When President Kennedy's *Profiles in Courage* won the Pulitzer Prize, there were at least two candidates who emerged as the likely ghostwriters. Arthur Schlesinger Jr and Ted Sorensen, both advisors to the president and speech writers. Years later, Sorensen wrote in his autobiography that he 'did the first draft of most chapters and helped choose the words of many of its sentences.' Many so-called prolific writers whose names appear in the record books for their phenomenal output used ghostwriters.

Leslie Charteris was one. Many of the detective fiction writer Ellery Queen's books were written by others. Before the franchise (James Bond, Bertie Wooster) took over, there was the book-churning industry. This was acknowledged by Mildred Wirt Benson, creator of the Nancy Drew series. Benson wrote for the Stratemeyer Syndicate in New York under the pseudonym Carolyn Keene. Her identity was kept secret until it was revealed in a court case in the 1980s. The books were translated into seventeen languages and sold more than thirty million copies. However, when she wrote under her own name, the books didn't sell as well.

Andrew Crofts is one of the most successful writers of our generation, but few books have appeared under his own name. He is ghostwriter to the stars, with over a hundred books to his name, which have sold over ten million copies and made him a millionaire many times over.

'Behind the title of ghostwriter, I could converse with kings and billionaires as easily as whores and the homeless, go backstage with rock stars and actors. I could stick my nose into everyone else's business and ask all the impertinent questions I wanted to. At the same time, I could also live the pleasant life of a writer ...,' he wrote in his *Confessions of a Ghostwriter.* His motto, as that of his profession, seems to be taken from something Harry S. Truman said: 'You can accomplish anything in life provided you don't mind who gets the credit.'

'Ghostwriting' was coined by Christy Walsh, an American who set up a syndicate in 1921 to bring sporting heroes to the public through the written word. He had a rule: 'Don't insult the intelligence of the public by claiming these men write their own stuff.'

Few sports stars can claim credit for writing their own autobiographies. The standard joke grew from an NBA star's response to a comment on his autobiography—he said he 'hadn't read it yet'.

Sachin Tendulkar, whose autobiography is the highest-selling sports book in India, said not long before the book appeared that 'he hadn't actually read a book yet' when asked what his favourite book was. There is an engaging honesty about this.

Sportswriters probably ghost more often than other professionals. Years ago, when a newspaper was carrying a regular column by the Indian hero Tiger Pataudi, he was happy to let me write it without going through the formality of discussing it with him. 'Enjoy yourself,' he said, 'but don't get me into trouble.'

The only time I was actually paid for ghosting was when Kapil Dev was invited to do the cover story for a magazine on the 1987 World Cup. I was paid a decent amount by the player, although I'll never get over the desperate late-night call from him: 'Hey, they want another 170 words, can you send it immediately?' Feeling like a grocer who had to home-deliver potatoes, I sent it immediately.

I once wrote when ghosting for another international: 'So-and-so dropped a catch anybody's sister could have taken.' It was meant to be funny (if sexist), and the player was mad. 'So-and-so is my friend,' he told me, 'and he will think I have written something awful about his sister.' All friendships survived in the end.

In those days, ghosting was seen as part of your job as a sportswriter. I knew only two Indian cricketers (they were mainly cricketers) who wrote their own stuff—Bishan Singh Bedi and Sunil Gavaskar. It wasn't great fun for us youngsters, but it ensured easy access, and that was the trade-off. Samuel Johnson said, 'No man but a blockhead ever wrote except for money.' We were a bunch of blockheads who had little choice.

Veteran ghostwriter David Bain said he thought of writing as a business, and had no ambition to be a Hemingway or a Grisham. Bain's favourite quote is from Charles Dickens—another writer who thought of novels not as high art but as avenues for money-making. 'When you have quite done counting the sovereigns received for Pickwick, I should be much obliged to you to send me up a few,' Dickens once wrote to his editor. Bain has one way of getting his name into some of the books he writes—he dedicates them to himself.

One Nobel Prize winner ghosting for another might seem unreal, but when it is Gunter Grass (Literature, 1999) writing for Willy Brandt, the German Chancellor (Peace, 1971), it becomes merely unusual. Their collaboration, *The Citizen and His Voice*, was published in 1974.

Credit was very much the topic of the day when the footballer David Beckham won an award for his autobiography *My Side*. Did the award belong to him or to Tom Watt, who actually wrote the book? Ghostwriting is big business. The vanity of the celebrity is the fuel that keeps the wheels turning, and the hack living a life that is the envy of those whose writings appear under their own names.

There is, too, the Association of Ghostwriters, a professional network to 'help writers connect with clients and refine their craft'. Sportswriters are some of the finest ghostwriters in the world. A grunt by a sportsman in response to a banal question routinely appears in the media as a profundity from Socrates knocked into shape by Márquez. It is called 'making the hero look (and sound) good.'

The ghost is the sieve through which the banal is converted into the brilliant for popular consumption. Ghostwriting, you might say, is a public service.

The writer's disease

It never ceases to amaze me all these years later how many of us who were headed in that direction did not become full-blown alcoholics. We drank to forget, we drank to remember, we drank to lament, we drank to celebrate, we drank on dares, we drank just because alcohol—the cheap, dangerous variety—was available.

We also drank because it was seen as necessary to the creative life which we believed was what we were leading, or about to lead. Some of us wrote poetry (I am confessing to this crime for the first time here); others stocked up on 'experiences' to be converted into literature in good time.

The writer as an alcoholic is one of the romantic images of the craft. Authors themselves have perpetrated this, with many claiming it is necessary to drink in order to work. Perhaps dentists and truck drivers feel the same way too, but there is no romance if *they* say it, only horror.

'Once drunk, a cup of wine can bring 100 stanzas,' the Chinese poet Xiuxi Yin claimed. Omar Khayyam, the eleventh-century poet, may have influenced generations into making the connection and acting upon it, but the myth has come down to us from ancient Greece. The great Urdu poet Mirza Ghalib was an alcoholic who gave the impression that alcohol was the great literary fuel; lesser writers chose the easier option, drinking rather than writing well.

'Too much champagne is just right,' said F. Scott Fitzgerald, who wrote *The Great Gatsby* in his twenties and was dead by forty-four, having imbibed huge amounts of alcohol in between.

'Always be drunk,' the French writer Baudelaire exhorted. It was advice many took to heart. 'I usually write at night,' William Faulkner told an interviewer. 'I always keep my whiskey within reach.' More than half the American Nobel laureates in literature were alcoholic. Across the pond, Dylan Thomas, Philip Larkin, Malcolm Lowry and Kingsley Amis were sometimes better known for their legendary drinking than for their creative bursts. 'Civilisation begins with distillation,' said Faulkner, putting it in perspective for the literary lushes.

Speaking for the other side is John Updike, who said his longevity and that of Philip Roth was due in no small measure to the fact that they were not alcoholics.

Biographers tend to pussyfoot around a writer's alcoholism, thereby missing out a major reason for their decline. Christopher Sykes's otherwise excellent biography of Evelyn Waugh is a good example of this.

In his study of alcohol and the American writer, *The Thirsty Muse*, Tom Dardis gives a list of alcoholic writers—Jack London, Scott Fitzgerald, Thomas Wolfe, Dorothy Parker, Ring Lardner, Tennessee Williams, James Jones, John Cheever, Truman Capote, Raymond Carver—and concludes, 'Alcoholism seems to be the American writer's disease'. The careers of Hemingway, Faulkner, O'Neill show that far from aiding creativity, alcohol ended careers prematurely.

Fitzgerald's last good book was *Tender Is the Night*, published when he was thirty-eight; Hemingway was forty-one when he wrote *For Whom the Bell Tolls*, and Faulkner forty-four when he finished *Go Down Moses*. O'Neill alone among them decided to stop drinking at thirty-seven, and produced *The Ice Man Cometh* and later, *Long Day's Journey into Night*.

In Alcohol and the Writer, Donald Goodwin shows that writers are more likely to veer towards alcoholism than any other professional. This is because, he says, the hours of work are good since there is no fixed schedule, it is more acceptable, even expected, and so writers are indulged, unlike, say, doctors. Finally, there is the romance attached to it: alcohol as inspiration.

Goodwin makes the following argument: Writing involves fantasy; alcohol promotes fantasy. Writing requires self-confidence; alcohol bolsters confidence. Writing is lonely work; alcohol assuages loneliness. Writing demands intense concentration; alcohol relaxes.

There is a superficial gloss to this till you realise you could substitute 'writer' with almost any other profession. Playing tennis, for example, involves fantasy, requires self-confidence and is lonely work. But the second part of the equation does not follow.

In *Cat on a Hot Tin Roof*, one of the characters says, 'I'm takin' a little short trip to Echo Spring', his name for the drinks cabinet. *The Trip to Echo Spring* by Olivia Laing describes the trips of John Berryman, Hemingway, Williams, Carver, Cheever and Fitzgerald.

There are no simple answers to the question: why do writers drink? Laing's journey in the book is physical (across America), intellectual (literary criticism) and emotional (her own experience growing up in a household 'under the rule of alcohol'). She suggests a number of answers—loneliness, diffidence, as a way to forget, to keep the future at bay—that are, again, applicable to non-writers too. There is no single answer, even if Cheever had a famous justification: 'The excitement of alcohol and the excitement of fantasy are very similar.'

It is sobering to realise that depression, blackouts, hospitalisation, DTs and electroshock therapy were the constant companions of such major writers as Faulkner and Hemingway. That they managed to actually write is a tribute to their ability to keep their original vision intact. Writing to Max Perkins, his publisher, Fitzgerald said, 'My work is the only thing that makes me happy—except to be a little tight—and for those two indulgences I pay a big price in mental and physical hangovers.'

Hemingway and Berryman committed suicide (like their respective fathers had), Carver died of cancer at fifty, Fitzgerald of a heart attack at forty-four.

Hemingway, who never considered himself an alcoholic because he had 'mastered the art of drinking in his twenties', wrote out his credo to his friend and biographer A.E. Hotchner: '[I] have spent my life straightening out (drunks), and all my life drinking, but since writing is my true love I never get the two things mixed up.'

Hemingway's is a particularly interesting case because he was clear-sighted enough to see how alcoholism was destroying the career of a man like Faulkner, but lacked the honesty to admit it was doing the same to him. 'He has that wonderful talent,' he said of Faulkner, 'and his not taking care of it to me is like a machine gunner letting his weapon foul up ...'

Perhaps Hemingway was talking about himself. After all, how many writers dependent on alcohol can say, like Winston Churchill, 'I have taken more out of alcohol than alcohol has taken out of me'? The rehabilitated O'Neill once wrote in a letter, 'I don't think anything worth reading was ever written by anyone who was drunk when he wrote it.' This is not a moral stand, merely a practical one.

Laing wrote an essay on female alcoholic writers too: Jean Rhys, Marguerite Duras, Patricia Highsmith, Elizabeth Bishop, Jane Bowles, Anne Sexton, Carson McCullers, Dorothy Parker and others. Warming up to her subject, she says Rhys was briefly in prison for assault while Bishop sometimes drank eau de cologne.

'I drank because I was an alcoholic,' Duras told *The New York Times*. 'I am a real writer, I was a real alcoholic. I drank red wine to fall asleep. Afterwards, Cognac in the night. Every hour a glass of wine and in the morning Cognac after coffee, and afterwards I wrote. What is astonishing when I look back is how I managed to write.'

Duras's childhood, wrote Laing, was marked by fear, violence and shame: common enough circumstances in the early life of the addict.

So perhaps that's why we dedicated drinkers of the past didn't become great novelists: our lives were marked by peace and pride. For a while I held it against my parents for giving me a happy childhood. Then I forgave them.

Crime and character

Detective fiction satisfies two kinds of readers. The first cries out 'Wow!' when the murderer is revealed and is happiest when his theories are shot to pieces by the detective in a French, Belgian, English, Swedish or Scottish accent. The second says 'Aha!' since everything merely confirms his own suspicions. One looks for surprise, the other for corroboration.

Style is the enemy of the development from the act to its perpetrator. So are backstories; these merely slow down the flow. The best, in the evocative phrase of Francis Wyndham, write 'animated algebra'. Agatha Christie, the queen of them all, in his words, 'dares us to solve a basic equation buried beneath a proliferation of irrelevancies. By the last page, everything should have been eliminated except for the motive and identity of the murderer; the elaborate working-out, apparently too complicated to grasp, is suddenly reduced to satisfactory simplicity.'

No one—not even the greatest fans of Sherlock Holmes—think detective fiction is literature. And certainly not if the detective appears in a series of books where, gradually, just as the reader begins to get the writer, he or she subverts all expectations. Even an intellectual writer like Umberto Eco is presumed to be goofing off when he writes detective fiction.

He called his huge bestseller *The Name of the Rose* 'upmarket Arthur Hailey'. *The Guardian* considered it an artful reworking of Conan Doyle, with Sherlock Holmes transplanted to fourteenth-century Italy. 'The book's baggage of arcane erudition,' it said, 'was designed to flatter the average reader's intelligence.'

Yet, there is something about detective fiction that unites people. Besides sportswriting, it is the one genre that is read by the semi-literate with passion and the intellectual without embarrassment. Eco memorably compared it to philosophy because both ask the same fundamental question: whodunnit?

'The charm of the genre,' wrote W.H. Auden, a fan, 'has nothing to do with literature: it is essentially magical and its effect is cathartic.' Edmund Wilson, however, called it 'sub-literary' and 'between a trivial pursuit and a wildly shameful addiction'. He wrote an essay in *The New Yorker*, 'Who Cares Who Killed Roger Ackroyd?' Fans of detective fiction have been publishing counter-arguments ever since. Christie, not surprisingly, has copped most of the criticism on behalf of her tribe. Wilson called her writing 'mawkish and banal'.

Raymond Chandler wrote: 'And there is a scheme of Agatha Christie's featuring M Hercule Poirot, that ingenious Belgian who talks in a literal translation of schoolboy French, wherein, by duly messing around with his "little grey cells", M Poirot decides that nobody on a certain sleeper could have done the murder alone, therefore everybody did it together, breaking the process down into a series of simple operations, like assembling an egg beater. This is the type that is guaranteed to knock the keenest mind for a loop. Only a halfwit could guess it.'

It was left to the contemporary French writer Michel Houellebecq to give it all a nudge towards balance with the declaration that 'She [Christie] understands the "sin of despair"' and calling one of her works a 'strange, poignant book; there are deep waters, with powerful undercurrents'.

With sales of over two billion copies of her books, Christie stands alone.

Some of her plots are unworkable; occasionally she feels the pressure of having created a Belgian hero (a confession she puts into the mouth of her fictional alter ego Ariadne Oliver, who writes books about a Norwegian detective and wonders why).

Perhaps the enduring charm of the Hercule Poirot books lies in their lack of depth. We are given character traits on a need-to-know basis. Poirot is fond of speaking of 'psychology', but he mentions it without acting upon it. In a neat reversal of Shakespeare, contemporary events cast their shadows back into the past in many of the mysteries.

Christie has not missed a trick. In one novel, the detective did it, in another the policeman, in a third, no one did it, in a fourth, everyone. Sometimes a murder is actually a suicide, and vice versa. Sometimes a line floating into her head provides a clue: *Why Didn't They Ask Evans*?

Then there is the one where every character is murdered, but the killer is not the sole survivor. The past throws a long shadow; a murderer is hanged and it turns out years later that someone else is the guilty party.

What of the murder glimpsed through the window of one train passing another? One on a flight, and another with the time and place of the murder announced in advance in a newspaper advertisement?

Then there is my personal favourite—*Cards on the Table*—where four people sit down to a game of bridge, an evil man is murdered and all of them had the detective's troika: motive, means and opportunity. Yet, only one of them could have actually done it. Much depends on the character of the suspects, and so the game is described in some detail with diagrams. Character is revealed by how a hand is played.

Someone once calculated that thirty-one of Christie's victims in sixty-six novels succumbed to poison. 'Poison has a certain appeal,' she wrote, 'it has not the crudeness of the revolver bullet or the blunt instrument.'

The essence of a Christie mystery is its simplicity. Complications are introduced only to throw the reader off track and make it difficult for him to distinguish between what is essential and what is merely incidental. It is a game in which readers co-operate, or need to, in order to enjoy the book.

As we grow older, certain authors we read—and enjoyed—in our childhood and youth place themselves beyond criticism. In my case, the list includes Christie, P.G. Wodehouse, G.K. Chesterton, R.K. Narayan, Arthur Koestler, Neville Cardus, Martin Gardner and a few others. It is difficult to be objective about such writers who provided hours of joy whether in the reading or in the rereading.

So what if it is seen as being below literature? Do we really need to read a Tolstoyan version of *Murder on the Orient Express*? Or work out if, with the injection of the right amount of characterisation and philosophy, we can convert a Rex Stout mystery into something Flaubert might have written? The detective story is its own philosophy. There is a finality about a murder which gives us a peep into the mind of the killer when he is finally revealed. That should suffice.

Still, the best of them are indistinguishable from literature—wherever the line is drawn between the genres, some writers cross over easily.

Whoever first called Keigo Higashino the 'Japanese Stieg

Larsson', a line displayed on the cover of the English translations of his books, got it wrong. Larsson lacks the pared-down sensitivity, the pregnant everydayness or the philosophical undercurrents of Higashino's works.

'People show their true nature in the act of committing a crime,' says Higashino, a perspective that might be straight from Dostoevsky.

And what crimes! If Christie had exhausted the possibilities of the standard murder mystery, Higashino renders irrelevant such a denouement.

The Loyalty of Suspect X begins with a woman killing her ex-husband; the rest of the book is about fixing alibis and reknitting the tapestry of the crime. In some senses, this is a wheredunit? *Malice* is a whydunit. Here, too, the killer is known within the first couple of chapters. But why would a writer of children's books murder an old school friend and popular writer? There is the whiff of plagiarism about, but the story is far more complex. Recollected in leisure, *Salvation of a Saint* can be seen as a whendunit. Higashino shows us that the whodunit is only one aspect of a mystery, and not always its most important or psychologically interesting one.

To keep the reader riveted after the identity of the killer has been revealed requires a rare self-confidence. It is as if Higashino is saying, let's get these distractions out of the way first and then settle down to a good yarn. There is a sense of crime and redemption, a cast of good bad people and bad good people moving in and out of the narrative.

In *Salvation*, the physicist Manobo Yukawa (called Dr Galileo), the solver of mysteries, tells a rookie detective, 'An imaginary solution is one that, while theoretically possible, is practically impossible. The trick is doable, but the pulling it off isn't.'

Detectives concern themselves with the pulling it off, physicists with the theoretical. The two strains come together in Dr Galileo.

'Some writers aim to move their readers,' wrote Higashino, 'others want to write beautiful sentences. I want readers to be continually surprised by my ideas.' In actual fact, he does all three.

Another personal favourite is Ian Rankin. His detective novels, featuring Inspector Rebus, use the setting of Scotland as a character. How many literary favourites do that? Or have his control, his economy, his ability to combine inevitability and surprise with such charm?

As for detective fiction's big sweep, here's John Updike: 'Nothing in Agatha Christie's brilliantly compact, stylised and efficient mysteries suggests that larger ambitions would have served her; the genre in its lean, classic English form fit her like a cat burglar's thin, black glove.'

Give me animated algebra any time.

A rare bird

The writer Ved Mehta once said of Muriel Spark that 'she went through people like pieces of Kleenex'. Mehta also told me that if ever a writer was neglected and deserved the Nobel Prize, it was Spark.

When she died in 2006, Spark was eighty-eight; this original voice was once regarded, alongside Graham Greene's, as the finest in English.

Spark said that writing novels was 'the easiest thing I had ever done', adding, 'because it came so easily ... I was in some doubt about its value'.

She was thirty-nine when her first novel, *The Comforters*, appeared. The heroine, who is writing her first novel, finds that she and her characters are being written into a first novel by someone else. Spark was a post-modernist before the term was invented.

That debut novel had to be worked on, rewritten, but for the rest, the words flowed 'directly into her pen'. *The Prime of Miss Jean Brodie*, her most successful novel, became a Hollywood hit and earned its star, Maggie Smith, an Oscar.

Spark's reputation as a de-familiariser of the commonplace, or elevator of the ordinary to the unique, was built on twenty-two novels, besides poems and short stories. 'He looked as if he would murder me and he did ...' begins *Portobello Road*, which goes in the opposite direction, rendering the supernatural normal.

Spark's originality and lack of predecessors in style, structure or sensibility unnerved critics at first. Malcolm Bradbury spoke of her 'great gift for being appalling'. As David Lodge said, 'A truly original writer is a very rare bird, whose appearance is apt to disconcert other birds and bird-watchers at first', while confessing that after initially being lukewarm to *The Prime of Miss Jean Brodie*, he later thought it was a masterpiece.

Like Greene, Spark converted to Catholicism. She dealt with the solemn issues of faith and evil and choice with humanism and unexpectedness, all with a brevity of expression that brought the narrative into sharp focus.

Sparkland was part of a literary landscape where the unexpected was the norm, cruelty was merely kindness extended and people who lived common lives reacted with uncommon severity to abrupt changes in fortune.

Spark's insistence that she loved her characters 'like a cat loves a bird' could be a partial explanation for the trials she visited upon them. Wickedness, violence and death were just waiting to be introduced.

Swimming through wet cement

At some point, after early years of reading a book through before taking on another one, I got into the habit of reading many books simultaneously. In every room of the house, there are books lying around half-read, almost-read, unlikely-to-be-read-in-the-near-future. Psychologists might see all sorts of connections between a former chain-smoker continuing as a chain-reader.

When I was young, finishing every book I started made me feel virtuous. I felt I owed it to the author; that was how well-brought-up lads behaved, it kept me free of guilt. I devoured series, all the Blandings novels, for example, or all the Father Brown stories of Chesterton. English teachers ensured some of us read everything by Jane Austen and Mark Twain and Charles Dickens in phases of competitive reading. Some we enjoyed, many we didn't, but it was always a start-to-finish affair. If I read more than one book at a time, the second book was usually for light relief: Agatha Christie, Erle Stanley Gardener, travel books. A glance at my bedside table as I write this shows books by Eduardo Galeano, Tim Parks, Janet Malcolm, James Wood, Amit Chaudhury, Penelope Fitzgerald.

These are books I know I will definitely finish reading. What about the ones lurking around on various shelves, taunting me, troubling me, teasing me? Books I once thought I would enjoy, but now seem unlikely to be read beyond whatever page it is I last read in each of them? Bryan Magee's *Confessions of a Philosopher*, Hillary Clinton's *It Takes a Village*, Gerald Durrell's *The Corfu Trilogy*, David Foster Wallace's *Infinite Jest* and so many more. *Infinite Jest* is particularly galling because I am a fan of Wallace's writings, especially his rambling essays. But a rambling novel of 1,079 pages immediately makes me think of alternatives.

So many books, so little time, surely I should be reading something else? In his foreword to the Wallace book, Dave Eggers asks, 'Will you be actually reading it?' I read the foreword while writing this, and now I suspect I will go back to the book and read it through after all. Or maybe not. These things depend on so many factors: inclination, circumstance, planetary positions, the occultation of Venus and a determination to punish (or reward) oneself. But that list is only the tip of the iceberg.

There are novels by Anthony Powell, James Patterson and Edith Wharton that I don't think I will even attempt. Perhaps I ought to give them away. Hell hath no fury like a reader scorned. You like an author's work, you begin to read him and then a book disappoints you. Joseph Heller is a good example. One great novel, and then, disappointment. 'Have you read Kafka?' is a fair question, an icebreaker of sorts. It is not, however, susceptible to a yes or no answer. By saying 'Yes', I am being truthful, but not entirely so. The more pointed question is: 'Have you finished a Kafka?' Here, if I am to be truthful, the answer has to be 'No'.

For long—at least in my mind—there was something reprehensible about incomplete reading. I imagined it reflected a character flaw; the terrible habit of leaving things undone. Robert Musil might have left *The Man Without Qualities* unfinished, and

Leonardo da Vinci might have picked up a reputation for leaving works incomplete, but that was no consolation. 'Soldiering through,' responded a friend when I asked him how far he had got through the Musil book. So that's what it was. One soldiered through. One put shoulder to the wheel, nose to the grindstone, ear to the ground and somehow read things through. Reading was an act of contortion.

You didn't understand a line of Stephen Hawking's *A Brief History of Time*, yet you soldiered through. It was the attitude that made Hawking's book the greatest unread book of all time. It gave us The Hawking Index—the measure of how far into a book a reader goes before giving up. Popularised by American mathematician Jordan Ellenberg in his blog, it is a fun way of checking out the books left only partially read. By this reckoning, only 25.9 per cent actually read through the bestseller *Fifty Shades of Grey*. *A Brief History of Time* gets 6.6 per cent and Thomas Piketty's *Capital in the Twenty-First Century* gets 2.4 per cent. Great fun, even if statistically unsound, because it takes into account only Kindle readers who highlight pages.

Author Nick Hornby once told the audience at a literary festival that they should give up reading a book when the going got tough. The writer and critic John Sutherland later wrote about his ten 'unfinishable' novels. It is an interesting list and includes my 'favourite' *Infinite Jest*. Reading it, he says, is like 'swimming through setting cement'. The list includes *Moby-Dick* and books by Italo Calvino, Howard Jacobson, Henry James, Vladimir Nabokov, Haruki Murakami.

Sutherland has written about Professor George Levine, who 'announced to the world that he was cancelling all his classes to lock himself away for three months to read *Gravity's Rainbow*. Eight hours a day. No remission. The professor was "giddy" at the end of it, but convinced that "Thomas Pynchon is the most important American novelist now writing".'

I can't see myself doing that. If I am locked up, I am more likely to write a boring book than read one. As one grows older, the choice is between making a full meal of one book or snacking on a number of them with the possibility that over time many will be consumed, till the final full stop. 'A half-finished book is like a half-finished love affair,' says the author David Mitchell. Why would you want a love affair to end by reading a book through?

As I grow older, I fantasise about other reasons for reading books simultaneously and leaving some unfinished. Perhaps it is a way of cheating death. Surely, I will not be called away when I still have half-a-dozen books to finish reading? That would hardly be fair. Unfinished stories, after all, kept the grand vizier's daughter alive in the Arabian Nights. And the one making the decision above is the same, by all accounts.

Sex and the pity

Whenever the discussion veers around to the inability of Indian novelists to write convincingly and unselfconsciously about sex, there is much tsk-tsking. Someone invariably points out that this is a comedown for a people who gave the world the *Kamasutra.* But have you read the *Kamasutra*? It is neither erotic nor pornographic, but a set of clinical instructions of the kind that might be seen in an instructions manual that accompanies a juice-maker ('Take A and push it into B, turn counterclockwise and switch on the apparatus.').

Where the human body is concerned, there are only so many ways you can take A and move it towards B; everything else is window dressing. And some of the greatest writers in the world have given us some of the most pathetic window dressings imaginable.

When sex is written badly, one of two or both reactions is guaranteed. Laughter or pity. I have always found the 'butting of the haunches' passage in D.H. Lawrence's *Lady Chatterley's Lover* hilarious. Lawrence expects us to read this with a straight face: 'The butting of his haunches seemed ridiculous to her and the sort of anxiety of his penis, come to its little evacuating crisis seemed farcical. Yes, this was love, this ridiculous bouncing of the buttocks & wilting of the poor insignificant, moist little penis'.

If he were to write that today—when there is a Bad Sex Award which celebrates 'poorly written, redundant or crude passages of a sexual nature'—he might have won a Lifetime Achievement Award. As it is, Melvyn Bragg, Tom Wolfe, Norman Mailer, Sebastian Faulks have already won the Bad Sex award while Márquez, Rushdie, Updike, Roth have been on the short list. The award, established by UK's *Literary Review*, might be literature's least coveted, but it must help sales in the same way a really terrible movie draws crowds—people are always curious to know just how badly one can do these things.

Manil Suri, who has won the award, is a Mumbai-born professor of mathematics in Maryland, USA. A few years ago, he was a delightful dinner companion of mine who spoke about his two fields with a rare intelligence. It may have been the mathematics that influenced the climactic passage in *The City of Devi* that won the award: 'Surely supernovas explode that instant, somewhere, in some galaxy. The hut vanishes, and with it the sea and the sands—only Karun's body, locked with mine, remains. We streak like superheroes past suns and solar systems, we dive through shoals of quarks and atomic nuclei. In celebration of our breakthrough fourth star, statisticians the world over rejoice.'

While picking up his award, Suri's publisher said, 'Take *the City of Devi* home to bed with you tonight and discover sex scenes that the *Times Literary Supplement* praised as "unfettered, quirky, beautiful, tragic and wildly experimental", written by an author who, according to the *Wall Street Journal*, "captures the insecurity, the curiosity and even the comedy of those vulnerable moments".'

While bad sex writing is easily recognised (and is more

common), nobody has satisfactorily defined what good sex writing is. In her book *The Joy of Writing Sex*, the novelist Elizabeth Benedict begins with four 'organizing principles' that serve as her guide: A good sex scene is not always about good sex, but is about good writing. It should always connect with the larger concerns of the work. The needs, histories and impulses of the characters should drive the scene. And, the relationship the characters have to one another should exert more influence on the writing than any anatomical details.

One would imagine that bad sex writing is the prerogative of novelists, but some years ago, the former British Prime Minister Tony Blair was nominated for a passage in his autobiography!

Here's his purple passage about the night spent with his wife Cherie following the news of the Labour leader John Smith's sudden death. 'That night she cradled me in her arms and soothed me; told me what I needed to be told; strengthened me. On that night of 12 May 1994, I needed that love Cherie gave me, selfishly. I devoured it to give me strength. I was an animal following my instinct.'

When Norman Mailer won posthumously (showing that where the award was concerned, you can hide but you cannot run) for his final novel, what swayed the judges was his description of the male organ as a 'coil of excrement'. It must have been a tough year, for Mailer had to beat this from Ali Smith: 'We were blades, were a knife that could cut through myth, were two knives thrown by a magician ... we were the tail of a fish, were the reek of a cat, were the beak of a bird, were the feather that mastered gravity ...'

Sex as a shopping list!

Sex scenes in most Indian novels are either perfunctory (the author is not particularly keen, he or she has been forced by the publisher to include a scene or two and gives the impression they hope the whole thing gets over quickly) or overwritten.

Here's an example of the latter, from Tarun Tejpal's *The Alchemy of Desire*: 'At times like these we were the work of surrealist masters. Any body part could be joined to any body part. And it would result in a masterpiece. Toe and tongue. Nipple and penis. Finger and the bud. Armpit and mouth. Nose and clitoris. Clavicle and gluteus maximus. Mons veneris and phallus indica. The Last Tango of Labia Minora. Circa 1987. Vasant Kunj. By Salvador Dali. Fraughtsmen: Fizznme.'

Embarrassment—the overriding emotion of the Indian writer—is often disguised by the use of clinical terms.

The explicit, the overstated, the unsubtle are the natural tools of the bad sex writer. For writing on sex to be gripping, it must suggest rather than draw pictures, for the human imagination is powerful, and feels cheated when it is brought down to earth.

So what did the man who did win a Lifetime Achievement award in bad sex writing—John Updike—think?

'Writing my sex scenes physically excites me, as it should,' he once said. Perhaps there is a lesson for Indian writers there. It is not enough to know the Latin names of body parts. Like good sex, good sex writing must involve passion too.

Writing a wrong

There is something almost other-worldly about writers who take a detour from their chosen field of specialisation to write with authority and passion on something just as close to their heart. Umberto Eco, the Italian semiotician and philosopher is, equally, a bestselling novelist. The evolutionary biologist Stephen Jay Gould has written a classy book on baseball. Ramachandra Guha, historian and anthropologist, is one of India's finest cricket writers.

And now here is Stephen Pinker, cognitive scientist, with his 'Thinking person's guide to writing in the 21st century'. This is the subtitle of his wonderful *The Sense of Style*.

Writing is an unnatural act. It follows, therefore, that any attempt to write better or differently is doomed to failure because that is simply a way of piling artificialities upon an original artificiality. And yet, every generation is told that language is 'degenerating very fast' (a line from a complaint in 1785) and that 'kids today are degrading the language and taking civilisation down with it'.

There is no need to panic. Clay tablets of the ancient Sumerians have complaints about the deteriorating writing skills of the young. In fact, 'Don't panic' might well be the subtitle of

Steven Pinker's elegant, calm (and calming) book.

Like Pinker, I love style manuals. You will find them all on my shelves: Strunk and White, Kingsley Amis, Ambrose Bierce, Bill Bryson, Stephen King, George Orwell, William Safire, Jorge Luis Borges, Eric Partridge, Lynne Truss.

Some of the instructions from these books have become clichés: 'Avoid needless words' (Strunk and White), 'Good prose is like a windowpane' (Orwell).

What they have in common is the belief that there is something called 'style', and a good style is worth striving for. Unnatural or not, writing is communicating; practice and an awareness of the craft can lead to a better style and greater clarity.

If we do get worked up about language and its usage, then it must matter, unnatural or not. If you think about it, acting before cameras is unnatural, leg spin bowling is unnatural. Yet, actors and bowlers hone their craft, enjoy it and pass on that enjoyment to viewers. Similarly with writing.

Style, says Pinker, matters for at least three reasons:

'First, it ensures that writers will get their message across, sparing readers from squandering their precious moments on earth deciphering opaque prose. Second, style earns trust. If readers can see that a writer cares about consistency and accuracy in her prose, they will be reassured that the writer cares about those virtues in conduct they cannot see as easily. Style, not least, adds beauty to the world. To a literate reader, a crisp sentence, an arresting metaphor, a witty aside, an elegant turn of phrase are among life's greatest pleasures.'

Pinker belongs to that class of scientists who write (or should that be 'writes'—the book tells us) exceedingly well. It is a class that includes the evolutionary biologist Richard Dawkins and physicist Brian Greene, who speak directly to the reader without the need to sieve their prose through jargon and mumbo-jumbo. One reason we write badly, says Pinker, is owing to the curse of knowledge: the writer's inability to put himself in the reader's shoes or to imagine that the reader might not know all that the writer knows.

The joy of Pinker's book lies in its tone of easy amiability, simple and logical explanations, and its use of examples from popular culture (including comic strips). In this, it is distinct from the books by most of those mentioned above, which tend to be hectoring and suggest that it is 'my way or the highway'. Lynn Truss, for example, says that people who misuse apostrophes 'deserve to be struck by lightning, hacked up on the spot and buried in an unmarked grave'.

Pinker is gentle in his admonitions, almost apologetic in his mild insistences. That is not to say that he believes in *laissez faire*. He is aware that language is constantly evolving, and what was a no-no for one generation is commonplace for the next. Language bibles get outdated quickly.

Pinker's bottom line is clarity. He is happy to use 'like' and 'as' interchangeably and tells us that 'between you and I' is 'not a heinous error'. But he does draw the line at 'disinterested', which is slipping across the divide to mean 'uninterested'. He prefers that we retain its original meaning of 'impartial'.

He argues that many so-called errors that purists get into a tizzy over are fine, and have been in use since at least Shakespeare's time. For example, the split infinitive and the split verb. 'Most mythical usage rules are merely harmless,' says Pinker. He adds mischievously, 'The split verb superstition can even lead to a crisis of governance.'

During the US presidential inauguration in 2009, the Chief Justice baulked at having Barack Obama 'solemnly swear that I will faithfully execute the office of the President of the United States' and made him read instead, 'solemnly swear that I will execute the office of the President of the United States faithfully.' Then they worried whether the transfer of power had been legitimate. They repeated the original oath in private later that day!

So why should we attempt to write better? Here's Orwell again: '[Language] becomes ugly and inaccurate because our thoughts are foolish, but the slovenliness of our language makes it easier for us to have foolish thoughts. That process is reversible ... '

Motivation for writing well comes from the same springs as the motivation for doing anything well. As Pinker puts it, writing is something that can be pleasurably mastered, like cooking or photography. It is fun, to begin with. And profitable as well.

Another joy of reading style manuals is provided by the occasional slips in them. Pinker quotes Strunk and White to show where that book has gone wrong. On page 191 of his own book, Pinker says, 'A subset of these conventions are less widespread and natural ... ' Nice to know that this other-worldly writer is human after all, and occasionally uses a plural instead of the singular.

Religion without atheists

Eduardo Galeano, the Uruguayan writer, is the poet laureate of the beautiful game; his *Soccer in Sun and Shadow* is a fabulous combination of a fan's homage and a social commentator's insights.

'Tell me how you play and I'll tell you who you are. For many years, soccer has been played in different styles, unique expressions of the personality of each people, and the preservation of that diversity seems to me more necessary today than ever before. These are days of obligatory uniformity, in soccer and everything else,' he wrote of what he called 'the only religion without atheists'.

According to legend, every four years, Galeano put up a sign on his door, 'Closed for Soccer', and didn't emerge for a month while he watched the World Cup in his favourite chair and wrote about it.

Galeano died of lung cancer in 2015. He has been compared with Gabriel García Márquez and Pablo Neruda; his *Open Veins of Latin America* is a textbook of postcolonial and capitalist studies.

The best writers on sport combine childlike fandom with professional maturity. Thus, Galeano is able to write of Pele: 'When he executed a free kick, his opponents in the wall wanted to turn around to face the net so as not to miss the goal.' But he can also write of the same player, 'Off the field he never gave a minute of his time and a coin never fell from his pocket.' Poetry in both praise and criticism!

In the section 'The Sin of Losing', he says, 'Football elevates its divinities and exposes them to the vengeance of believers.' Colombian player Andres Escobar, who scored a self-goal in the 1994 World Cup, was shot dead on his return home. That was an extreme case, but as Galeano says, 'We are because we win. If we lose, we no longer exist ... in football, as in everything else, losing is not allowed; failure is the only sin that cannot be redeemed.'

Galeano's profundity is masked in humour, his knowledge in the wry, throwaway line. The French writer Albert Camus was a goalkeeper—a fact recycled every World Cup year. Yet, it took Galeano to explain why. Camus came from a poor home and played in that position because 'your shoes don't wear out as fast'.

It is possible that Galeano's classic on football could outlive his more political books where, too, the epigrams and succinctness startle the reader into recognising an original. A line that gives a flavour of his work and a glimpse into his soul is, 'In 1492, the natives discovered they were Indians; they discovered they lived in America.' He was fond of saying, 'History never really says goodbye; history says "See you later".'

Calling out the cons

'When people learn no tools of judgement and merely follow their hopes,' wrote Stephen Jay Gould, 'the seeds of political manipulation are sown.'

In March 2020, just as the authorities in India were beginning to start to commence to embark on acknowledging the dangers of the coronavirus, the cure was being simultaneously publicised by the usual gang of frauds, cons and shams.

Garlic, homoeopathy, acupuncture were the early favourites. The most dramatic, inevitably, was the claim by the president of the Akhil Bharat Hindu Mahasabha that cow's piss was the answer. This remedy has been touted in recent years for everything from cancer to misplaced library books. A 'Gaumutra' (cow's piss) party was held in order 'to neutralize the effect of coronavirus.'

Professor Edzard Ernst was quick off the block. The German researcher is the world's first professor of complementary medicine, a debunker of non-scientific approaches to alternative medicine. He had just three words to say about the cow piss approach to the coronavirus: 'ineffective and disgusting'.

Ernst and Simon Singh co-authored *Trick or Treat: Alternative*

Medicine on Trial where they looked at the scientific basis for popular treatments like homoeopathy, acupuncture (there is none), beginning their book with a quote from the father of medicine. 'There are in fact two things,' wrote Hippocrates, 'science and opinion; the former begets knowledge, the latter ignorance.'

When US President Donald Trump suggested that injecting disinfectant into the body might be a cure, a leading disinfectant firm was forced to issue a clarification as people began to experiment or check with their doctors if it was prudent.

Why do clever people believe stupid things, asks Ben Goldacre in *Bad Science*. Simon Singh, Ernst, Goldacre are among the well-known debunkers of medical nonsense that seems only too well-entrenched in our world.

Debunkers owe a debt to the man who first popularised the question: Martin Gardner. In 1957, he published *Fads and Fallacies in the Name of Science*, and spent more than a half-century thereafter exposing the frauds and fools, the deliberately convinced and the merely gullible.

Pseudo-science was one of Gardner's varied interests—in 1981, he published *Science: Good, Bad and Bogus*, which carried this wonderful line, 'Cranks, by definition believe their theories, and charlatans do not, but this does not prevent a person from being both ... ' And then, as an aside, giving us a glimpse into the man's range and style: 'It was Elizabeth Browning's passionate faith in spiritualism that almost wrecked an otherwise happy marriage.'

Gardner wrote over seventy books on philosophy, physics, mathematics both recreational and creative, literature, magic, fiction, and the delightful *The Annotated Alice*, which opened up a whole new field in literary criticism.

When he passed away in 2010, aged ninety-five, I felt I had lost a friend. I had known him since I was eleven or twelve, through the pages of *Scientific American* available in the school library. I didn't fully understand the articles in it, but Gardner's *Mathematical Games* (on the last page I think it was) was usually fun and simple.

It also ensured that I could, in a blink, answer questions adults asked about maths and logic. Invariably they simply lifted these from Gardner's columns (later put together in books), and I knew the answers even before the question was asked fully. It earned me a reputation as a whizkid, and who doesn't like that moniker at that age?

'If you look over all my columns (they are collected in fifteen books), you'll find that they steadily become more sophisticated mathematically. That was because I was learning math,' said Gardner. Generations of mathematicians grew up on that column. Gardner had no training in maths but did more to popularise it than anybody else. Recreational mathematics, an apparent oxymoron, slid easily into our lexicon.

The 2014 Fields Medal winner Manjul Bhargava has said Gardner inspired him 'a huge amount' when he was a schoolboy. 'Recreational mathematics often leads to serious research in mathematics as well, and it certainly has for me,' he said in an interview.

Gardner's writings were also a platform for mathematicians to get acquainted with progress in their specialised fields. Benoit Mandelbrot's fractals, Roger Penrose's aperiodic tile and John Horton Conway's Game of Life were popularised there. When he wrote about M.C. Escher, it brought that Dutch artist's works to a larger audience.

In his autobiography *Undiluted Hocus-Pocus*, Gardner wrote:

'One of the pleasures in writing the column was that it introduced me to so many top mathematicians, which of course I was not. Their contributions to my column were far superior to anything I could write, and were a major reason for the column's growing popularity. The secret of its success was a direct result of my ignorance ... I had to struggle to understand what I wrote, and this helped me write in ways that others could understand.'

In his book *Fear No Evil*, the Soviet dissident Natan Sharansky has written about how the only book he was allowed in prison was a collection of Gardner's logical puzzles. A study of these helped Sharansky outwit his interrogators.

When I met Roger Penrose, the physicist and philosopher of science, some of the excitement was caused by the fact that there was now just one degree of separation between Martin Gardner and me. Gardner had been a schoolboy hero, continued to be one as I took fledgling steps towards a career in science, and became an even bigger favourite when I switched to the arts in university.

He taught me, too, the first lesson of journalism—the need to develop a healthy scepticism.

Gardner's answer to the Goldacre question can be found in his explanation for William James's weakness for psychics and mediums. 'James though a brilliant writer was too ignorant of the methods of deception to understand the ease with which intelligent persons can be flim-flammed by crafty charlatans,' he wrote.

James Randi, the magician and debunker of pseudo-science, frequently had to explain to audiences that Gardner actually existed and was not four people, an amalgamation of Isaac Asimov, Arthur C. Clarke, a famous magician and a well-known literary critic. For such was Gardner's range. He also wrote learned essays on G.K. Chesterton, Coleridge, Eliot and Joyce.

Gardner was both hugely amused by the mysteries of the world and hugely amusing about them. For those who ask themselves, What Would Martin Gardner Tweet?, the answer is on @WWMGT. A recent tweet asks: What letter is not in the name of any number from 0 through 99, yet is in the name of every number greater than 99 and less than 1 million?

Among Gardner's fans were the artist Salvador Dali, the poet W.H. Auden and the novelist Vladimir Nabokov. There is a playful reference to Gardner in one of Nabokov's novels. Dali was intrigued by Martin's writings on the four-dimensional cube, a feature of his own painting, *Crucifixion*.

'I wrote a book on relativity mainly to teach myself the theory,' says Gardner in *Undiluted Hocus-Pocus*, and in those twelve words you get a glimpse into the mind of the man. Some of us learn by reading, others by writing. He brought to everything he wrote a wide range of cultural references, literary enthusiasms, and the lucidity that either comes naturally or not at all.

Yet, for all his achievements as a debunker of pseudo-science, sceptic and literary sounding board, Gardner's autobiography is a strange mix of the banal and the brilliant. This is partly because events that seem hilarious when they occur often lose their froth when recalled out of context, and partly because the attempt here is not to tease and explain concepts—as some of Gardner's best writing does—but to explain himself. And that, for an essentially modest man, is clearly a difficult task.

Gardner is at his best when he shines the light away from himself and enlivens discussions on maths and magic, on philosophy and cheating, in the name of science. For the true autobiography, there is *The Whys of a Philosophical Scrivener*, a 'book of essays about what I believe and why'. There is no compulsion here to speak of birth and background, military training and early jobs, just a series on why he is what he is and not something else.

Thus, Gardner tells us why he is not a pragmatist or why he is not an anarchist or, indeed, why he is not an atheist. This last caused a few eyebrows to be raised when the book appeared—a sceptic who believed in god? But Gardner's argument was far more nuanced than that.

This 'essential' Gardner was given a scathing review by George Groth in the *New York Review of Books*: 'He defends a point of view so anachronistic,' said Groth, 'so out of step with current fashion, that were it not for a plethora of contemporary quotations, his book could have been written at the time of Kant.'

The last sentence of the review said: 'George Groth is one of Martin Gardner's pseudonyms.' How can you not admire a writer who takes a hatchet to his own book under an assumed name?

The best introduction to Martin Gardner is his collection of essays, *The Night Is Large*. Here, sieved through Gardner's exquisite mind are essays on symmetry, quantum mechanics, relativity, string theory, Werner Heisenberg, H.G. Wells, cultural relativism, artificial languages, the irrelevance of Conan Doyle, Sigmund Freud, William James, George Perec, fractal music, Newcomb's paradox, free will, Isaiah Berlin, god and much more.

The title is from the Irish playwright Lord Dunsany and captures Gardner's philosophy: *Man is a small thing,/ and the night is very large/ and full of wonders.*

'If there is any aspect of our culture,' he writes in one of the essays, 'that one might suppose lie outside the folkways, grounded in a reality independent of cultural processes, it is mathematics ...'

The Whys of a Philosophical Scrivener tells us what Gardner is not. 'I am a mysterian,' he says in the prologue. Mysterians (a list which includes Penrose and Noam Chomsky) 'share a conviction that no philosopher or scientist living today has the foggiest notion of how consciousness, and its inseparable companion free will, emerge, as they do, from a material brain.'

Gardner begins perhaps the most philosophical of his books with a simple question—'Why does a mirror reverse only the left and right but not up and down?'

From such fun questions do mighty theories grow. Two of the most stupendous scientific events of the twentieth century—the physicists' overthrow of parity and the biologists' discovery of the DNA—are intimately connected with the nature of mirror reversals. 'In the end,' says Gardner, 'our investigations will plunge us straight into some of the deepest, least-charted waters of contemporary science.'

Disinfectant, cow piss and more—Gardner might have found these lacking in challenge. Too easy, too easy.

Wodehouse, the mystery writer

Fans will remember the only Bertie Wooster story narrated by Jeeves. Owing to a concatenation of circumstances, Wooster, contemplating living with his nieces, is tricked into making a speech at a girls' school. Nonplussed, he begins with the usual hems and haws and says, 'I'll tell you something that has often done me a bit of good, and it's a thing not many people know. My old uncle Henry gave me a tip when I first came to London.

'"Never forget, my boy," he said, "that if you stand outside Romano's in the Strand, you can see the clock on the wall of the Law Courts down in Fleet Street. Most people who don't know don't know it's possible, because there are a couple of churches in the middle of the road, and you would think they would be in the way. But you can, and it's worth knowing. You can win a lot of money betting on it with fellows who haven't found it out." And by Jove, he was perfectly right. Many a quid have I—'

At this point, the principal interferes, but that is of no import here. The key is, 'You can win a lot of money betting on it with fellows who haven't found it out.'

For here's another bet you can win—you can bet that P.G. Wodehouse once wrote a murder mystery, and listen to measured discussions on humour writers, performing fleas, Jeeves, Mulliner's Buck-U-Uppo, Cuthbert and the golf stories, Psmith and Madeleine Basset before running out of patience and whipping out *The Education of Detective Oakes.* Or, if you have *The Uncollected Wodehouse* edited by David A. Jason, turn to page 178 and point out *Death at the Excelsior*, which is the name for the same story used in that edition. It was written in 1914 and first appeared in *Pearson's*, a monthly magazine.

It is a classic mystery of the 'locked room' variety—the victim is found in a locked room on the second floor, there is an open window with a bar across it that nobody could have squeezed through and there are the classic red herrings. Detective Oakes is young, full of himself and cocksure; he has theories, and he has 'proved' them.

His boss, Paul Snyder, who runs the Detective Agency in New Oxford Street, is an indulgent man despite being patronised by the junior. The denouement is interesting, considering what Wodehouse thought of mystery stories and the role of women in them, for it is a woman, the owner of the boarding house, who solves the case.

And what did Wodehouse think of murder mysteries and their characters?

'For though beautiful, with large grey eyes and hair the colour of ripe corn,' wrote Wodehouse, a great fan of mysteries, 'the heroine is almost never an intelligent girl ... she may know perfectly well that the blackbird gang is after her to secure the papers. The police may have warned her on no account to stir outside the house. But when a messenger calls at half-past-two in the morning with an unsigned note that says, "Come at once" she just reaches for her hat and goes.'

Then there is the 'heavy' or villain, who, when he was a boy was told by his parents he was clever, and 'it has absolutely spoiled him for effective work.'

And finally, the clincher. 'If I were writing a mystery story, I would boldly go out for the big sensation. I would not have the crime committed by anybody in the book at all.'

Wodehouse proceeds to tells us, in a dozen short paragraphs, how he would do this. He would unmask the crooks thus: 'The fiends were too cunning to let themselves get beyond the title page. The murderers were Messrs. Hodder and Stoughton.'

Hodder and Stoughton being, of course, the publishers of the novel!

Still, Wodehouse resisted all these temptations and wrote a straightforward murder mystery which could stand beside anything Poe or Chesterton wrote without looking out of place.

Wodehouse was a great fan of the Sherlock Holmes stories, and many of his early novels and stories had Holmesian references. Later, he became a friend of Arthur Conan Doyle and a teammate at The Authors Cricket Club. It may have been Psmith who first used the expression, 'Elementary, my dear Watson,' although I am yet to find an authority to endorse that view. Here he is in *Psmith Journalist*: 'Sherlock Holmes was right. You may remember that he advised Doctor Watson never to take the first cab, or the second. He should have gone further, and urged him not to take cabs at all. Walking is far healthier.'

This is the tone Wodehouse uses in his early affectionate parodies of the Sherlock Holmes stories (about a detective named Burdock Rose and his sidekick, Dr Wotsing). In the *Adventure of the Split Infinitive*, for instance.

The connection between humour and mystery (certainly of the Wodehouse type) is—technically—an obvious one. Both use cover-ups, misdirection, poor communication, misunderstandings, blackmail, audio or visual misinterpretations to achieve their ends. Wodehouse was a master at all of the above, whether it is the stealing of the cow creamer, Egyptian scarabs or sundry hearts.

The Wodehouse expert Richard Usborne has suggested the possibility that the Jeeves character might have been inspired by fictional butlers in Doyle's works—Ambrose, valet to Sir Charles Tregellis in *Rodney Stone*, and Austin, Professor Challenger's servant in *The Poison Belt*. The name, of course, came from the Warwickshire cricketer, medium pacer Percy Jeeves.

Wodehouse was also a fan of Agatha Christie, who was a great fan of his work too. Her Poirot novel *Hallowe'en Party* is dedicated 'to P.G. Wodehouse—whose books and stories have brightened my life for many years. Also, to show my pleasure in his having been kind enough to tell me he enjoyed my books.'

A month before he died, Wodehouse received a letter from Christie which ended, 'Goodbye for now and thanks for all the laughs.'

A gentle truth-teller

In a study of George Orwell, his friend George Woodcock wrote, 'What made Orwell such an excellent journalist and often gave his books a touch of that reality that goes beyond mere verisimilitude was his intense interest in the concrete aspects of living, in "the surface of life", as he would say.'

It is a description that applies equally to Mike Marqusee, author, activist, poet, whose philosophy of humanism and support for the underdog was expressed through books as wide-ranging as studies of Muhammad Ali and Bob Dylan, cricket from the colonies to the corporates, Zionism, Neil Kinnock and the Labour party, William Blake, and finally, on living through cancer, to which he succumbed aged only sixty-one.

Marqusee borrowed from Orwell the title of his classic on the 1996 cricket World Cup in the subcontinent, *War Minus the Shooting*, one of his two contributions to the list of top cricket books. The other is *Anyone But England*. 'Only an outsider who has come to the game late in life could articulate its peculiarities so well,' wrote a reviewer. Marqusee, born in New York, came to England at eighteen, and reopened debates in many areas thanks to his unique worldview as he sieved the ordinary, the accepted, the taken-for-granted through his own experience and gave us new ways of looking at them.

Many saw Marqusee as the spiritual successor to C.L.R. James, the Trinidadian Marxist who wrote *Beyond a Boundary*, and there is an argument there. But I always thought of Marqusee as a latter-day Orwell, passionate and generous as well as objective and compassionate. Orwell had to deal with tuberculosis and Marqusee with cancer, both leading to premature death, Orwell's at forty-six.

Marqusee was a truth-teller and a disturber of the smug and unthinking. And even, as he demonstrated early in life, a questioner of other radicals' long-held beliefs. He described himself as a 'deracinated Jew', and in *If I Am Not For Myself: Journey of an anti-Zionist Jew*, wrote about his father at the dinner table calling him a 'self-hating Jew'. It was 1967 and Marqusee was fourteen.

Both his parents had been active in the US civil rights and anti-war movements. Jews were expected to celebrate Israel's success in the Six-Day War, exult in the spoils of victory, the many square miles of land. Marqusee, who felt it was 'wrong for one country to take over another by military force' offered the following analogy: 'If the US was wrong in Vietnam—and that was a given around our dinner table—then Israel was wrong in taking over all that Arab land.'

That was when Marqusee's father made his remark and the boy 'burning from head to toe, threw down knife and fork and left the table in a huff.' In adult life, Marqusee was able to rationalise: 'If I am not for myself, then the Zionists will claim to be for me, will usurp my voice and my Jewishness.' Jews can be anti-Zionists, just as Hindus can be anti-Hindutva, a connection Marqusee himself makes in a later chapter.

'In many respects,' he says, 'Hindutva and Zionism are natural bedfellows. Both depict the entities they claim to represent as simultaneously national and religious, territorial and transcendent. Both claim to be the sole authentic spokespersons for these entities (Hindu and Jew). Both share an ambivalent historic relationship with British colonialism. Both appeal to an affluent diaspora. And most important at the moment, both share a designated enemy ("Muslim terrorism").'

When he turned sixty, I sent him a message. 'Yes, I made it to 60,' he wrote back, 'which was a little miracle, as when I was diagnosed (with multiple myeloma at fifty-three), I was given 3 or 4 years to live. Things are up and down, but I'm still here, still writing, still watching cricket (mainly on TV these days).'

A few months later, we sat in his living room in North London and talked cricket; he was working out a piece in his mind: 'Why cricket?' It was the last essay he wrote; it was for *Wisden India Almanack*, which I was editing.

'Cricket,' he wrote, 'offers all the pleasures of sport in general, plus a highly distinctive appeal of its own, to which many elements contribute. One of the chief of these is the way it treats time and space ... it keeps its own archaic kind of time ... cricket is a game with a determined centre and an indeterminate periphery ...'

That morning Marqusee made the coffee—his companion and fellow traveller Liz Davies had to leave for a meeting—and we also spoke of Chola bronzes, the Carnatic music season in Chennai and his forthcoming book on William Blake. He signed for me a copy of his poetry collection, *Street Music*. 'In friendship,' he wrote, adding, 'See page 80.'

On page eighty was this wonderful paean to an Opening Pair:

One of us drops anchor
While the other gets off to a flyer.
It's not because one is more impetuous
Or cautious than the other.
The assault, like the defence, is calculated.
We play the same percentages
to different rhythms, following
our own sequence
of stressed and unstressed beats,
each of us fashioning
our own departure from the norm.
After the crescendo, the rest,
after the rest, the crescendo.
One of us foil for the other, as it should be.
Personality will out.
We perform in our styles
Because that is our function.
We never get in each other's way.
We perform who we are
Because that is what the situation demands—
But at a pinch we can swap roles,
One coming out of the shadow of the other.'

At the door, we shook hands in a formal goodbye, and then, as if we realised something, we hugged. We performed who we were because that was what the situation demanded.

Close and out of reach

Indian writing in English has been hijacked by the semi-literate, by novels that merely aspire to chicklit, by writing that is over-explained, single-layered and under-done. Yet—and this says something about the readers—the practitioners of such writing are much feted. They are also sought out for their opinions on subjects beyond their ken, presumably on the assumption that if you are capable of writing a bad novel you must be an authority on nuclear disarmament or economic theory.

Into this milieu has arrived a novel that restores faith in the English novel as an Indian convention too. The author, Poile Sengupta, is well known as a playwright, poet and children's author. *Inga* is her first adult novel.

Set in the 1960s, *Inga* is the story of two female relatives—Inga and Rapa—and how they deal with their oppressive lives. This, against the background of some of the most casually vicious relatives in contemporary literature—from aunts and grand-aunts to parents and uncles and siblings.

Rapa lives in Delhi, is educated, immerses herself in English literature, keeps a journal, writes stories. Inga, who stayed behind, is a brilliantly carved out character, central as well as tangential to the story, which is an incredible achievement.

Rapa's story is about Inga, but the reverse is not necessarily true. The narrative uses three devices: Rapa's journal, Inga's letters, and the stories Rapa writes from the age of twelve. There are, too, the notes by Rapa's husband which bookend the novel.

Inga is a common Scandinavian name, but here it is possibly a Tamil abbreviation of a longer word, thangachchi (younger sister), as articulated by a child. The word that comes to mind when discussing the novel is another Scandinavian one: smorgasbord.

Like some of the best works of fiction, Inga is difficult to classify. Family drama. Social commentary. Mystery. Historical. Love story. Forbidden love. Thriller. Feminist. Comic. Coming-of-Age. Revenge saga. Redemption tale. All fit.

Sengupta, the playwright, handles dialogue deftly; in prose she is mistress of what is left unsaid. The genius of the unwritten is that it is both poetic and shows a healthy respect for the reader's intelligence. Writers in control of their craft don't have to illuminate the obvious with the light of their overwrought clichés.

There is unspoken, misunderstood, unrequited love, unsatisfactory marriages and ironies which depend for their effect on the nearly said. The family stories reveal both character and the author's passion for language, and control over English, Tamil and Malayalam.

Blood flows—in more ways than one—betrayals abound, yet the tone is non-judgemental. A weapon against suffering is humour. Inga has the comic energy of Naipaul's *A House for Mr Biswas*, for even while ridiculing the actions of a character, the author shows deep sympathy for and understanding of how things are and why they cannot be otherwise.

'Did I like being there?' Rapa asks at one point, of her

extended family. 'I could have rebelled against its authoritative temper, but strangely I didn't. Why didn't I? When Inga was with me, I did not ask myself that question. When she wasn't nothing else mattered.'

Like Don Quixote, who raises the ordinary to the level of the heroic, Rapa's father, an otherwise pragmatic man, confuses the handicapped with the divine when a deformed child is born in the house. It is both typical and out of character, and one of the novel's strengths is this ability to reconcile apparently contradictory qualities. The comedy is both situational and in the descriptions. ('She had the voice of a woman who triumphed at bargaining.')

It is the comedy of forgiveness; but laughter, we realise, is a catalyst for both clemency and cruelty. There is much violence too here, great viciousness and emotional churning. Much of it is offstage (the playwright's influence again, perhaps), and all the more powerful for that.

The growth of the family, the gradual revelation of long-kept secrets, the tantalising clutch of what-might-have-beens universalises an individual experience. Tolstoy's Anna Karenina Principle (he didn't call it that, of course) applies: 'All happy families are alike; each unhappy family is unhappy in its own way.'

Inga is a page-turner; again, the reverse is also true. You often linger over a page just to absorb the language, and the passion for the written word. One of Poile's plays is entitled *Keats Was a Tuber*, a commentary on the mechanical way lessons are taught in our schools. Students memorise 'Keats was a tuberculosis patient' by breaking the sentence up into two meaningless halves. Clearly, this is a writer who loves words and is pained by faulty usage.

Rapa writes her stories in various styles: from Enid Blyton and

Jane Austen to Oliver Goldsmith, Conan Doyle, Thomas Hardy, Christina Rosetti. Literary styles mark the ageing of a book-loving character subtly but memorably.

Inga fascinates because she seems to be just out of reach. Like a Scott Fitzgerald heroine, she is there, but not there. Her letters to Rapa ground her in reality, but you are never certain that you too are not being pulled into the conspiracy. For the family, to quote Penelope Fitzgerald's description of the Waughs, 'formed a conspiracy against the outside world, not feeling the necessity to explain itself'.

In an essay on Fitzgerald, the critic James Wood wrote, 'Her fictions sit on the page with the well-rubbed assurance of fact, as if their details were calmly agreed upon, and long established. And though you might expect work of irritating certitude, Fitzgerald's confidence in her material is oddly disarming; she seems somehow to take life as it comes, as if we were always entering her novels in the middle of how things just are.'

It is a wonderful description that fits Poile Sengupta equally well. The writers have one other thing in common (apart from their gender): both wrote their first novels after the age of sixty.

Perhaps that explains the maturity, the depth and the complete absence of any gimmickry.

India's bookman

At a bookstore, I am first drawn to the 'Books on Books' shelves. This is a broad church comprising volumes on reading, collecting, rare editions, bibliomania.

Alberto Manguel's *A History of Reading* rubs shoulders with Rick Gekoski's *Nabokov's Butterfly*, John Carter's *ABC for Book Collectors* and essays by Michael Dirda, Tim Parks, Italo Calvino, Anne Fadiman. There is fiction too: A.S. Byatt, Jasper Fforde, Carlos Zafon, Umberto Eco ...

The Book Hunters of Katpadi by Pradeep Sebastian, India's most refined bibliophile, fits smoothly into that special shelf. As does *The Groaning Shelf* by the same author.

'The pleasures of bibliophily for me,' Sebastian once wrote, 'lie in fully embracing the book as material object; its bibliographical aspects—binding, edition, condition, rarity, and typography matter to me as much as their literary content.' It is a pleasure he communicates effortlessly.

Emerson said a man is known by the books he reads. Equally, I think, a man is known by the books he writes. One informs the other, which is why *The Book Hunters* is a delightful romp through a whole literary subgenre.

From his columns, we know that Sebastian is obsessed with

Salinger, collects first editions, has visited more bookstores physically and virtually than most and understands the esoteric world of antiquarian books. He is an authority on books about books.

By channeling all that knowledge and passion into his first novel, Sebastian has given us a double treat: the fictional story of a manuscript coveted by collectors (which may or may not have been authored by the explorer Sir Richard Burton) as well as factual stories of the book world. There is action, suspense, adventure.

The antiquarian world can be fun too, as Neela and Kayal, the women who run the fictional bookstore set in Chennai, suggest.

Sebastian also puts into the mouths and actions of his characters enough material on the antiquarian trade, methods of authentication, printing, auctions and stories of intrigue and thievery to keep the reader interested both in the business of books and in the mystery itself.

Not all collectors are as crazy as Nallathampi Whitehead and Arcot Templar, the major bidders for the Burton manuscript. Some are crazier! In *A Gentle Madness*, Nicholas Basbanes tells us about the Spanish monk Don Vincente, who, in the 1830s, committed eight murders in order to grab copies of rare books owned by his victims.

Perhaps India's first bibliomystery will inspire the creation of India's first proper antiquarian—as opposed to the second-hand—bookstore. Sebastian has shown, with empathy and humour, how it can be done. Perhaps he ought to do it himself! Build it and they will come.

In *A History of Reading*, Alberto Manguel makes the point that reading precedes writing. Yet, although whole libraries have been written about writing, there is not enough on reading, the more common activity.

Perhaps this is because it is possible to be coldly objective, even clinical about writing, with nods in the direction of deconstruction and semiotics and a bagful of literary theories. But any readable book on reading must necessarily be personal and brimming with passion. Few writers read that well and even fewer readers write that well.

There are scholarly, academic books on reading which are worthy efforts that, for the average reader, barely balance on the verge of meaning. These tend to be dry and humourless. Written for (and read by) other academics, such books, like how-to manuals on sex, ignore the essential feature of the activity—its sheer joy.

'Reading or making love,' writes Manguel, 'we should be able to lose ourselves in the other, into whom we are transformed: reader into writer into reader, lover into lover into lover.' As with all passions, the relationship between the reader and the book is, as the critic George Steiner says, 'intimate, possessive and very private. Every consummation has its perils and specific register of excitement.'

It takes a special type of bibliophile to understand this; the popular writer who signposts the path to excitement is worth a thousand scholars who squeeze the juice out of an experience. Such a one is Sebastian, who has been writing about books for years and is easily our most cultured writer on the subject. His essays, brought together in *The Groaning Shelf*, are not just about reading, though.

He recalls the time the late T.G. Vaidyanathan, Bengaluru's legendary English teacher and columnist, bought a book for its physical beauty alone. He had no intention of reading it; he merely caressed it and put it back on the shelf. On another occasion, he taped the edges of a book he was smitten by so it would never be opened.

Sebastian discusses Diderot, C.S. Lewis, Amar Chitra Katha, Shakespeare & Company and other bookshops, Umberto Eco, antiquarian books, the first editions of J.D. Salinger's novels, Nabokov, book thieves, collectors and much more with easy familiarity.

Steiner's description in another context aptly sums up Sebastian, who 'celebrates the diversities of desire—tempestuous, hidden, intermittent, lapsed—which relate us to a literary text.'

The Groaning Shelf is not a paean to the 'good old days' before television and the internet replaced books; it is not a cry for help from a book lover who sees readership dwindling and takes it upon himself to right the balance.

There is no place for clichés here; nothing judgemental or admonitory. This is about one man's obsession with, and involvement in, the culture and tradition of bibliography. That it carries the reader along is a strength, but the effect, powerful though it may be, is, in a larger sense, purely incidental.

It is about, as the author says, 'the inner life of one reader: from re-reader to lapsed reader to (when all you can read are books about books) meta-reader.' This is not an inevitable path followed by bibliophiles, of course, but merely a portion of Sebastian's journey—exciting, educative, pleasurable, but incomplete.

The strength of *The Groaning Shelf* lies in its attraction not just for the bibliophile, but the non-reader whose library comprises a couple of Readers Digest condensed books, four DC comics and the *Complete Works of Oscar Wilde* presented by a favourite uncle in the distant past.

There is a double treat in store for them. The unalloyed joy of Sebastian's romance with books in the short term, and a long-term association with the books and the life in books he discusses.

'I often envy non-readers for all the wonderful books that they have never read,' says Sebastian. 'Imagine the joy of encountering these great works for the first time. A literary fantasy of mine has been to turn amnesiac for a year and read all my favourite books as though for the very first time.'

Getting Pico to write on cricket

We met at the Jaipur Literature Festival at a party thrown by a publisher on the terrace of a ramshackle building which you reached through a narrow, winding, never-ending staircase. This, presumably, for the writers from abroad searching for the authentic India experience.

It was cold, especially when the wind blew in the wrong direction, but he provided the warmth. For years I had been a fan of Siddharth Pico Raghavan Iyer, and when I told him that, he bowed with grace as if he were hearing this for the first time.

I had just read *The Man Within My Head*, and if I didn't have an agenda in mind, our conversation would have touched upon the Dalai Lama, Leonard Cohen, Graham Greene and the places Pico had visited and written about so wonderfully.

But those days, all meetings, even with one's heroes—in fact, especially with one's heroes—were agenda-driven. I was the editor of *Wisden India Almanack*, the 'Bible' of cricket, and hoping to attract my favourite writers to contribute. This was a perk of the job, to be able to read my favourite authors writing about my favourite game!

Pico said he might write if he could think of something and if he had the time. I was happy to wait. And we left it at that. I recalled the response by Graham Greene to Pico's letter asking for an interview for *Time* magazine. If any letter could make him succumb, Greene had replied 'in just the courteous, elegant tones I'd expected,' Pico tells us in *The Man Within My Head*, 'it would be mine'. But 'time was short and he had much to do'.

I began bugging him soon enough. When I wrote saying he had made a promise to write, he gently reminded me it wasn't so. 'I seem to remember saying something like, "If anyone could ever persuade me to write about cricket, it would be you." No one could be more fun, more persuasive and more engaging. I so hugely enjoyed our meeting, and yours was among the most literate and thoughtful and charming company I found in the city ...'

It was a promising start, but it was a 'No'. Gentle, kind, charming, but a 'No', nevertheless. 'We may have to wait for a more propitious moment—or for a six from the Ashes series to hit me on the head so as to ensure a memorable article. But once that happens, it would be a great honour to contribute to the cricketer's Bible, especially in the country where cricket is more of a religion than anywhere else, in some future year.'

Editors get rejection letters from writers too, but they don't get to their posts by giving up at the first sign of rejection, however charming. I apologised for my unsubtle attempt at railroading, and suggested that something he had said himself about 'boyhood reminiscences' (Pico had written he had nothing other than boyhood reminiscences) would fit the bill perfectly.

Four days later came the most exciting letter I received in the job. 'You're simply too irresistible,' wrote Pico. 'I think I might be able to offer a 1500-word reminiscence of the cricket I knew as a boy, at school, played with dice, or around me in the Oxford Parks, if that might be something you could use.'

Had Pico written to say he would have rearranged the names in a telephone book and sent it under his name, I would have accepted. My reply probably had more 'Yes'-es in it than Molly Bloom's in *Ulysses*.

Pico's next letter, about a fortnight later said, 'Inspiration struck quite quickly after our exchange. I'm sure it will be many, many years (if ever) before anyone displaces you as the champion of gracious, kind and eloquent solicitations.

'And if you see anything that looks wrong to you here—let alone any recidivist American spellings—please feel free to correct. Somehow, all these years, I've remembered Clive Lloyd effortlessly stroking sixes in the Oxford Parks when I was a boy. But when I accessed just now the West Indies tour of England in 1969—which must be what I remember—I find Michael Carew was the star and Lloyd wasn't even in the team that day.

'The tricks that memory (or else cricket lore) plays!

'I'm so glad you didn't give up on me, and this would certainly be a feather in my cap, to be a cricket writer for the first (and surely last) time in my life.'

Pico began his essay thus: 'The great open space between the trees is a perfect elegance of green and white. You can smell the fresh-cut grass. The pavilion in one corner, now empty, speaks for a near-vanished world of clapping and tea. The chairs are arranged in a ceremonial circle, as if the conducting of a group discussion in which no one can hear anyone, so everybody speaks very softly. If you are lucky, this is one of the three days the British government allows every year for sunshine.'

Pico describes his day in the sun watching the touring West Indies team taking on Combined Universities at the Parks, Oxford. Cricket, he wrote, was the best way we could turn life into something sweet.

'I know 1500 words about cricket, and now I have given them all to you,' he wrote to me. Clearly this is not true. For, like so many of us, he had played 'dot cricket' as a boy, 'rolling the dice again and again to complete whole Test matches between our favourite teams (a 5 meant you were out, as I unreliably recall).'

And he had been, briefly, scorer at his school's second XI ('the almost-best position for a non-athletic nerd other than captain of the Chess Club'). He read *Wisden*, 'the scripture we consulted when we were meant to be reading the Gospels'. There was even a memorable catch he once took accidentally on the boundary line where he had been sent to field by 'someone wise enough to try to place me as far as possible from the ball, or any chance of action.'

There's more than 1500 words on cricket in that superbly organised mind. Pico's piece, titled 'A Midsummer's Daydreams' told us just what cricket writing has lost in moving away from the charm and gentle cadences of the game itself—apart from suggesting what cricket lost in not having Pico write about it more often.

A crash course

Clive James is finally dead. He was on death row for nearly a decade—with terminal leukaemia and emphysema—and towards the end preferred the company of books. There was a website where you could check if James was still alive. Morbid, but cheerful in a way.

James was not just reading, he was writing too. Essays, poetry, criticism. The *New Yorker* once called him 'a brilliant bunch of guys' for being a TV critic, novelist, autobiographer, rock lyricist and documentary maker.

In the first book of his I read—was it *Unreliable Memoirs*?—he began by quoting the poet Rilke, and in the next sentence said, 'In many respects, Rilke was a prick.' Which schoolboy could resist such a dramatic preamble or fail to be charmed by that combination of erudition and coarseness? It was, too, a fine introduction to both James and Rilke.

I discovered James was an Aussie living in England; it gave his literary judgements an edge missing from polite English writers. 'I have never been convinced,' wrote James, 'that a lust for anonymity is a better guarantee of seeing the world as it is.'

James will live on in his essays, his autobiographies and *Cultural Amnesia: Notes in the Margin of My Time,* a cultural history of the twentieth century told through essays on its main actors. 'A crash course in civilization,' J.M. Coetzee called it.

James was a gatherer and sorter-out of existing ideas rather than an originator of them. He served youngsters well as a ride through the bookish world. Writers who attract you in the early years are not necessarily the venerated ones but those who write provocatively, with passion and with manifest enjoyment, like James.

In 2014, he wrote a poem beginning, 'Your death, near now, is of an easy sort'. It is about a Japanese maple his daughter had planted in his garden and about wondering whether he would live to see the leaves flame red. 'I am in the slightly embarrassing position where I write poems saying I am about to die, and I don't,' he told an interviewer later.

There is something heroic about a man waiting to die while distilling a lifetime's experience into his writing. As he says, 'The childish urge to understand everything doesn't necessarily fade when the time approaches for you to do the most adult thing of all: vanish.'

In a London bookstore once, I came upon two copies of the same edition of one of his books. One was signed by him. Yet—and James would have loved the irony—the unsigned copy was the more expensive!

Time lost and regained

In the seventh and last book of *Remembrance of Things Past*, Proust comments casually that one forgets the duel one nearly fought but remembers the yellow gaiters one's opponent wore as a child in the Champs-Elysees. *Remembrance* is a paean to memory, to everydayness, to loss of innocence, the vanity of human endeavour and more. Or to growth, maturity and cessation, if you will.

Even those who haven't read the book know of one scene in it: the flood of memory released by tasting a madeleine dipped in tea. Proust insisted that only involuntary memory is significant in art. Which probably means, if you think about it, that method acting isn't art—but that's not an area we need to get into.

For two decades, the asthmatic Proust stayed in his cork-lined room, going out but rarely, and wrote his only novel in some 1.5 million words. It may be one of the great works of literature, but it's not greatly read. Marcel's brother, a doctor, once commented, 'The sad thing is that people have to be very ill or have broken a leg in order to read the book.'

Polish writer and painter Josef Czapski qualified on both counts; he had a broken heart, and an attack of typhoid that enabled him to read the novel in its entirety. He was a Bohemian who, while living in Paris knew Gertrude Stein and Picasso, had an affair with Vladimir Nabokov's younger brother Sergey, and possibly with the poet Anna Akhmatova too—he appears in one of her poems.

Czapski first came to *Remembrance* a year after Proust's death and was initially put off by what he called an excess of style. He went back to it after his failed romance, and this time recognised that it was a masterpiece. He was one of the first to write a review of the collected volumes. Soon, as his circle in the Parisian art and literary world expanded, he came to know many of Proust's friends.

When Germany invaded Poland in 1939, Czapski was captured and handed over to the Soviets, who executed over 20,000 Polish officers. Czapski was among the 395 who survived (he died aged ninety-six, having lived through nearly the entire twentieth century). In prison, relying on nothing more than memory (there were no books available), he gave a series of lectures on Proust. Later, two inmates helped him transcribe these into a book.

To remember in intimate detail the quintessential book of remembering is a stunning effort. You can't get more meta-literary than that.

Czapski could recall whole passages and relate the novel to the prisoners' current situation. 'After a certain length of time,' he wrote, 'facts and details emerge on the surface of our consciousness which we had not the slightest idea were filed away somewhere in our brains.

'These memories rising from the subconscious are fuller, more intimately, more personally tied one to the other. I came to understand why the importance and the creativity of Proust's involuntary memory are so often emphasised. I observed how distance—distance from books, newspapers and millions of intellectual impressions of normal life—stimulates the memory.

'Far away from anything that could recall Proust's world, my memories of him, at the beginning so tenuous, started growing stronger and suddenly with even more power and clarity, completely independent of my will.'

Czapski's lectures on Proust in the prison camp have been brought together in *Lost Time,* translated by the American Eric Karpeles, a biographer of Czapski and like his subject, a painter and writer.

It is an extraordinary effort for the context, the substance and the way Czapski draws lessons, personal and universal, from the master book on memory, nostalgia and death. It is an intimate evaluation that brings alive both the novel and its author.

Imagine the scene: 'Freezing, exhausted from overwork, on the brink of starvation, the men hardly thought of themselves as survivors (they were known as the former officers of the former Polish army). They struggled to keep their spirits alive and their morale strong. The men devised the plan for talks in the evening to be given by speakers on subjects close to their heart.'

There were no books to refer to; memory was all.

'Every great book is profoundly tied to the very matter of the life of the author,' begins the lectures, which are contained in some ninety pages. Czapski kept 'pulling passages out of the air,' says the translator Eric Karpeles.

Surrounded by death, the prisoners heard of Proust's relationship with it. He had been born sickly and was ill through most of his life. As he lived in its shadow, death had become, said Czapski, a matter of indifference to him. Death is a subtext to the lectures, as indeed it was to the existence of the listeners.

There is, too, the cry for making the most of the time available, whether waiting to find out if a death sentence is coming your way, or in the comfort of your life in general. Even though our lives wander, wrote Proust in the final volume, our memories remain in one place.

Czapski brought to his talks a casual, chatty tone that only someone truly obsessed can. He could quote from memory rather like Proust himself could quote Balzac. Great writers are brought alive by great interpreters, even if in this case, that was merely a by-product. The prospect of death focusses the mind, and memory is a safe haven: Proust's implied theory is confirmed afresh by Czapski.

'There is some Proust in me,' wrote Czapski, 'and through Proust, bit by bit, I become aware of my own possibilities.'

Having read the book in French, Czapski recalled it in French and lectured in that language.

The effort of remembering also provides necessary oblivion, however brief and however misplaced, in times of extreme stress. Arthur Koestler has written about his time in a Spanish prison when he felt cheered while recalling Euclid's proof that the number of primes is infinite.

In *Survival in Auschwitz,* Primo Levi writes about trying to remember the Canto of *Ulysses*. 'Who knows how or why it comes into my mind?' he asks. He felt 'as if I was also hearing it for the first time: like the blast of a trumpet, like the voice of God. For a moment I forget who I am and where I am.'

The act of remembering brings to Levi the gift of forgetting.

Czapski recalls a less-celebrated moment in Proust's book in his lecture. 'At the moment he passes under the archway in the courtyard, he must step aside to let an automobile pass; his feet land on two paving stones that are uneven. At this most unexpected moment, the author recalls having felt the same sensation years ago in Venice, and all at once he has a clear and electrifying vision of Venice and all that he saw and experienced there. He has the sudden conviction of a book existing within him, with all its details, only waiting to be realized ...'

Marcel Proust wrote that 'remembrance of things past is not necessarily the remembrance of things as they were.'

What is fascinating also is the plan that Czapski drew for his lectures, a hybrid of writing and drawing, called 'a cosmology of Proust' by Karpeles. It is a work of art in itself. Czapski made some mistakes too—minor ones, but interesting ones of both omission and commission—that tell us as much about the man and the process of tapping into memory. The process of remembering may corrupt the product of memory, and while Proust has been studied by neuroscientists for this, Czapski, whose effort probably took greater skill, has been spared the unweaving of the rainbow.

Mind, your language

As I walked into the auditorium, there was a buzz around me. The ego quickly finds a reason for such behaviour: I was hugely popular. And as if to confirm this, someone who looked formal and official came up to me and said, 'Welcome, doctor, it's an honour to have you with us.' Perhaps it was a local custom, this manner of addressing someone respectfully as 'Doctor'.

And then realisation dawned. I was being mistaken for someone else.

The official-looking person thought I was the man all of us had come to hear speak, Dr Vilayanur Ramachandran. My fifteen seconds of fame lasted exactly that long. Apologies made, embarrassed laughter ensued and I was asked if I could introduce Dr Ramachandran to the audience when he arrived. My qualification being, I suppose, that I was so nearly him that day!

When Dr Ramachandran finally wins the Nobel, I told the bemused audience, you will recall today, and exactly where you were sitting. Some of you might even remember the man who was mistaken for him.

That first meeting with Dr Ramachandran led to others. I

went for other speeches, we sometimes had a meal together in Chennai. The man who was among the few to have revolutionised his field, once described by Richard Dawkins as 'a latter-day Marco Polo, journeying the Silk Road of science to strange and exotic Cathays of the mind,' remains a fun-loving, mischievous boy with a booming laugh and a wicked sense of humour.

The British scientist J.B.S. Haldane once wrote that the world shall perish not for lack of wonders, but for lack of wonder. Ramachandran's sense of wonder is not just his greatest quality, it is also responsible for some of the most startling discoveries in the neurosciences.

Around the time we sat down for a formal interview in Chennai, god had been much in the news. Stephen Hawking had said god might play dice after all, regardless of what Einstein thought. And, apparently, Ramachandran had isolated the 'god module'—the portion of the brain that deals with religion and god. But that was an oversimplification. 'Unfortunately, that aspect of my work has received more publicity than anything else,' he said.

We are at his Mylapore residence in Chennai, and Dr Ramachandran's rust-coloured T-shirt and unkempt hair suggest he is a mischievous undergraduate rather than one of the foremost authorities on the human brain in the world. The ready smile reaches his eyes with a regularity that puts his guest at rest. He has just turned fifty, and speaks with an energy and verve that might have caused comment in someone half his age.

Ramachandran is quick to point out that he is not reducing god to mere neurophysiology. Certain kinds of epilepsy are associated with a heightened sense of religiosity. After an episode, patients may speak of having had a 'religious experience'. Ramachandran asks why, in *Phantoms in the Brain*. 'I can think of four possibilities,' he says. 'One is that god really does visit these people.' The scientist's effort to bring in god through the backdoor grabbed media attention, but Ramachandran laughs it off. The director of the Center for Brain and Cognition, University of California, San Diego, has moved on.

'We are currently working on synesthesia, which for years was considered a mere curiosity,' he explains. 'Here a patient literally "tastes" a shape or sees colour in sound or in a number. Poets and artists who deal in metaphors are prone to synesthesia.'

Nabokov saw the letter *t* in pistachio colour, his *b* was the colour of burnt sienna, his *w* a combination of dull green and violet. Richard Feynman saw the *n* in his equations as 'mildly violet-bluish'. Kandinsky said of a Wagner opera, 'I saw it all in colours, wild lines gorging on the insane forced drawings before my very eyes.'

The condition was first written about by Sir Francis Galton, a nephew of Charles Darwin, in 1880. But, says Ramachandran, it was seen as an oddity. 'It was like explaining a mystery in terms of an enigma,' he points out.

By attacking it, Ramachandran tells us as much about the problem as about himself. 'What is important is not necessarily what is difficult,' he says. Moving from the clinic to the laboratory gives him insights denied to most, while the ability to devise simple tests to confirm his theories places him above everybody else in his field. 'God is not conspiring against us,' he says with a smile. 'Why should he?' In any case, he says, it is better to pursue ten outlandish ideas than play safe with the commonplace.

Ramachandran suggests that a cross-wiring of specific neural pathways might lead to synesthesia. Specific regions of the brain process information about specific things. There are areas for colour, texture, nouns, verbs, softness, hardness and so on.

A primary colour area lies next to an area that handles letters and numbers. If these regions were connected, they might fire simultaneously and produce synesthesia. Another colour area is next to an auditory area, which could explain why some people see colours when they hear sound.

According to Ramachandran, 'perception precedes meaning'. He devised a simple experiment—devising simple experiments is one of his strengths—to demonstrate this. When an image in the periphery of our vision is surrounded by similar images, the brain has trouble registering its presence despite the eye picking it up. But even when synesthetes can't 'see' a peripheral image—say a 5 in a group of 3s—they can see the colour associated with that number. 'This is red (or green, blue, yellow as the case might be), and therefore it must be a 5,' they argue, correctly. That suggests that synesthesia occurs in the earliest stages of perception—before the brain stamps meaning on what the eye reports.

The theory also seems to explain the origin of language. 'Language could have evolved,' says Ramachandran, 'through a sensory-to-motor synthesis. Sensory-to-motor is not difficult to understand. Think of dancing. Here, our movements (motor rhythm) mimic the sound and visual rhythms.'

While onomatoepic sounds (bow-wow for the dog) and imitation have roles to play, it is synesthesia that is at the bottom of Ramachandran's theory of language. 'Three elements fell into place before a proto-language could develop,' he explains. 'For example, if you show people a figure with sharp points and another curved like an amoeba and tell them these are bubka and kiki, but ask which is which, 96 per cent will say the curved one is bubka and the other is kiki. This is because the abrupt visual changes in "kiki" mimic the sharp inflections of that word.

'Secondly, when you watch someone doing something (or

starting to), the corresponding mirror neuron fires in your brain, allowing you to read the other's intentions. Thirdly, lip and tongue movements are synesthetically linked to what they refer to. For example, the word "suck" mimics the tongue movements used in sucking.

'These are the three stages of the "language" triangle. They were in place before language was invented. The bootstrapping between these elements culminated in the vocal proto-language. The rest was refinement.

'Far from being an oddity, therefore, synesthesia allows us to proceed (perhaps) from a single gene to a specific brain area (fusiform or angular) to maybe William Shakespeare in one sweep,' says Ramachandran, the smile never leaving his eyes.

He switches easily to Hindu philosophy, and the story of the lotus which lives in muck but displays only beauty. 'Scientists must be obsessed, knowing that insights come unexpectedly,' he says. 'My way is to choose a problem and throw all my energies into it.' The technique saw him resolve the problem of phantom limbs.

When Lord Nelson lost his right arm, he experienced phantom limb pains in that arm, including the sensation of his fingers digging into his non-existent palm. This he saw as 'direct evidence of the existence of the soul'.

Ramachandran's work gave it a less esoteric neurological explanation involving the shifting of the 'brain map' (we know which part of the brain is responsible for what sensation, but that can change).

He made phantom limbs disappear in many cases by using a simple mirror box which tricked the brain into seeing the phantom limb and manouevering it. He later called it the 'first successful amputation of a phantom limb'.

The thread of humour that runs through his work and his books shows that metaphorically, Ramachandran performs a unique feat of contortionism: his head is in the clouds but his feet are firmly on earth.

When his son comes rushing into the room with a VCR problem, Ramachandran does what all of us do in similar situations. He says, 'Go ask your mother.' He met his American wife Diane Rogers (a psychologist who has published papers with Ramachandran) at a conference in Florida. His children, Chandramani and Jayakrishna, get the full Indian treatment every year when the Ramachandrans take a break in India.

Ramachandran is working on the 'science of art'; not the first time a scientist is attempting this. But this scientist has a consistent, measurable, neurological theory for the universal grammar underlying all visual aesthetics.

It begins, as these things so often do, with rats. You can get a rat to choose between a square and a rectangle by placing food behind the rectangle. If you alter the proportions of the rectangle, the rat will still go for it, and more vigorously. What it has recognised is 'rectangularity'. This is known as the peak shift. 'Amplifying a specific rule and eliminating irrelevant detail makes a work look attractive,' explains Ramachandran.

Ethologists have known for some time about seagull behaviour. The young ones follow the mother's beak which has a red spot on it. From here it gets regurgitated food. If a beak is painted onto a long stick, the chicks follow that too, having eliminated the unnecessary detail. If then a stick with three dots is held up, the chicks get highly excited.

'In an art gallery for seagulls,' says Ramachandran, 'a stick with three dots on it will be viewed as high art—a Picasso of the seagull art world.'

'Picasso did much the same thing, bringing different perspectives onto the same plane. Hence the two eyes on the same side of the face. The Chola bronzes, where the female figure is exaggerated with hourglass figures, big hips and big breasts, achieve the same effect. The "rasa" or essence of femininity is isolated and irrelevant detail eliminated. We enjoy a Picasso for the same reason we appreciate a Chola bronze. All art is hyperbole. The artistic amplification produces a super stimulus to which certain brain circuits respond.'

Ramachandran proposes a list of eight laws of artistic experience that artists use to titillate the limbic system in the brain.

1. The 'peak shift' principle makes exaggerated elements attractive.
2. Isolating a single cue helps to focus attention.
3. Perceptual grouping makes objects stand out from the background.
4. Contrast is reinforcing.
5. Perceptual 'problem-solving' is also reinforcing.
6. Unique vantage points are suspect.
7. Visual puns or metaphors enhance art.
8. Symmetry is attractive.

The peak shift principle can be tested with the skin conductance response (SCR), the technology used in lie detectors. It measures the limbic (emotional) activation produced by an image.

Ramachandran says that one could also compare the magnitude of an SCR to caricatures of women with the SCR produced in response to a photograph of a nude woman. It is conceivable that the subject might claim to find the photograph more attractive at a conscious level while registering a large 'unconscious aesthetic response—in the form of a larger SCR—to the artistic representation.' That art taps into the subconscious is not a new idea, but SCR measurements are the first attempts to test the idea experimentally.

'This is only a starting point,' says Ramachandran, who earned his MD from Stanley Medical College in Chennai and a doctorate from Trinity College, Cambridge, and was nominated one of *Newsweek*'s 100 men to watch in the new century.

Talking to Ramachandran is like viewing a kaleidoscope—the contours of the conversation change rapidly, shifting from the Gita to Shakespeare to Newton to Van Gogh to his botany teacher in Vaishnav college and his friend Francis Crick.

In his foreword to *Phantoms in the Brain*, Oliver Sacks says, 'The great neurologists and psychiatrists of the nineteenth and early twentieth centuries were masters of description, and some of their case histories provided an almost novelistic richness of detail.' It is a fine description of Ramachandran's own books, which require no knowledge of technical detail and are thus easily accessible to the common reader. Only a few top scientists—George Gamow, Peter Medawar, Stephen Jay Gould, Richard Dawkins—have this extra gift.

The Emerging Mind, the book of Ramachandran's Reith Lectures for the BBC, is dedicated to his parents, wife and children as well as to Semmangudi Srinivasa Iyer, the doyen of Carnatic music. That says something about the scientist too.

Love and language

Language, lore, learning, laughter, lyricism, loss, lust, labour, labyrinths, lament, lightness, literacy, loneliness, loyalty, luminescence and, of course, love. In fact, mainly love. There is, too, ecology, environmental degradation, folklore and the orcaella brevirostris, the sea mammal being followed by Piyali Roy, a Seattle-based cetologist of Indian origin. To weave these threads together requires exceptional skill in three areas—structure, language and imagination. Amitav Ghosh is in control of these elements; in fact, they are important themes as well in *The Hungry Tide*.

The structure is deceptively simple as the reader is led by the hand through the past, present and suggested future by Kanai Datta, his uncle Nirmal and Piyali. Nirmal is dead before the book begins, but leaves behind a notebook. The setting is both real and conceptual, for the Sundarbans is 'an immense archipelago of islands ... interposed between the sea and the plains of Bengal'. Floods submerge the land. Forests appear and disappear. Fresh and salty channels flow into each other. The only permanent thing is the water. It can be seen as the theme of the novel too, where forces beyond their control eliminate characters, where other characters appear and disappear while the sophisticated and unsophisticated cut into each other, the apparently sophisticated learning from the apparently unsophisticated.

Anthony Burgess had said of Ghosh's *Shadow Lines* that 'it smells of cow dung fires and it tastes of chillies.' *The Hungry Tide* shows something primeval in both man and nature; tides and storms and relationships arrive and depart, replacing memories and even calling them into question, like the central uncertainty in Forster's *Passage to India*.

Kanai speaks six languages and runs a translation agency. The illiterate boatman Fokir barely speaks his own, Bengali, yet there is a strength in what he knows and what he doesn't that makes him attractive to the two young women in the book, Piyali and Moyna, his wife, an aspiring nurse.

Of all the loving and almost-loving and pretend-loving that fill the book, it is Moyna's for Fokir, a man she ignores when he is around, that is the most passionate. And it is a measure of Amitav Ghosh's skill that this is also the least mentioned, the least obviously apparent and the least commented upon. The writer conveys the love in words that are never articulated, gestures that seem to signify the opposite of what they mean and virtually offstage, as it were, with the two appearing together in the novel just once. This subtlety is in sharp contrast to the over-defined and over-explained scientific portions.

There is something refreshing about the fact that true love slips into the narrative tangentially; it is not the prerogative of the protagonists Kanai or Piya; it is not the preserve of Nirmal, a failed revolutionary, and his wife Nilima. The other implied combinations do not even come close. In fact, everybody falls in love in this book, which is quite an achievement. And in the process, each discovers just what that means. From the smug, city-bred Kanai, who can't begin to comprehend how the American Piyali can even contemplate any feeling for Fokir, to Nilima, who suspects her husband might have had an affair with Fokir's mother Kusum, a young girl for whom Kanai himself nursed feelings warmer than those of mere friendship in his teens.

All this is not as convoluted as it sounds, for the important thread in the narrative is consistency. Perhaps this is at once the book's strength and weakness, for the characters tend to do what is expected of them in the situations in which they find themselves. An exception is the retired school headmaster Nirmal, who throws his weight behind the emancipation of the people of Morichjhapi years after he thought he would end his life as a useless revolutionary with a bark worse than his bite. The Rilke-loving Nirmal is the less obvious link between the book's themes of love and language.

Ghosh wrote in an earlier book, *In an Antique Land*, in another context, 'I had no alternative; I was trapped by language.' This could just as easily have applied to *The Hungry Tide*, which can be read as a complaint against the tyranny of language or as a paen to pre-language even. In *The Seven Pillars of Wisdom*, T. E. Lawrence uses the expression 'not filtered through or made typical by thought' to explain the purity of an experience. This thought is reflected in an early passage, when Piyali thinks of her parents (and the reason why she didn't learn Bengali: because they always quarrelled in that language): 'The accumulated resentments of this life were always phrased in that language so that for her its sound had come to represent the music of unhappiness. As she lay curled in the cupboard, she would dream of washing her head of those sounds; she wanted words with the heft of stainless steel, sounds that had been boiled clean, like a surgeon's instruments, tools with nothing attached except meanings that could be looked up in a dictionary—empty of pain and memory and inwardness.'

This vagueness, this shadowy quality, this undefined something in Piyali finds a natural ally in Fokir, whose actions too are not filtered through or made typical by thought. In this, there are echoes of the other Lawrence, D.H., and the gamekeeper's attraction for Lady Chatterley. It is a world apart from Kanai's expertise in many languages which ultimately weighs him down and keeps him from soaring towards an unsaid, unexpressed but felt affinity for Piyali. Fokir eschews words and language for music, singing songs learnt in childhood ('in a difficult meter,' according to Kanai) that fascinate Piyali. When Kanai gives Piyali a gift, it is the translation of the myth behind his song and an echo that is found in Rilke.

Kanai himself has a pre- (or is it post-) language experience when face to face with a man-eating tiger: 'His mind was swamped by a flood of pure sensation. The words he had been searching for, the euphemisms that were the source of his panic, had been replaced by the thing itself, except that without words it could not be apprehended or understood.'

But through it all, Fokir apart, it is Moyna who understands language and the fact that not all poetry is written in words. Worried that she might be losing her husband to another woman, she tells Kanai to advise both Fokir and Piyali (between whom he is the interpreter). 'Words are just air, Kanai-babu. When the wind blows on the water, you see ripples and waves, but the real river lies beneath, unseen and unheard. You can't blow on the water's surface from below. Only someone who's outside can do that. Someone like you.' Kanai is an outsider in a larger sense too, as the man who knows too much but feels too little; as the man who has all the answers, but doesn't understand the questions.

There is an overlapping of love stories which is intriguing. There is the innocent first love of Kanai and Kusum, the filial love of Kanai, Nilima and Nirmal; the (possibly) forbidden love of Nilima, Nirmal and Kusum; the love triangle of Kanai, Piya and Fokir, as well as Piya, Fokir and Moyna. You can peel away the layers that represent Piya's compulsive love for the mammal, her obsession with ecology and environment, Kanai's self-love and Nilima's love for her neighbours. Nilima is a social worker who is committed to bettering the lives of those around her. She builds a hospital, trains nurses and so on, but is not a major character in the book. She knows why, though: 'The dreamers have everyone to speak for them. But those who're patient, those who try to be strong, who try to build things—no one ever sees any poetry in that, do they?' This technique of stepping outside the narrative to comment on it works well.

There is passion on one side—especially of the understated love—and on the other there is the clinical, as in the descriptions of the sea mammals. The passion does not mingle with the clinical, which is fine; but sometimes the clinical mingles with the passionate, diluting it, robbing it of soul.

Of the three skills we started with, language, structure and imagination, we are in the presence of a top-class practitioner where the first two are concerned. Ghosh's language is direct, confident, learned, in superb control of his material; the structure, as we have seen, is well constructed and hides its joints well. Imagination? The subtlety of the love story apart (and that is a major achievement), it does not match the other two elements. Perhaps it is because the characters are do-gooders and lack the otherness that makes for unusual but fascinating people.

Sports, literature and COVID-19

What did the coronavirus pandemic do to sport? Did it make us realise how unimportant it was, or the reverse? Do we now understand how vital it is, how closely linked to our sanity? Do we remember who the Wimbledon champion in 2002 was? Maybe not. But we do appreciate how necessary that tournament was at that time of the year in that place at that venue. It was a sign of normality.

And that's what sport is—an assurance of normality. It is a meaningless exercise that is the most significant thing we can do. Or watch. Or comment on. Or argue over. Events have to take place in a predetermined order, giving us a chance to both cheer and complain. That is what we were largely deprived of.

We can trust sport. We might look suspiciously at economic figures or the COVID-19 statistics. It may be that one of them is exaggerated while the other is understated. But when Ajinkya Rahane makes 112 in a Test match, we know that is a fact. Not one run more, not one fewer. If Lionel Messi goes scoreless in a match, his public relations team does not tell us that he scored a hat-trick. Sport is the statistical comfort of our times.

Watching great gymnasts or swimmers or athletes perform at the peak of their powers is a reminder of what we are capable of. Not each of us individually, but humanity as a whole. About seven billion and a bit of us have no hope of dribbling past defenders and scoring goals or running the 100 metres in nine and a half seconds. But Maradona could do the former and Usain Bolt the latter. We are confident they represent us, the unfit, the unconcerned, the no-hopers. And that is deeply satisfying.

It inspires a few of us to run or compete on the sports field; the majority can sit back, content that we don't have to put in all those years of training and sacrifice. It is enough that we can enjoy the efforts of those who actually do these things.

Football is not a matter of life and death, said Liverpool manager Bill Shankly, 'it is more important.'

COVID-19 has scooped out both the essence and the humour in that. Nothing is more important than life. Nothing more than death.

But sport is important—both to enhance life and to get over death. That is why we look forward to sport. It is a sign of life.

For long, the sports section of the newspaper was called the Toy Department. It was a place for misfits and oddballs and for squeezing in relatives of the owner's spouse who couldn't be accommodated anywhere else. Some called it a backdoor entry into real journalism.

Then people realised that the best writers tended to be misfits who saw the world from an acute angle. Covering sports was merely an excuse to write about life.

'The game doesn't change the way you vote or comb your hair or raise your children,' said Don Delillo. 'It changes nothing, but your life.'

Great sportswriting transcends bats and balls to display the qualities of literature: incision, wit, force and vision, suffused with style and substance. As with the words 'love' and 'happiness', experts are still trying to find an all-encompassing definition for 'sport'.

My favourite is by the American philosopher Bernard Suits: 'Sport,' he wrote, 'is the voluntary attempt to overcome unnecessary obstacles.' Why do we try to strike a small ball into a hole far away when we could, if we wanted, easily walk to it to do so? Or throw a ball into a hoop past people trying to grab the ball from us? The idea itself seems bizarre, and to top that, we create obstacles by laying down rules that are inviolable and pretend they mimic natural laws.

And then we attempt to overcome these of our own volition. If a Martian landed on earth, it is likely that sport will confuse him more than any other human activity.

I read about Suits later. When I joined the sports department of *Deccan Herald* in Bengaluru, the motto was laid out by sports editor Rajan Bala, a writer known for his acerbic writings on cricket. 'You can do anything here,' he told me in all seriousness, 'so long as you don't fuck on my table.' It was easy enough to agree—another example of a voluntary attempt at overcoming unnecessary obstacles.

I was straight out of university, hadn't been to journalism school and didn't know about 'the four Ws and H' (what, where, why, when, how) in writing. It was a great advantage. From the start, unencumbered by unnecessary obstacles like that, I was left free to write my way, so long as the message got across. My models were Ray Robinson, John Arlott, Ernest Hemingway. There were others too: men who had specialised in sportswriting and had found the idiom in which to communicate. In time, the models having done their job recede into the background and you are on your own.

I was aware of sportswriting-as-literature, but the familiarity came later. There has existed a tenuous relationship between the two. Some venerated writers have been sports fans and introduced sport into their fiction to make larger points about life.

George Plimpton evolved the Small Ball Theory to assess the quality of literature about sports. According to this, there is a relation between the standard of writing about a particular sport and the ball it uses. The smaller the ball, the greater the literature. The theory is interesting, but little else. Most of us can find books that either support the theory or trash it. Perhaps boxing has produced some of the finest literature because the balls involved are smaller than a basketball, which has no literature to speak of. But I am being facetious.

Literature and sport have come together in unexpected ways. From 1912 to 1948, poetry was an Olympic sport. The poems had to be 'inspired by the idea of sport'. You won't find the poems on the Olympic website, though—perhaps they were too embarrassing.

Did the early sportswriters think of themselves as literary figures? The first reports of cricket matches, in the eighteenth century, were written in Latin verse. The form was heroic, but the actual match details were sketchy, many of them omitting scores altogether.

The first cricket writer in the sense we understand the term today—in prose, and with match details—was a woman, Mary Russell Mitford, otherwise remembered for her sketches of rural life. 'I doubt whether there be any scene in the world more delightful than a cricket match,' she wrote.

Mitford's sketches began to appear around the same time as the first great piece of sports literature, 'The Fight', by William Hazlitt, essayist, art critic, philosopher and friend of Wordsworth and Coleridge. Boxing was merely one of Hazlitt's interests. When Norman Mailer wrote about the Muhammad Ali–George Foreman bout in Zaire, he called his book *The Fight*, using the title and the structure of Hazlitt's essay in tribute.

From the mid-eighteenth century to the mid-nineteenth, the rules of various sports were codified: cricket, football, boxing, tennis, hockey, rugby and other sports in Britain, and in America, football, baseball and basketball. As these became popular, they attracted writers, both the journeyman who recited scores and details and the writer who looked beyond the here and now. The passion for watching sport and reading about it ensured the development of both fields. Sports journalism came into its own.

In Britain, Daniel Defoe, author of *Robinson Crusoe*, went around the country in the eighteenth century and wrote about horse racing at Newmarket, while the essayist and playwright Joseph Addison extolled the virtues of exercise.

In 1857, Thomas Hughes wrote *Tom Brown's Schooldays*, which C.L.R. James later called the 'sacred text of Victorianism', with its muscular Christianity, moral certitude and the development of boys into men through cricket and other sports. This was the beginning of the philosophy of sport as character-building.

Wordsworth wrote on skating, Coleridge on climbing and Byron on swimming before a new generation of writers both played and wrote on the sport they loved: Arthur Conan Doyle, P.G. Wodehouse and J.M. Barrie were all cricketers and fans, although once he shifted to America, Wodehouse began to focus on golf stories.

Daily newspaper reporting and literature came together in one man, Neville Cardus, who saw the humanity of sport, its humour, its ironies and wrote colourfully about the players. When challenged about some of the quotes he responded, 'I put words in his mouth that God intended the player to utter.' You can see in that a love for the truth above mere fact, or a convenient way of romanticizing the players who are, after all, the tools of your trade.

Sport was also a vehicle for another literary device, the anti-hero. In the American David Storey's *This Sporting Life,* rugby league and social realism told the story of a victim of the exploitative world of sport. It wasn't all honey and roses and aspiration, but something darker. Sport had its victims too. Allan Sillitoe's *The Loneliness of the Long Distance Runner* about its non-conformist hero deliberately losing a race had been published a year earlier.

In *Ravelstein,* Saul Bellow tried to put the basketball great Michael Jordan in perspective: 'Ravelstein's young men were well up on basketball. In Michael Jordan, of course, they had a genius to watch. Ravelstein felt himself deeply and vitally connected with Jordan, the artist. He used to say that basketball stood with jazz music as a significant black contribution to the higher life of the country—its specifically American character.'

American writers took sport seriously, not seeing it at the other end of the cultural scale from, say, the opera. Philip Roth, Bernard Malamud and Don DeLillo set novels in sport. Ring Lardner and Paul Gallico began as sportswriters. Hemingway, Damon Runyon, Ring Lardner, Norman Mailer and Jack Kerouac all worked as sports journalists. Hemingway once got $30,000 from *Sports Illustrated* for a 2,000-word piece on bullfighting. Richard Ford wrote a novel called *The Sportswriter.*

Nabokov was a chess fanatic, composing complex problems in the game. 'Puzzling out chess problems and solutions,' he wrote, 'demands from the composer the same virtues that characterise all worthwhile art: originality, invention, conciseness, harmony, complexity and splendid insincerity.' *The Luzhin Defense* was an early novel of his with a chess player as protagonist.

In 1935, R.K. Narayan wrote *Swami and Friends*, where Swami forms a cricket team, the MCC (Malgudi Cricket Club), whose second order of business is to write a letter to the suppliers of cricket equipment.

'Dear Sir,' begins the letter, 'Please send to our team two junior bats, six balls, wickets and other things quick. It is very urgent. We shall send you money afterwards. Don't fear. Please be urgent.'

Following the example of Gallico, Plimpton made a name as a 'participatory journalist', getting into the boxing ring to take on light heavyweight champion Archie Moore and then write about it in *Shadow Box*, spending a month as a quarterback with the Detroit Lions, and so on.

However, being established writers or great philosophers was no guarantee that when they turned their attention to sport, they wrote literary classics. A.S. Byatt, winner of the Booker Prize and a football fan, was once commissioned by *The Observer* newspaper to report some games. Her output was ordinary. Likewise with the Tottenham Hotspurs fan and philosopher of logical positivism, A.J. Ayer.

One reason is that they were literary people writing about a populist activity, and could not resist the temptation to force deeper life lessons into their sportswriting, linking sport to all manner of significant things. This works sometimes, but often a missed goal is simply a missed goal.

Great sportsmen inspire great literature too. It has been said often that Muhammad Ali may be the most important figure in the history of sportswriting. Some of the finest literature in sport is centred on Ali in particular and boxing in general. Ali was unique. A top sportsman with a conscience and an enormous, almost comic self-belief. David Remnick, Mike Marqusee, Hunter Thompson, George Plimpton, none of them professional sportswriters, have written brilliantly on Ali.

Outside of Britain and America, the Trinidadian writer and Marxist C.L.R. James wrote what, in many people's reckoning, is the finest sports book: *Beyond a Boundary*. It is a wonderful mix of autobiography, social commentary, colonialism and class struggle, and begins by asking the question: 'What do they know of cricket who only cricket know?' V.S. Naipaul, who has himself written on cricket, called it 'one of the finest and most finished books to come out of the West Indies.'

I never got to share a press box with James, but I did with Donald Woods, during the 1992 cricket World Cup in Australia.

As a strong voice against apartheid and author of powerful books on that period, Woods was a hero to many. I had read excerpts from his biography of Steve Biko, the Black leader. His beliefs were hard on his family. There were threats, and on one occasion, T-shirts sent with Biko's image turned out to be poisoned and scalded his children. That's when he decided to leave his country.

Woods was in Australia to report cricket. 'You have an enviable job, travelling the world to watch cricket,' this man who had played a role in changing the world told me. 'It had once been my ambition.' Somewhat startled—it was a bit like hearing Che Guevera say it had been an ambition to get into fashion design—I asked if he was enjoying himself. 'You are living my ambition, and I am living yours,' I joked.

Masterpiece on toilet paper

For so long had Ngugi wa Thiong'o been in the mix at the annual Nobel Prize conversations that many believed he had already won the prize. But the Kenyan consistently missed out, while even Bob Dylan and Kashuo Ishiguro were honoured.

At an intimate, animated, worshipful gathering in Bengaluru, I toyed with the idea of asking him how he felt about this. Midway through the session I suddenly knew what he would say: *Success is the work itself, not the prizes it attracts.* The greatest writer of our generation might, like Tolstoy and Dostoevsky and Joyce and Nabokov, miss out. It would be an honour, though, for the Nobel to have him in their list.

Ngugi changed the language of discourse in African literature, wrote the textbook on decolonising the mind and language as power, but he remains in essence a teller of stories and a monument to the undying spirit of man. 'What's good about writing is that when you write novels, people can see that the problems in one region are similar to problems in another,' he told a rapt audience.

Ngugi, who had written his early plays and novels in English, decided—while in prison—to write only in his native language: Gikuyu. It didn't limit his audience; it gained him the admiration and gratitude of his own people. Language is not merely a tool of communication, he said, it is a carrier of culture. It wasn't commercial suicide as widely anticipated; instead, his works were absorbed into popular culture, as a reviewer pointed out.

It scared the authorities. President Daniel arap Moi even ordered the arrest of Matigari, one of Ngugi's fictional characters, the asker of troubling questions!

The term in prison followed a play (*I Will Marry When I Want*) and the questioning and satirising of local oppressors who had replaced the colonial oppressors. 'One day, I was this successful author, next day I was in maximum security prison,' Ngugi said. 'The walls were grey all around; it was meant to break our spirit.'

Ngugi wrote *Devil on the Cross* while in prison. Secretly, and on toilet paper!

Great writers have passion and energy; Ngugi, a generous man, has more: an enormous gift for happiness. He was the one who was sent to school (thanks to his mother), he was the one who was chosen to write an original play in an inter-collegiate competition, he was the one who survived a horrific physical attack in Kenya. The gratitude shines through. His eyes have an unusual mix of sadness and gaiety; it hints at a profound understanding, which his books confirm. He could be bitter and cynical, he has chosen instead to be gregarious and affable.

'Time always extends itself to accommodate what you want to do,' Ngugi, then eighty, said in response to a question. Will time extend itself to accommodate his Nobel? Perhaps *we* need him to win—if only to restore our faith in the rightness of things.

Reading suspiciously

I read Enid Blyton before the golliwogs were expunged, and Mark Twain when Injun Joe hadn't metamorphosed into Indian Joe and 'slave' hadn't replaced the N-word. I am not sure being exposed to the original had a lasting negative effect on any of us who read these authors at that age. But it is the normalising of such usages that is pernicious and calls for action.

Political correctness is not literary criticism, it is a later age imposing its values on an earlier one. It is possible to imagine—and you don't need a particularly active imagination—the QAnon coming to power in America, say, and restoring the N-words and the golliwogs and a host of such charged words to the works in which they appeared. And the cycle could continue. One generation's poison is another's elixir.

QAnon might be an extreme example, but how do you hold someone guilty of a literary misdemeanour decades after she is dead? Novelists cannot be held responsible for the direction the world takes to arrive at what is acceptable and what is not decades after their death. They don't even have the responsibility of being true to their own times—what originates in the mind need not be inspired by what they see or hear around them.

If, in some of her writings, Enid Blyton was merely reflecting the language and attitudes of the White Western person of her times, then her fiction is probably closer to social history, just as Twain's was before her. When UK's Royal Mint decided in 2019 not to have Blyton's profile on the 50p coin, it was a reaction to her 'racist, sexist and homophobic' views. But her writings were, her defenders averred, merely a reflection of the 'casual racism' of the 1940s and 1950s in her country.

Just as one does not advocate exposing children to pornography in the name of free speech and social commentary, they don't need to handle the N-word in casual reading either. Not every change, however, is necessary and not every new layer of meaning on a word or expression calls for abandoning the original. Unless we say that some changes—however wrong they might feel philosophically or intellectually—are necessary, we evade an important question in literature. What is literarily acceptable can be morally degrading, and we have to make a choice.

The year 1922 is particularly significant in modern literature. It saw the publication of James Joyce's *Ulysses* and Virginia Woolf's *Jacob's Room*. Eliot's *Wasteland* appeared, as did the first published works of Blyton, a collection of poems. Blyton has probably sold twice as many copies of her books as the other authors put together. This is not to suggest that quantity is a guarantee of quality, merely that if you took a critical trowel through those novels, you would come up with enough examples of political incorrectness in them too.

The question of Eliot's anti-semitism has exercised critics. His poetry is one of anti-Semitism's few literary triumphs, wrote Anthony Julius. 'It is dangerous to pronounce from a position of partial comprehension' was Craig Raine's response. Joyce has been accused of being anti-feminist (and so too, strangely, has Woolf).

How seriously are we to take critics and how important is criticism? What are the rules?

At one level, it is a straightforward matter. A critic is explaining what he finds interesting (or not), and thus piquing (or stubbing out) the interest of the reader. He can be persuasive, bland, provocative, annoying. The reader learns to build a relationship with such a person and works out just how much of a margin to leave for extreme views, how certain things don't work for him as a reader and just what portions to ignore as being irrelevant.

For some readers, the author's personal life and loves is irrelevant; the work is all. Others like a bit of gossip, the telling anecdote, the sexual episodes. 'The story of a life,' writes Muriel Spark in her novel *Loitering with Intent*, 'is a very informal party; there are no rules of precedence and hospitality.' Does the sexuality of Henry James matter? It does to a certain type of reader. Is it necessary to know that Thomas Wolfe wrote his novels standing up or that Norman Mailer shot his wife?

John Updike drew up the following rules when he set out as a critic: a) try to understand what the author wished to do, and do not blame him for not achieving what he did not attempt; b) give enough direct quotation so the reader can form his own impression; c) confirm your description of the book with a quotation from the book rather than proceeding by fuzzy precis; d) go easy on the plot summary and do not give away the end; e) try to understand failure. Sure it's his and not yours?

How quaint and old-fashioned all that sounds now, although you cannot dismiss any of the rules out of hand. Today's reviewer often either uses the platform to show off (hinting that he would have written a better book if only he cared to sit down and do it) or to praise/dismiss with a passion that is suspicious.

'The only sensible procedure for a critic is to keep silent

about works which he believes to be bad, while at the same time vigorously campaigning for those he believes to be good ...' That is advice from W.H. Auden in *The Dyer's Hand.* If a book is bad, ignore it, don't waste time explaining why. That is convenient, but cannot be a policy.

When did good behaviour become more important than interesting writing? The critic's job is to defend language, using it skilfully, even reverentially, if he expects the same from the writer he is discussing.

Martin Amis once pointed out that art critics, when they review art shows, don't paint pictures about those shows, film critics don't review movies by making movies about them. 'But,' he said, 'when you review a prose-narrative, then you write a prose-narrative about that prose-narrative.' Writing words about words is fraught with danger, therefore, and needs to be handled with both care and compassion.

Tolstoy wrote to a critic thus on *Anna Karenina*: 'Your judgment ... is true, but not all of it.... What you have expressed does not express all that I meant.... It is one of the true things that can be said. If I wanted to express in words all that I meant to express by the novel, then I should have to write the same novel as I have written all over again.'

This reads like something out of Borges.

The critic tells us what is not there, what could be interpreted differently and why certain things work or otherwise. He points to the symbols and explains the codes so the reader can appreciate the richness of the creation. 'To read suspiciously' was the accepted notion, and generally works for the reader.

Rita Felski, in her brilliant *The Limits of Critique*, suggests going beyond that to post-critical reading. While expanding on the role of suspicion in criticism, Felski says that to read suspiciously is to maintain that a text's real meaning is always hidden.

But this implies a limitation in the role of the writer while the critics 'unmask, expose, subvert, unravel ... in the assurance that the text is withholding something of vital importance and it is the critics' job to ferret out what lies concealed ...'

Instead of looking behind the text for hidden causes and noxious motives, Felski asks us to 'place ourselves in front of the text, reflecting on what it unfurls, calls forth, makes possible.'

Felski writes with a clarity that, despite the use of jargon, seems to have bypassed some other theorists. There has always been a suspicion that critics write for other critics while writers write for readers. Fleski argues in *Uses of Literature* that the rise of theory did not necessarily lead to the death of literature.

In *Better Living Through Criticism*, A.O. Scott says, 'Art is durable and mutable whereas criticism is fixed and therefore perishable. The job of criticism is about art; the job of art is just to be.' Criticism is what supplies art its lifeblood. 'The critic is a creature of paradox, at once superfluous and ubiquitous, indispensable and useless, to be trusted and reviled.'

The key, of course, is to develop a relationship. Even the worst critics tell us something—usually point us away from a book that is not worth the time. The best take us into the very synapses of a book, inviting us to understand how it was done, and what the meaning beyond the obvious might be. But the average reader deals with the critic in-between, neither the purely impressionistic nor the overly intellectual.

This is the relationship that matters. Does the critic recommend a Dan Brown or a Rohinton Mistry? Does he criticise one or the other, and why? Now superimpose your own reactions on the critic's. Place the critic's 'whys and why nots' over your own. It is almost a physical activity.

Over a few reviews and such overlaps the relationship is built.

Now you know how much of what he says you can accept and how much to ignore. The critic has to be consistent, the reader not so much.

One reason a book reads differently to us at different times of our lives is the manner in which each reading places on it another level of meaning, another set of experiences through which we see it.

Contrary to popular belief, Keats was not killed by a bad review. He didn't read a review, turn to the wall and give up the struggle against tuberculosis. The American critic Elizabeth Hardwick writes, 'Later evidence has shown that Keats took his hostile reviews with a considerably more manly calm than we were taught in school, and yet the image of the young, rare talent cut down by venomous reviewers remains firmly fixed in the public mind.'

So there we have it, the tropes of criticism: the noxious reviewer, the young talent snuffed out, the moving personal story embroidered by succeeding generations of students, and an anecdote that somehow adds to the greatness of a poet. The aching heart and the numbing drowsiness, truth, beauty and all.

Premier blossom for the bookworm

In the 1970s, I bought Jean Paul Sartre's *Being and Nothingness* at the Premier Bookshop in Bengaluru. Setting aside for the moment the question of why a schoolboy might want to read such an inaccessible book, let's move on. When I was at Premier some thirty years later, its proprietor T.S. Shanbhag pulled out a book from under a pile and asked if I wanted this recent edition. It was *Being and Nothingness.* I was startled he should remember.

'Actually, I haven't read the last one I bought here,' I mumbled as Shanbhag broke into his familiar hearty laugh. He hadn't laughed when I had first bought the book, a tribute to the civility of the man, and his sympathy too, for a youngster who deserved pity rather than admonition or admiration.

Rather like the protagonist in James Hilton's *Goodbye Mr Chips*, he was just Mr Shanbhag for us. I didn't know his first name for a long time. Then the internet supplied the information: Sarvotham. It means 'the finest'. Few names are so appropriate. When he succumbed to COVID-19 in May 2021, he took away with him a chunk of my growing years.

As a journalist, when I was working in Delhi and came to Bengaluru for a day, my editor who wanted to get in touch told a colleague, 'Go look for him in that bookshop, he'll be there.' He did. I was.

Soon the bookshop itself was no longer there—Premier shut down in 2009. A part of Bengaluru died when that happened; a part of me too. Many felt that way, for like Lalbagh and Cubbon Park, Premier had been a part of our growing-up years.

Even in the old Bengaluru known for its hospitality, grace and charm, Shanbhag stood out for these qualities. He was personally acquainted both with his customers and his books. He encouraged the browser, although at Premier, browsing was a contact sport. Informal rules had to be observed. It was best to leave the actual pulling out of the book you wanted either to Shanbhag or one of his assistants to whom he was constantly reeling out names, positions, directions and occasional anecdotes.

Regular visitors tended to walk around in a fixed pattern. In three decades and more, I don't think I changed mine once. It began with a quick glance at the latest arrivals near the door, and was followed by a more measured look at the science and art sections. Then it was onwards till the sports section to the left of Shanbhag at his table. Anticlockwise every time.

My friend Ram Guha preferred the alternative route, walking clockwise and finishing with the new arrivals. There were only two routes, and if you hoped to avoid someone, it could be easily managed; Shanbhag would help you, unless he was in one of his wicked moods, in which case he would contrive to bring you face to face with the person you had been hoping to avoid.

Shanbhag played the jolly host, introducing customers to one another, getting them to discuss a recent event or bringing all arguments to a close with a sudden faraway look in his eyes.

I was in junior school when I first walked into Premier. I had a gift coupon. Other bookstores in the area looked at schoolboys not as customers then or for the future, but pesky adolescents who needed to be followed around suspiciously and asked questions till they left the store in sheer annoyance.

At Premier, Shanbhag waved a genial 'Hello' and carried on with whatever he was doing, leaving you to your devices. Loyalty came from being treated like adults.

Importantly, when he occasionally sensed that only a shortage of funds kept this schoolboy from buying a book, he either gave ridiculous discounts or didn't take any payment at all, saying vaguely, 'We can do that later,' and looking (I imagined) like a smaller version of Wodehouse's Lord Emsworth.

Premier was the most welcoming and wildly stocked bookstore and a meeting place for both young lovers and storied intellectuals, many of the former hoping to grow into the latter in time.

Through our school and university, Shanbhag watched us grow while he himself hardly changed. He didn't lose more hair because there wasn't much to lose. His full-throated laugh never softened. Nor did his sense of mischief diminish.

The finest bookstores in Bengaluru today are those which deal mainly in second-hand books. They stock new books too, and give marvellous discounts on them. Over the years, I have found greater excitement in stores around the world that surprise. The Strand in New York, Skoob Books in London, for example.

Used-books stores promise the unexpected. They (and their customers) thrive on serendipity. How civilised a city is can be gauged by the number of bookstores it has; especially used-book stores. It takes a certain refinement to invest in used books.

It is a humane trade which is not capable of being vulgarized beyond a certain point, wrote George Orwell, and it's a sentiment I share.

Virginia Woolf best captured the creative madness in such a store:

'Books are everywhere; and always the same sense of adventure fills us. Second-hand books are wild books, homeless books; they have come together in vast flocks of variegated feather, and have a charm which the domesticated volumes of the library lack. Besides, in this random miscellaneous company we may rub against some complete stranger who will, with luck, turn into the best friend we have in the world.'

There is a sense of urgency too—you must buy the book the first time you see it. It may never be replaced, unlike those in large chain stores where books are like ducks in a shooting gallery and an identical one pops up when one is removed.

The spirit of Premier lives on in Bengaluru. Blossom Book House's Mayi Gowda and The Bookworm's Krishna Gowda are genial, knowledgeable men who gave up the professions they were trained for (engineering and management, respectively) to sell books.

Even if unknowingly, they might be paying tribute to another professional—a lawyer—who established what was for long the best-known and best-stocked such store in the city, Select, in a lane just off Brigade Road.

Select was established in 1945 by a lawyer from Andhra, K.B.K. Rao. Rao's son, K.K.S. Murthy, an aeronautical engineer, carried the family business forward. Select is now run by the third-generation bibliophile, Sanjay, who trained as an accountant.

Select is the place for rare and antiquarian books too. Murthy once had a first edition of *Alice in Wonderland*. It was, according to Pradeep Sebastian, India's leading authority on books, 'the first true printing of *Alice in Wonderland,* the scarce 1865 copy that preceded the authorised 1866 first edition from Macmillan. Only sixteen copies of this 1865 Alice are known to exist, most of them in institutional collections.'

A hop, step and jump away from Select is Church Street, *the* books street, the finest in the country. This is the place for the latest books, used books and everything in between.

Mayi Gowda's Blossom began in a tiny space where you had to step out to think. Today it deals in books from two buildings on the same street—one a three-storey, tightly packed area and the other a sprawling space, similarly packed. That's a huge increase in real estate, never mind number of books, in less than two decades.

Close to the new Blossom is Krishna Gowda's The Bookworm, of roughly similar area. If you walked down from Koshy's, you entered Bookworm first.

Independent bookshops in the age of large chain stores and Amazon are doubly special. Not just for what they are, but for what they symbolise. Sheer guts, for one. Passion, for another.

'If what a bookstore offers matters to you,' wrote the novelist Ann Patchett in a charming essay on opening a bookstore in Nashville, 'then shop at a bookstore.'

More lasting friendships are made in a bookshop than in a bar. For all are equal in the presence of books. Also, as someone said, you can always find what you are looking for online. But it takes a bookstore to find what you were not looking for. This is something Mayi Gowda is keenly aware of. Blossom is the establishment that changed the texture of Church Street.

Here is his story in his own words: 'I was born in a small village called Rangasamudra, around twenty-five kilometres from Mysore. My parents were agriculturists. After I finished school

I did a diploma course in Mysore. After the final exam, I told my father I wanted to do engineering, but he said he couldn't afford it.

'He gave me Rs 300 and said that was all he could spare. I came to Bengaluru with that, and found a job in a factory. I shared a room with a friend from my village. After three months, I got my diploma results. I had finished seventh in Karnataka state. I now joined the University Visveswaraya College of Engineering.

'It was college in the day and work at night. For the first two semesters, results were bad. Meanwhile, my friend moved back to the village and I didn't have a place to stay. I gave up both my studies and my job. I found a room in a hostel near the Majestic bus stand.

'This was the turning point. Near my hostel, I saw people selling second-hand books and started helping out. I borrowed some books from them and sold them on the pavement on Mahatma Gandhi Road. Business was good, so I went back to engineering and did well.

'After completing my course, I started Blossom Book House in 2002, with around 1,500 books in a 200 sq. ft place. Today Blossom has two locations—3,000 sq. ft and 8,600 sq. ft—with around 500,000 books.'

The Bookworm's Krishna Gowda has a remarkably similar story. He too hails from Rangasamudra. He too sold books on the pavement on M.G. Road, switching between college in the morning and work in the evening. He too moved into a building at the turn of the century.

Let Krishna take over here: 'My father was a farmer and mother a housewife. I am the sixth child. I helped out by selling vegetables and by doing housework too.

'I completed my pre-university course with the highest marks in the village. My father insisted I find a job, but when friends told him I should study further, he relented, and I attended evening college.

'One day, in June 1997, I met Mayi Gowda. Later, he asked if I was willing to work in Bengaluru and continue in an evening college. Since my family respected Mayi Gowda, they didn't ask anything about the job or salary. I was just over sixteen years old.

'We started by selling books in front of Higginbothams on M.G. Road. After graduating in commerce from Vijaya Evening College, I began a management course. I quit the job with Mayi after three and a half years. I started selling books outside the Shrungar Shopping Complex near the earlier spot.

'After my MBA, I was unsure of what to do. I read a lot; I was fascinated by old books and vintage covers. We had a beautiful edition of *Of Human Bondage.* Mayi told me to sell it for at least Rs 100. A customer offered Rs 110, but I didn't sell. I didn't want to part with such a beautiful edition.

'Mayi was angry, but I said it's a beautiful edition, just keeping it in the shop makes me happy. Today I have a good collection of such books at Bookworm.

'I opened a shop inside the Shrungar complex. Word of mouth gained us customers. Now Bookworm has over 1,50,000 books (and more than 3,00,000 books in the warehouse).'

Some years ago, Krishna Gowda organised a function at his shop for book lovers of Bengaluru to meet the legendary Shanbhag, who by then had even been the subject of a documentary. It was a nice gesture, and a way of paying tribute to a man who had inspired a whole culture in the city.

Shanbhag had pulled the shutters down seven or eight years earlier. 'I gave away the name board and some old furniture to a scrap dealer,' he told his audience, many of whom were seeing him in the flesh for the first time. 'Only intangible memories have heritage value,' he explained, 'not the tangible accessories.'

As a schoolboy, it had been my wish to see my books on Shanbhag's shelves. But my first book appeared two years after the closure. Intangible memories I have plenty of ...

The great catalyst

Many years ago, when I finally got my hands on Colin Wilson's *Introduction to the New Existentialism* at the British Library in Bengaluru, I decided to keep it. I paid the 'lost fees' to assuage my conscience. Books were hard to come by then.

It was a fascinating book made more fascinating by the writing on the inside back cover. These were notes for a short story tentatively called 'A Joyous Death' (and below it was the instruction to self: change title; get rid of whining tone). I recognised the handwriting. It was that of my friend and schoolmate Anil Kuruvilla. We had discovered Colin Wilson more or less at the same time while in school; now he was living abroad, we had lost touch, but here he was in my life once again. The later Wilson would have loved the coincidence and theorised endlessly about it. But it was the unsentimental, hard-nosed earlier Wilson who had initially attracted us.

Rather like Aldous Huxley, Colin Wilson died on the wrong day. In Huxley's case, this was 22 November 1963, when John F. Kennedy was shot. Wilson died on the same day as Nelson Mandela, and was thus largely ignored by the media. Yet, there was no guarantee that a better choice of date might have got the world to take notice. Wilson was eighty-two, and a far cry from the '24-year-old genius' who had burst on the literary scene as England's home-grown existentialist and answer to Jean-Paul Sartre. He wanted to live for as long as his hero, George Bernard Shaw, who died at ninety-three. On another occasion, he told Iris Murdoch that he wished to live to be 300.

In his first autobiography, *Voyage to a Beginning*, Wilson said he regarded himself as the most important writer of the twentieth century, adding, 'I'd be a fool if I didn't know it, and a coward if I didn't say it.' Many agreed, others didn't but, ironically, both sets used the same argument.

Some saw him as a crank, author of books on the paranormal and criminology, on serial killers and booze, and biographies of mystics and Jack the Ripper. Older readers remembered him as one of the 'Angry Young Men', a group of working-class authors who found success around the same time in the mid-1950s. Men like John Osborne, Kingsley Amis, John Braine, Stuart Holroyd, Bill Hopkins: talented writers who were squeezed into a media invention.

Wilson was self-taught and by twenty-four had read more than most might in a lifetime. He spent his nights in a sleeping bag in Hampstead Heath and wrote by day in the reading room at the British Museum. *The Outsider*, a journey through alienation, first spoke of a 'positive existentialism', a counter to what Wilson thought was the negative approach of Sartre and Heidegger. Wilson saw the problems raised by the Continental philosophers as genuine, but found their solution, or lack of one, both depressing and unnecessary.

I must have been fifteen or sixteen when I first came across *The Outsider* and was stunned to know that philosophers asked the same questions that adolescents did—some of them then went on to look for answers, others let the idea of there being no answer overwhelm them.

But this was not so much an introduction to philosophy (although it was a fine introduction to philosophers from Locke and Hume and Descartes to Nietszche and Schopenhauer and Kierkegaard) as a drive through literary criticism. Artistic alienation was a broad enough category to include T.E. Lawrence, Vincent Van Gogh, Vaslav Nijinsky, Ramakrishna Paramhansa, Gurdjieff, T.E. Hulme, Dostoevsky, Eliot and Kafka.

It was a fascinating read at that age. We—Anil and I—were old enough to understand that pessimism was more stylish, and more likely to impress girls, but young enough to hope for hope.

There was something both dismissive and intimate about the line that defined our growing years, which Wilson was fond of quoting and by extension so were we. It was the ultimate romantic philosophy and appeared in Auguste Villiers de L'isle Adam's play *Axel*, which neither of us had read then.

Count Axel lives in an isolated castle in the Black Forest where he is training to discover the solutions to ultimate mysteries. The castle holds a vast treasure in its basement. That attracts a young woman, Sara, who is intent on stealing it. Sara is as beautiful as Axel is handsome, and, inevitably, the two fall in love.

They make plans for the future, which beckons in that special way it does for couples like them—couples who have everything: love, youth, social position, power and enormous wealth. Sara speaks of 'all the dreams to realise'.

Axel introduces an element of doubt by asking, 'Why?' He tells his love, 'Sara, we have just exhausted the future. All the realities, what will they be tomorrow in comparison with the mirages we have just lived? To consent to live would be sacrilege ...'

And then the stirring line that excited the two teenagers in Bengaluru: 'As for living, our servants can do that for us ... '

Axel convinces Sara, they drink poison and die in rapture.

This is not a diversion into a discussion on Symbolist heroes (*Axel* was written in 1890), but the apparent power of a single line that Anil and I kept repeating to ourselves, first as a short-cut to Colin Wilson's world (*The Outsider* introduced us to the concept), and then as a cheery greeting, as between two old friends recalling an important, if slightly embarrassing time in their lives.

As for living, our servants can do that for us.

Even bad books can influence you—years later, I made a brave attempt to read *Axel* but could not complete the book. As for reading, our servants can do that for us. As for playing cricket for India, our servants can do that for us. As for writing the great novel, our servants can do that for us. It had become a shorthand for shortcomings in later life, the grand excuse, the overarching justification for everything, a sort of the-dog-ate-my-homework explanation for lives not lived.

It was some years before we could slot Wilson correctly. He was not the philosopher we had thought he was, but a literary critic with a fascinating theory and a wide range.

But all that was in the future. We devoured the *Outsider* series (six volumes, plus a summing up: *Introduction to the New Existentialism*). We accepted or rejected a writer based on what Wilson had to say about him. There was something exhilarating in the message that we could change the world. Or, at least, become rich and famous just by thinking and writing.

The everyday world might be boring and trivial, but the wider world of art and literature had infinite interest. We tend to forget the latter, and get trapped in the former. If Wilson developed a cult following, it was because he confirmed many of our suspicions at an age when 'philosophy' and 'literature' were still things that other people did.

Ultimately it was the literature that mattered. Wilson's books of criticism, *Eagle and the Earwig, The Craft of the Novel, The Books in My Life, Poetry and Mysticism* retain their freshness and originality after all these years. Amazingly, the *Outsider* cycle was completed when Wilson was just thirty-four. It was too early to become the grey eminence of philosophy (for one, Bertrand Russell was still alive, as was Karl Popper); Wilson chose the alternative, spreading himself over a range of subjects and arriving at the same answers through different routes.

He could not shake off the biggest criticism of his oeuvre of 181 books (someone had actually bothered to count): that he wrote the same book 181 times. The actress Mary Ure, wife of John Osborne, called *The Outsider* an anthology of other people's ideas. But, at a certain age, that's what you want: an intellectual tourist bus that takes you through various personalities and their ideas en route to one big idea.

There was, too, the attraction of the Wilson coda: 'Every day I realize that an ironic nature has given us everything we could desire—and has omitted to give us the ability to enjoy it.'

Writing the same book so many times meant that generally speaking, any one of them delineated Wilson's philosophy in full or near-complete terms. Wilson was not unaware of where he stood or what was being said about his work. He used Isaiah Berlin's classic distinction between foxes and hedgehogs in an interview with Geoff Ward in 2001: 'The fox knows many things; the hedgehog knows just one thing. So, Shakespeare is a typical fox; Tolstoy and Dostoevsky are typical hedgehogs. I am a typical hedgehog—I know just one thing, and I repeat it over and over again. I've tried to approach it from different angles to make it look different, but it is the same thing.'

The reviewers who had called Wilson a genius when *The Outsider* appeared—like Byron, he awoke one morning and found himself famous—seemed embarrassed by their high praise and tore into his next book. While that did not guarantee instant anonymity, it gave Wilson the time and space to work without any intrusion. It also might have caused him to take on some commissions just for the money.

In 1956, the critic Philip Toynbee gave *The Outsider* a ringing endorsement in *The Observer*, calling it 'luminously intelligent', but probably embarrassed by this, panned its sequel, *The Religion and the Rebel*, as 'a vulgarizing rubbish bin' and backtracked on his earlier enthusiasm for the first book by calling it 'clumsily written and still more clumsily composed'.

It didn't discourage Wilson. In fact, he displayed a kind of heroism in keeping at his work despite years of neglect following the years of criticism. 'I suspect that I am probably the greatest writer of the twentieth century,' he told an interviewer modestly. 'In 500 years' time, they'll say, "Wilson was a genius", because I'm a turning-point in intellectual history.'

In an interview following the release of his 2004 autobiography, *Dreaming to Some Purpose*, Wilson was asked if he'd had much influence as a philosopher. His reply is revealing: 'Oh no!' he told the interviewer. 'None at all. Daphne Du Maurier said to me that everyone who has a great success finds that the next 10 years are very difficult—they have a period when people take no notice of them. And I thought, No, not 10 years, I couldn't bear it! But I've been forgotten for almost 50 years. It's been a bit discouraging.... But when I'd done this new autobiography, I looked at it and thought my God, this is a bloody good book! Now they'll see what I'm getting at!'

How wonderful it is to keep a vision alive for half a century and to continue to believe in personal genius till the end. For me and others who woke up one morning and found ourselves a friend in Wilson, he is like a favourite uncle. We know his weaknesses, but we don't care. Boyhood heroes are beyond criticism.

Well, up to a point. Wilson gave us two gifts when we were growing up; neither made him a great philosopher, or indeed a writer for the ages. The first was the casual introduction to the virtual canon of Western philosophy, from the ancient Greeks to the modern Europeans. From Socrates to Sartre. The introduction to the literary giants meant many happy years were spent in reading their works.

Wilson was the great catalyst—initially for lighting up interest in his own work, and then as the writer who led you to other writers: Shaw, Eliot, Hemingway, Kierkegaard, the Lawrences D.H. and T.E., Yeats, Auden, Camus, Beckett, Wells, Wilde, Dostoevsky. Few writers stood at the meeting point of philosophy and literature with such self-confidence and such conviction as Wilson did.

And that was his second lesson. He told us that the two most important things for a writer were passion and conviction—the first had to be authentic, and the second a consequence, and it didn't matter if the conclusions were wrong so long as the problem was laid out correctly.

'Existentialism, like romanticism, is a philosophy of freedom,' he wrote in *Introduction to the New Existentialism.* 'It has reached a standstill because no existential thinker can agree that there are any values outside man—that is outside man's everyday consciousness. Man is free, says Sartre, but what is he to do with his freedom? Man is free, but the world is empty and meaningless—this is the problem.'

Stated like that, we come to a dead end. Wilson's solution is a 'positive' existentialism that makes the leap from this Sartrean negativity.

This he first stated in *The Outsider,* studies of different kinds of outsiders from fiction and life—the underdeveloped (Roquentin in Sartre's *Nausea*), the romantic (Nietschze), artistic (Van Gogh) and then the visionary (Ramakrishna). The route from the neurotic to the transcendent is lit by the lives and works of such men. I wasn't mature enough to see that the men in *The Outsider* (there were no women; the creative angst seemed exclusive to one gender) had little in common except a vague dissatisfaction with their world. This they tried to overcome by sometimes attempting suicide and occasionally succeeding at it.

Wilson himself was an outsider—an 'uneducated' (in the sense of university) working-class lad who believed he was the most significant writer of the twentieth century, and had a reading list to prove it. Alienation was not an original theme by the time he sat down to write *The Outsider* (published in 1956); it had been the central theme of modernism from T.S. Eliot to F. Scott Fitzgerald. Jean Jacques Rousseau wrote about it in the eighteenth century; many see portions of the Old Testament too as studies in alienation. The concept has a well-recorded history.

While academics laid out an argument using other people's words, Wilson did the reverse—using his own words to show what was common to a disparate range of writers. It showed more than a talent for gathering quotations and anecdotes; what it revealed was the confidence to let other people light your path while you had your say.

He did the biographer's job superbly too—his biographies of the psychologist Abraham Maslow and George Bernard Shaw are not just wonderful introductions to the works of these men, but equally, extensions of his own work.

While tasting the madeleine dipped in tea, Proust's hero says, 'the vicissitudes of life had become indifferent to me, its disasters innocuous.... I had ceased now to feel mediocre, accidental, mortal ...'

It was an important lesson to learn while growing up.

Six decades after *The Outsider*, has Colin Wilson regained respectability? Respectability that he himself worked so hard at destroying by publishing books about the paranormal and supernatural and what can only be described as tabloid novels and pulp fiction?

In a review of his *Collected Essays on Philosophers,* the *Philosophy Now* magazine said, 'This collection should cast aside once and for all the spurious notion that Wilson was not a philosopher. Here he comes across as a serious thinker about other serious thinkers, analytic or existentialist, and spends less time on expostulating his own agenda, although his prime focus, the expansion of human consciousness via an examination of our mental states, is never far away.'

In the more recent *At the Existentialist Café*, the story of the birth of Sartrean existentialism, Sarah Bakewell notes, '*The Outsider* certainly is an eccentric book, revealing hasty and partial readings of its sources. Yet it has flair and conviction, and it had a deep impact on many readers ...' The list includes Bakewell's father, who found the book one of the 'few sources of light during a drab period in post-war Britain'.

India in the mid-to-late 1970s wasn't quite as drab, nor in need of the kind of light Bakewell Sr speaks of, yet *The Outsider* stood for something. It was one of the most borrowed books from the British Library. You couldn't buy it in any of the bookstores. I bought my first copy in 1980, a Picador edition with a wonderful cover illustration by the American artist Robin Harris.

The *Guardian* obituary called Colin Wilson 'Britain's first, and so far last, homegrown existential star', thereby almost reluctantly acknowledging a part of Wilson's self-view (although Iris Murdoch might have objected to this were she alive; she was an existentialist thinker, biographer of Sartre—and a supporter of Wilson's).

Perhaps unintentionally, the obituarist endorsed another Wilson self-image: 'I would like my life to be a lesson in how to stand alone and to thrive on it.'

In his introduction to the edition of *The Outsider* twenty years later, Wilson wrote: '[*The Outsider*] still produces in me the same feeling of excitement and impatience that I experienced as I sketched the outline plan on that Christmas Day of 1954. Why impatience? Because it aroused enormous anticipation. At the time, I mistook it for anticipation of success. Now I recognize it for what it was: the realization that I had at last settled down to the serious business of living ... I had ceased to waste my time ... I was starting to do what I always intended to do. There was a feeling like leaving harbor.

'It made no difference that the critics later tried to take back what they'd said about the book. They couldn't take back the passport they'd given me.'

What you take from *The Outsider* may be less, or in my case, more than the author put in. That happens sometimes. It was a passport—and not just for Colin Henry Wilson.

Book of unexpected gifts

Cricket teases out character in those who play it. Also in those who write about it. To love cricket is one thing, and necessary, as is a more demanding love, for language itself.

There is yet another love, rarer and more precious. Sidhanta Patnaik had it. He felt personally responsible for the game. If anything went wrong, if the game was brought into disrepute, it hurt him physically. He asked himself: What could I have done to prevent this?

'Cricket is my source of energy,' he said in the last piece he wrote, one that ended mid-sentence with the word 'and ...' The symbolism is inescapable. Patnaik was only thirty-four when he succumbed to cancer. He brought together in one person qualities that go into the making of sports journalists: passion, energy, empathy for the underdog, an eye for the unusual, searing honesty, a phenomenal memory and a nose for where the real story lay.

When he first walked into my office at *Wisden India Almanack*, he said international cricket could take care of itself, he was focused on the neglected: juniors, under-19 and, above all, women's cricket. He soon became the country's go-to man in these areas. His book on the history of women's cricket in India, *The Fire Burns Blue* (co-authored with Karunya Keshav) is a seminal work. He was working on a book on the Ranji Trophy even as his strength ebbed away and pain and frustration became his chief companions.

I was in England during a Test series when I received a message: doctors had given Sidhanta two hours to live. But he hung on with that combination of mind and heart that characterised everything he did. Soon he was out of intensive care—he had asked for an 'extension' so he could complete his *Almanack* work—and back home. 'I can live for two months, two years or twenty years,' he said casually.

To live each day as if it were your last is sound advice. With Sidhanta it was just pragmatism. He couldn't live any other way. Loved ones gained strength from his attitude—his wife Aishwarya and Anantrika, his four-year-old daughter, his sister, his parents.

Sidhanta probably did more work in and around intensive care than most people in plush offices in the same period. There were the books and articles to be written. There was a cricket magazine, *Women's CricZone*, to be launched—he was the editor-in-chief. Youngsters had to be encouraged, fires lit under those who favoured status quo over progress.

He wrote final letters to friends: thank you for everything, there are no regrets. He travelled to Bhubaneswar to prepare his grandmother for the bad news to follow. He wrote down a plan for women's cricket. He left no loose ends except for that dangling sentence.

He loved the game; his writings earned him the love of anonymous people. 'Cricket kept me protected,' he wrote. He did the same for cricket.

And he left behind the book he co-authored: *The Fire Burns Blue*. On first reading it, my mind went back to a (men's) cricket Test at the KSCA Stadium in Bengaluru when the crowd began the chant: 'We want Shantha, we want Shantha.' This was Shantha Rangaswamy, the best-known woman player then, maker of India's first Test century. She was articulate, and a beacon for the sport.

At a talk she gave soon after, someone asked: 'What's the difference between men's and women's cricket?'

'That's easy,' she replied, deadpan. 'Women don't need to wear boxes.'

Women needed a sense of humour to survive then. Things changed gradually. The Board of Control for Cricket in India finally took over the administration, and players had annual contracts.

It was a sign of progress that players developed the confidence to go public with their grievances. Earlier, an Indian captain was slapped by an official for no fault of her own. Another captain, the well-spoken Mamatha Maben, was dropped for ten years for missing a catch!

Harmanpreet Kaur's 171 in the World Cup against Australia quickly assumed legendary, even mythical proportions. She had, according to *The Fire Burns Blue*, walked out to bat 'with a serious expression, a clear mind, an aching shoulder and a borrowed bat.'

The marvellous economy, the telling detail and the research implied in that short sentence make for a wonderful introduction to the book. The qualities are sustained. It is, one of the finest written on cricket history in India.

The authors might well be asking, borrowing from Kipling, 'What do they know of women's cricket who only women's cricket know?' For women's cricket needs to be seen in the context of sport, women's sport, the place of women in society, the challenges of breaking through hardened cultural and psychological attitudes and much more.

'When we started out reporting on women's cricket,' said the authors, 'it was hard to ignore how almost every person of any relevance was single.'

This consciousness of context gives the book the feel of a Renaissance painting—where the background and foreground are both in focus simultaneously; there is both depth and detail here.

It means when the large issues are discussed, they gain significance in the story of the individual, while an individual's story illustrates a bigger point.

The Fire Burns Blue is the story of the players great and small and the gradual emergence of a sport from the sexist cartoons ('All they want during the drinks break is the make-up kit') to the back pages to the front pages and live television and the highest sign of acceptance today—social media trolling.

The stories of struggle—'Thoughts of suicide crossed my mind,' confesses one player—and the sacrifices of the pioneers make the turnaround that much more rewarding and heart-warming.

It is a far cry today from when the women travelled in unreserved railway compartments, learnt how to pull the chain without getting caught and time their run to the food carts on the platforms so they didn't have to get a teammate to pull the chain. There was little administrative interest, hardly any money, few matches, fewer international engagements, but as one official said, 'The girls just wanted to play.' Still the fire burned.

At one point in the book, former captain Purnima Rau says, 'Initially we had great individuals: Shantha, Shubhangi (Kulkarni),

Diana (Eduljee), but India never gelled as a team.' That could have been taken straight from a history of men's cricket, when despite some great players—C.K. Nayudu, Amar Singh, Vijay Merchant, Vijay Hazare, Lala Amarnath—'India never jelled as a team.'

Perhaps that is the Indian way. Perhaps that is the burden pioneers have to bear. A reading of the history of women's cricket informs our understanding of men's cricket too.

The Fire Burns Blue is a book of unexpected gifts. Virginia Woolf puts in an appearance, as does Emily Dickinson. Women's issues seldom spoken about are discussed intelligently: menstruation, pregnancy, sexual harassment, sexual preferences. There is a plea for a progressive pregnancy policy. Post-career counselling is crucial too, as another former captain, Pramila Bhatt, says.

Of India's narrow defeat in the final of the 2017 World Cup, the authors say, 'The Japanese art form of *kingtsugi* repairs broken and flawed pottery with gold, silver or platinum. It doesn't hide the cracks, but embraces them, seeing them as integral to the object's history, and rebuilds something new. (Had India won), the cracks would have remained unexposed. The margin (nine runs) is the perfect mirror to look back at the gains, learnings and areas that still need work.'

That is an unusual but thought-provoking take. It puts that 171 in perspective.

And it leaves behind for the girl who was four years old when her father died, a legacy she can be proud of.

Making it clear

In school I earned a reputation as a scientist. Not that I was very good at laboratory work—in fact, my specialty was to work backwards from the expected result and note down the figures; reverse engineering in fact, although we hadn't heard the expression then. No, it was for my habit of borrowing mainly science books from the school library. George Gamow, Martin Gardner, Isaac Asimov, Peter Medawar and others.

These writers communicated an excitement and a sense of possibilities that was unique. I resolved to be a scientist, a physicist.

Strangely, I was never interested in science fiction, although later in school I did read the science novel, as the story of Sigmund Freud by Irving Stone was called. The book was *Passions of the Mind* and it introduced me to a whole set of new ideas and a new kind of scientist.

Science was glamorous. I once attended a lecture by India's then lone physics Nobel laureate, C.V. Raman, at the institute named after him. An uncle who worked there arranged it. I must have been nine or ten, and shook the great man's hand. I even told him I enjoyed his talk. I didn't understand a word of it, but didn't want the scientist to feel bad.

The first book on science I owned was *One, Two, Three ... Infinity* by George Gamow. I see by the date on the book that two more soon joined Gamow on a shelf I had in my bedroom: *Relativity Made Simple* by James Coleman and a second-hand copy of *The Expanding Universe* by Arthur Eddington. Perhaps books on physics were relatively easier to get then; I can't remember reading much about biology, for example. It was many years before popular books on science became easily available, and many books I bought—including later editions of the George Gamow books—are with me still.

C.P. Snow's *Varieties of Men* introduced me to the mathematician G.H. Hardy and his Indian friend Ramanujan. Hardy's *A Mathematician's Apology* remains among the books I reread often. Hardy was a cricket fan, as was Ramanujan's grandson, whom I met in Chennai. That made it just one degree of separation from another great Indian!

When I find myself in the company of scientists, wrote Auden, I feel like a shabby curate who has strayed by mistake into a drawing room full of dukes. In the half-century and more since he wrote that, a generation has matured that has been throwing a bridge between shabby curates and handsome dukes. This includes both scientists and science writers who write confidently and with lucidity, ensuring they don't alienate the informed reader or dumb down for the novice.

It is a delicate balance, but men with the varied backgrounds of Richard Feynman, Stephen Jay Gould, Richard Dawkins, John Gribbin, Brian Greene, Oliver Sacks, V.S. Ramachandran, Steven Pinker and Roger Penrose have achieved it.

In recent years, research has become so specialised that sometimes even scientists in the same field fail to understand one another. The media has added to the confusion by using a journalistic shorthand that neither explains nor describes. 'Everything is relative,' is, according to some, the most complete survey of Einstein's theories.

Britain's Astronomer Royal Martin Rees put it in perspective when he said, 'I'd personally derive far less satisfaction from my research if it only interested a few other specialists. It is a real challenge to explain clearly and without technicalities even a concept that one understands well.'

With the publication of *A Short History of Nearly Everything,* a third type entered the fraternity: the popular writer in another field. Bill Bryson's book made a splash when it appeared, for making concepts accessible to the reader without a background in science. Bryson confessed he had less than the intelligent man's working knowledge of science, and so he set out to educate himself. He passes on the knowledge to those who have neither the time to meet, nor the access to, top scientists who answer his questions. The information gathered through a close reading of texts and sharp questioning of scientists is sieved through the clarity of his prose.

As in all writing, this involved choice. What do you leave out? How deeply do you go into a subject? Bryson the travel writer gives us a travelogue through science, finding the balance between oversimplification and necessary technical language.

How well has the popular science book educated the average reader? It is certainly a useful catalyst to kindle interest at a young age. Many modern scientists have written about the debt they owed to writers like Michael Faraday, who first opened up to them the excitement and fun of science.

But there is a danger in this that I was first alerted to by my son Tushar when he was in university. For a reason I never understood, while he was doing his undergraduate course in science, he had no time for the large number of popular science books that we had at home. He argued that these, especially in physics, tended to distort.

In a magazine article about this, using the example of Brian Greene, physicist and author of popular books on the subject, he wrote: 'Greene's books are more reader-friendly and therein lies the problem. It isn't as much the clarity of the prose that makes his books readable as the encouraging but deceptive effect of understanding they produce. It isn't Greene's fault. The fault, dear reader, is not in ourselves, but in the stars, the strings, the quarks ... the rest of physics. The fault is that physics is described in its unique language—mathematics. Any attempt to translate mathematics into English or any other language is doomed. Popular books subscribe to the idea that every equation in them will halve sales. But the caveat is that every equation dropped halves the authenticity, a trap Greene falls into.

'"Popular physics" is an approximation. While it is a good introduction and has inspired many young scientists, it isn't complete. In ignoring this, we leave ourselves open to charlatans, such as those who tell us of the so-called spiritual aspects of quantum mechanics and its links to ancient eastern philosophies. The only thing worse than people claiming that spirituality tells us more about the universe than physics is people who believe they are somehow connected. They are not. They can be made to seem connected because of a widespread fallacy—that quantum mechanics can be described in the same language as philosophy.'

That is a strong argument. Now that he is a research fellow in philosophy at Cambridge, he may have mellowed somewhat. But I doubt it.

I shall, however, continue to enjoy Dawkins and Gould, Venki Ramakrishnan and V.S. Ramachandran, Carlo Rovelli and Gribbin,

Michio Kaku, Lee Smolin, David Bodanis, James Gleick and a host of others. As the poet Houseman said, 'Perfect understanding will sometimes almost extinguish pleasure.'

Some of us need to dismantle the toy car to see what makes it run. Others are happy to enjoy the run.

Le Carre's spin

Quite the most startling sentence in John le Carre's 2019 novel *Agent Running in the Field* appears on page 167: '... in my persona of British Commercial Counsellor (I) discuss with our daughter's future parents-in-law such issues as Britain's post-Brexit trade relations and the tortuous bowling action of India's spin bowler Kuldeep Yadav ...' The first issue is important, the second isn't, but often the apparently casual is significant in Le Carre's world.

It is a unique world, both personal and universal at once, like in the finest art, and with its own vocabulary—mole, lamplighter—later adopted by spies in the real world.

It has long seemed to me illogical, if not downright insulting, that Le Carre should be seen as a genre writer of 'mere' spy novels. I am in good company here. *A Perfect Spy* was described by Philip Roth as 'the best English novel since the War.' Ian McEwan says he should have won the Booker Prize long ago. 'Growing up in Spain in the 70s, I remember that even the self-appointed literati were in awe of his books,' says the Spanish writer Carlos Ruiz Zafron.

'The tropes of espionage—duplicity, betrayal, disguise, clandestinity, secret knowledge, the bluff, the double bluff, unknowingness, bafflement, shifting identity—are no more than the tropes of the life that every human being lives,' wrote the novelist William Boyd of Le Carre's world, pointing out that 'literary' writers Graham Greene, Muriel Spark, Norman Mailer, Ian McEwan, Sebastian Faulks and John Banville have written spy novels too. As, of course, have Joseph Conrad, Somerset Maugham and Graham Greene.

On the other side of the divide are Salman Rushdie's early criticism and Clive James's lament about the 'coagulated style'. Anthony Burgess said, 'Le Carre's talents cry out to be employed in the creation of a real novel.'

Is Le Carre a great talent who has limited himself, or a writer who has managed to rise above his subject matter? I think he is neither; he is a modern master holding up a mirror to our times.

Part of the reason for the ambiguity is that Le Carre's characters must necessarily carry incomplete descriptions or risk premature unmasking. That is the nature of the genre. But the fluidity of his writing, and its economy, is something the best strive towards without always succeeding.

Agent Running in the Field, read in a certain way, can be seen as the mirror image of his first big success, *The Spy Who Came in From the Cold*, where an agent is betrayed and killed. Betrayal is a Le Carre specialty, as is the revelation that there is little to choose between 'Us' and 'Them', either in the Cold War period or in the battles against capitalism and corruption in his post-Cold War novels.

Kuldeep Yadav may not know this, but he is guaranteed immortality of sorts.

On form

Most sportsmen—in fact, most performers—understand the concept of 'being in the zone'. It is an expression balancing on the verge of cliché.

Here's the footballing great, Pele, speaking of the 'strange calmness' he experienced during the 1958 World Cup final against Sweden. 'It was a type of euphoria; I felt I could run all day without tiring, that I could dribble through any of their team or all of them, that I could almost pass through them physically. I felt I could not be hurt. I have felt confident many times (before) without that strange feeling of invincibility.'

Here's the novelist Don DeLillo: 'It's a state of automatic writing, and it represents the paradox that's at the centre of a writer's consciousness. First you look for discipline and control. But there's a higher place, a secret aspiration. You want to let go. It's a kind of rapture ... '

'One is raised beyond the prosaic or the everyday to an orgasmic or spiritual level.' This last quote is from Mike Brearley, former England captain, in his book *On Form*.

Cricket, one would imagine, is best deconstructed by someone who has played at the highest level or is a psychoanalyst or perhaps a philosopher. So what happens when someone who is all three writes a book? Will the mixture get too rich? Do different parts of this unique personality get in one another's way or do they enhance the insights these bring?

'Cricket helped me to be psychologically more aware,' says Brearley, this unique personality in his unique book. The warning comes early, however: 'There is no simple narrative logic to this book.'

It is neither prescriptive nor fully descriptive. It is like a guided tour through the realms of psychoanalysis as it bears upon cricket. But unlike on a guided tour, you are left to your own devices—you take a path or ignore it, you meander, you spend time in certain areas, you may even lose your way, for the wonderful thing is, not all these paths actually lead to a destination.

Losing our way, says Brearley, is an opportunity for serendipity, and ends the book with the delightful instruction: 'Get lost!'

Perhaps a guided tour is a false analogy. Brearley seems to be wilfully avoiding any attempt at joining the dots, leaving it to the reader to do so. It is impossible to know whether your final pattern agrees with his, for you may have joined the dots differently. This is either charming or irritating, depending on how you approach it.

The essence of *On Form* is digression. Brearley is being deliberately discursive, and if he didn't already have a reputation as one of the finest captains in the game and probably its greatest thinker today, you might even be tempted to think he was showing off.

But wait! Brearley read classics and moral sciences at Cambridge, was briefly a lecturer in philosophy (following his retirement from cricket) before becoming a practising therapist. So when he evokes Wittgenstein or Descartes or Hume or

Huizinga, or the Hungarian psychologist Mihaly Csikszentmihalyi (who wrote about 'flow', synonymous with 'zone'), Sartre's *mauvaise fois* (bad faith) is definitely not involved.

Writers, actors, movie directors, even a tree-cutter from India have lessons for us; cricketers too. There is Greg Chappell, who talks about focus: 'The conscious mind can be involved with the big picture stuff such as strategy, but once the bowler approaches, one must trust the subconscious and the years of training to do the rest.'

Technique is vital. As Brearley says, with good technique you can forget technique.

The philosopher David Papineau pointed out in *Knowing the Score* that there is little time for conscious decisions in batting. The ball moves too fast, everything has to be instinctive. And instinct is developed through practising technique. And sticking to it under pressure. The body and mind have to be in harmony.

So what of form? Brearley recalls England player and coach Tiger Smith asking him, 'Do you think frowning helps you hit the ball harder?' Years later, Brearley inspected a batting glove of Ian Botham and discovered its fingers were almost unmarked by the bat. Relaxation is key. As is enjoyment.

Brearley shines a light on cricket (even if he suspects it is not all about form), on his profession and, above all, on himself. *On Form* is a quasi-autobiography. Forty years ago, when Brearley wrote his first book, co-author Dudley Doust commented on his temperament that made him look at ideas from different angles. Brearley's autobiography should be called *On the Other Hand*, Doust suggested. Brearley sees both sides of that too.

On Form can be read in many ways. For the average victim of television commentary, who has had it drilled into his head that 'form is temporary, class permanent', it is a door to a challenging new world full of the unexpected.

The insider

Albert Camus begins *The Myth of Sisyphus* with 'There is but one truly serious philosophical problem, and that is suicide. Judging whether life is or is not worth living amounts to answering the fundamental question of philosophy. All the rest—whether or not the world has three dimensions, whether the mind has nine or twelve categories—comes afterwards.'

It is nearly as famous as his other opening paragraph: 'Mother died today. Or maybe yesterday, I don't know.' That is from *The Outsider* (or *The Stranger*, as it is known today, but here I shall call it *The Outsider*, which was the title when I first read the book).

The latter is a novel in which its anti-hero, Meursault, finding himself bored and with nothing in particular to do, shoots and kills an Arab on a beach in Algeria. That was published in 1942. Camus didn't think it was necessary to flesh out the story of the Arab, who had served his purpose by being shot and killed. Edward Said later pointed out that in Camus's best-known novels, nameless, faceless Arabs have to die in order for Europeans to have fancy philosophical reflections. That seems to be the privilege of colonial rulers.

Kamel Daoud, an Algerian journalist, set about filling the holes in Camus's story, and more importantly, telling it from the Arab perspective seven decades later in *The Meursault Investigation.* 'Mama is still alive today,' begins the book, and a little beyond the halfway mark turns the Camus philosophy on its head with, 'Whether or not to commit murder is the only proper question for a philosopher, the only one he ought to ask. All the rest is chit chat.'

Harun, for that is his name, gives the dead Arab a name (Musa), a family (it's his brother) and a history, and by backgrounding anti-colonialism introduces a tension and dimensions missing from Camus. Algeria became independent of France in 1962, by which time Camus, who had been against independence, had died in a car accident.

The book is brilliant, it is funny, it is surreal and as much of a philosophical tract as *The Outsider*. It is like no other reimagining of a classic, and now you cannot—must not—read *The Outsider* without following up with *The Meursault Investigation.* Murderer and victim are tied together by fiction; so too are the murderer and the victim's brother, who steadily finds himself acting like Meursault, down to the pointless murder and an argument with the priest who wants him to seek god.

The premise of Daoud's novel is as startling as it is imaginative. It presumes that Musa's murder is a true story, and that Camus is the murderer. Daoud then establishes that Meursault, the fictional killer, is the author of the novel. And, of course, just as the name of 'the Arab' is never mentioned in *The Outsider,* Camus is never mentioned in *The Meursault Investigation.* The book is about Harun speaking to a Frenchman at a bar.

Camus summed up *The Outsider* in one sentence: 'In our society any man who doesn't cry at his mother's funeral is liable to be condemned to death.' But is that a limited reading of his classic?

The novelist Daoud is telling us that this is indeed so. For it is as much about ignoring the colonial as a person of no significance; it is about Arab identity; it is about what Said called Camus's 'incapacitated colonial sensibility'. As Harun points out, the word 'Arab' appears twenty-five times in the original book, but there's not a single name, not once. How could so little importance be accorded to a dead man, he asks.

In connecting the past with the present, the political with the personal, the faith with the lack of it ('What would become of me in this country, between Allah and ennui?'), the author simultaneously lights up the riches in the later book with a torch so powerful that the outlines we missed in the earlier one are silhouetted too. It is both profound and great fun, a combination that has excited philosophers for centuries.

When an Imam tries to talk to Harun about god, he makes an attempt to explain that 'I had so little time left, I didn't want to waste it on god.' By now Harun is indistinguishable from Meursault, who had told the chaplain in *The Outsider*, 'I didn't have much time left. I didn't want to waste it on god.' The Harun-Meursault transformation underlines the absurdity in both situations, and all situations in general.

Meursault had killed an Arab, Harun killed a Frenchman. The police officer tells Harun, 'You should have killed him with us, during the war, not last week.' Both killers got their timing wrong. For all is forgiven in love and war. A wartime murder of the enemy is heroic and leads to medals; in peace, such a murder is criminal and leads to the gallows.

'The story we've been talking about,' Harun tells his companion, 'should be rewritten from right to left.' Not very subtle, perhaps, but poignant all the same; after all, an unjust fate had befallen his brother 'who died in a book'.

The idea of reimagining is not new. Jane Smiley reimagined King Lear on a farm in Iowa (*A Thousand Acres*), for instance, and more famously, Tom Stoppard built a philosophical play around two minor characters—Rosencratz and Guildenstern—from *Hamlet*. Every narrative, wrote Stoppard, has at least a capacity to suggest a metanarrative. He once declared that the inscription he wanted on the door of his study was: 'No symbolism admitted and none denied.'

The Meursault Investigation succeeds because it causes us to question the truth of the original, suggesting powerfully that there is another way of looking at things, even if, as in this case, it is a fictional narrative. Camus, who expounded the absurd, would have loved it.

Concealing art

When I first read *Swami and Friends*, I realised novels need not be all dark and depressing and Dickensian; it was a startling revelation for a twelve-year-old who swore by Dickens. Swami played cricket in the maidan and in his mind. So did I. Swami wrote letters to the MCC in London, and I marvelled at his confidence. I was always planning to write, but never did. Swami became a close personal friend, and Malgudi a familiar town. I knew where the post office was, where the big banyan tree and the Sarayu river, the Albert Mission college, the statue of Fredrick Lawley and other landmarks were.

Malgudi might not have been on the geographical map of India, but it was certainly on its psychological map. You identified with it even if you didn't entirely recognise it. And Narayan kept confusing us by altering the details occasionally. Fiction demands no 'factual' consistency; it doesn't matter, for instance, whether Dr Watson was shot in the leg or the shoulder in the Sherlock Holmes stories. Enough to know that he was injured in battle.

I tried to read everything by and about Narayan; his autobiography, his *Dateless Diary*, his friendship with Greta Garbo and his travails in the US.

Meanwhile, I was told by a teacher in school that Narayan

didn't write well at all, his language was all wrong. It was unfashionable to like him. If you wanted to be taken seriously, the first thing you had to do was renounce Narayan and his 'small-town' mentality. And never mind what Graham Greene said. Or Faulkner wrote about.

This is what an 'English' education in India does to you sometimes. You develop a kind of foolish literary snobbery and turn your back on old friends and comforters like Swami. I can't remember if that was a period of revisionism in general, but there were articles in magazines around the same time about the 'simplistic' and contrived style of the writer and his limited vocabulary. All very unfair, but we bought into it because schools were training us to be brown sahibs three decades after Independence.

Looking back now, I wonder how many Indians who wrote in English were dismissed thus. A whole generation, possibly more, of Indian writers in English was rejected. Mulk Raj Anand, Raja Rao, Kamala Markandeya were attempted only much later, and even now I don't feel they were identifiably of our world.

G.V. Desani was different, however. He was funny, we knew people who spoke like his characters and, in any case, hadn't the poet Eliot told us he was like-worthy?

In Desani's obituary, Amitav Ghosh put his finger on what ailed what was then referred to as IWE: Indian Writing in English. 'Desani was, I think,' he said, 'haunted by the incommensurability of what he wanted to say with the language he was saying it in. This is, of course, an awareness that haunts many of us who write in English. But Desani was unique in that he alone had the courage to follow his perceptions to their natural conclusion—into the unreachable otherness of silence.'

Apparently, it was a crime to write the English language

in any way other than the manner in which the English-born did. I am slightly ashamed of some of our teachers, who were wannabe Englishmen and women and couldn't countenance anything Indian even decades after Independence. But Narayan has endured better than some of their heroes.

Still, I was influenced by such dismissal to keep off Narayan for a while. It wasn't until my critical faculties were better developed and I began to have greater confidence in my own opinions that I reread him. In my mind I apologised to Swami and went back to him.

And what a treat it was! It didn't matter what the critics thought. I realised Narayan's art lay in concealing art; that despite his own confession ('I am an inattentive quick writer who has little sense of style,' he once told Ved Mehta), he was a master craftsman for whom the story was the thing, and the nuances came in the telling of it.

On Vijayadasami Day in 1930, Narayan wrote the first line of his first novel, 'The train had just arrived at Malgudi station.' But that's not how *Swami and Friends* begins. In his essay on Narayan, Mehta tells us that was revised to: 'It was Monday morning.' That was unusual, for Narayan seldom revised anything, believing that 'writing is a dovetailing process'.

I don't know if others have a similar experience. But sometimes I get nostalgic for a time or a place that never was. Now there is a word for it. Anemoia. It was invented by John Koenig in his *Dictionary of Obscure Sorrows*. Malgudi—none of us has lived there, but all of us know the place and identify with it—is such a place, where time has changed nothing.

People who live there think they are in charge, but they are actually at the mercy of forces they don't understand and can't control. Heroism is limited to the small things; no one is larger than life. If anything, they are smaller. People leave in frustration or disgust, like Mr Sampath or Chandra (*The Bachelor of Arts*). The majority simply give up and give in. Acceptance is the first sign of maturity, even if sometimes that maturity is a long time coming. The stories are remarkably non-judgemental and non-preachy, qualities one realised in retrospect.

Hope and hopelessness are two sides of the same coin. Today's hopeful is tomorrow's despairing. Changes happen, but there is comfort in the unchanging. Jagan's sweet emporium and other landmarks are both symbols of agelessness and hint at the possibility of change. Above all, lives, seen from a particular angle, are filled with humour; individual sorrows and happiness belong to the village. Privacy is neither heard of nor encouraged.

That last is something many of us could identify with. Everybody knew everything about everybody in the villages and small towns. There were no secrets among friends. Or foes. Especially foes. Privacy was an alien concept.

The last train to Malgudi has gone, but generations to come will continue to visit the town, leaving their own vehicles parked outside. The office of the Banner newspaper, Margayya the financial expert and all the landmarks of Malgudi, human and human-made, are frozen in time forever.

And somewhere, Swami is getting ready for his next cricket match.

Astigmatic pedantry

The writer and translator Norman Thomas di Giovanni wrote of co-operating with Jorge Luis Borges thus: 'We agreed that a translation should not sound like a translation but should read as though it had been written directly in the language into which it is being made.'

This might sound like a universal truth, but not everyone agrees. Nabokov held that a translation should sound like a translation. His translation of *Eugene Onegin* strips the original of all poetry. 'The clumsiest literal translation,' he wrote, 'is a thousand times more useful than the prettiest paraphrase.'

This difference in perspective between the literal translation and the poetic has kept translators busy for generations and critics falling on one side of the argument or the other, knowing they would always have the support of one or the other of the great writers of our time. A bridge across the two cultures was thrown by Susan Sontag, who wrote in an essay that translation was 'ethical, one that mirrors and duplicates the role of literature itself ...'

Trust, ethics, beauty, harmony, smoothness, aesthetics all enter into it. As Borges explained to di Giovanni, 'In spite of (my) poems, the translations must be good.'

Mark Polizzotti's *Sympathy for the Traitor: A Translation Manifesto* talks of translators who kill enjoyment through 'astigmatic pedantry'. They belong to the literal school which favours information over interpretation.

Translation is never finished; nor can there be a final, irreducible version of a work of literature.

All this makes translation one of the least understood of arts, and translators the least celebrated of writers, when they should be literary heroes, admired for the sheer scale of their work. There is first the business of a straightforward reading in one language. There has to be a deep appreciation of the nuances and cultural underpinnings of the original and the attempt to duplicate that in the language the work is being translated into. A knowledge of the author's other works, their place against the background of works in his time and place is a given. Obviously, the writing must change, but equally, it must remain the same.

As Conrad wrote to Scott Moncrieff, the translator of Proust's masterpiece, 'I was more interested and fascinated by your rendering than by Proust's creation. I am speaking of the sheer mastery of language; I mean how far it can be pushed—in your case two languages—by a faculty akin to genius.'

Translations have to conquer both text and context. And this is where the literal school gets it wrong. And why translation never ends. A response to a book is a bit like a response to a painting—the reader/viewer brings to it his own experiences while seeing things the writer/artist might not have been aware of himself, at least not consciously. To that extent, everybody is right about a book, just as everybody is right about a work of art.

Anyone with an interest in translation will know where the 'Traitor' in Polizzoti's title comes from. The Italian expression *traduttore, traditore* is an aural pun, implying the traduttore (translator) is traditore (traitor). The cultural, psychological, semantic, philosophical implications of that have kept translation experts busy for decades.

Cervantes has written somewhere that reading a book in translation is like looking at a Flemish tapestry from the back. I am not entirely sure what he meant by that, but it does conjure up an intriguing image. Did he mean the process is as confusing as the threads seem to be, following no easily discernible order or syntax? Or did he mean that it would be like revealing a magician's trick, and would therefore lose its charm? Perhaps he meant that a work should only be read in the original because translation either distorts or diminishes.

What of writers who translated their own works? Samuel Beckett wrote in French and English, and translated from one to the other. Writers who self-translated into English include Nabokov (from Russian), O.V. Vijayan (Malayalam), Girish Karnad (Kannada), Italo Calvino (Italian), Rabindranath Tagore (Bengali), Karen Blixen (Danish). It is like 'sorting through one's own innards and then trying them on for size, like a pair of gloves,' wrote Nabokov. There is something about translation that inspires great imagery from our finest writers.

The English version of Nabokov's *Speak, Memory: An Autobiography Revisited* began its life as an essay written by him in French, which was translated by Hilda Ward (and revised by Nabokov himself) for publication in *The Atlantic Monthly* in 1943. Seven years later, the American version of the autobiography, *Conclusive Evidence: A Memoir*, grew out of a series of articles Nabokov wrote for *The New Yorker*. The same year, *Speak, Memory: An Autobiography* was published in Britain.

Now it becomes more interesting. Nabokov himself translated that into Russian (*Drugie Berega*). Then Nabokov retranslated portions of the Russian version into English for *Speak, Memory: An Autobiography Revisited.*

He wrote in this final version: 'This re-Englishing of a Russian re-version of what had been an English re-telling of Russian memories in the first place, proved to be a diabolical task, but some consolation was given me by the thought that such multiple metamorphosis, familiar to butterflies, had not been tried by any human before.' And we'll leave it at that!

When Jhumpa Lahiri, the American writer, first wrote a book in Italian, a language she had to learn and one she was in love with, she chose Ann Goldstein to translate it into English. It was a fascinating exercise. Lahiri, born in London to Bengali parents, raised in the US, wrote in her Italian book (translated into English as *In Other Words*) that she felt 'exiled even from the definition of exile.'

She spoke an alien language at home (the rule was she could only speak in Bengali to her parents) and another at school. Neither belonged to her. That was circumstance. But Italian was a choice, something she had chosen for herself and was thus more intimate, more personal.

'When I write in Italian, I think in Italian; to translate into English I have to wake up another part of my brain. I don't like the sensation at all,' she wrote of her decision not to self-translate.

Also, it was important to render 'my Italian honestly, without smoothing out its rough edges, without neutralizing its oddness, without manipulating its character.' Hence, Goldstein, a *New Yorker* editor and translator of Elena Ferrante.

In Other Words is both the experiment and the explanation, a writerly book on writing, like some books on science written by scientists. Lahiri then wrote a slim reflection, *The Clothing of Books,* in Italian. It was translated into English by her husband Alberto Vourvoulias-Bush.

Then she went one step further, translating her Italian novel (*Dove Mi Trovo*) into English (*Whereabouts*) herself.

How successful was Lahiri's effort? It is impossible to tell unless you are familiar with both Italian and English (the American edition of her book, in fact, was published with the original and the translation on facing pages). Tim Parks, the British author and critic who has lived in Italy for forty years, thought there was an element of hubris in this. 'What Lahiri writes,' he says of *In Other Words*, 'is little less than an account of her attempt to escape English. At no point does it draw energy from Italian culture ... there are no Italian characters in the book ... the book is somehow not written *for* Italians; rather, the achievement of Italian becomes a trophy to show off to the reader.'

What did Parks think of Lahiri's Italian novel?

Parks begins by sounding positive (I think) about the effort, saying, '(the novel) offers an altogether more interesting solution to the dual nature of her bilingual texts. It's a novel with radical ambitions: it seeks to be inside and outside two literary traditions, neither here nor there.'

Thematically she invokes Italo Calvino and Cesare Pavese, he says. 'But,' he continues, 'the complete immersion in Italian culture evident in Calvino and Pavese is missing in *Whereabouts*, and it's this absence that conveys to the reader the disorientation of the book's title. The clothes don't quite fit.'

Parks increasingly appears unconvinced, saying, 'In her translation, Lahiri avoids Goldstein's quaintness, rearranging the syntax and sometimes adjusting the meaning to make the speaking voice more fluent and convincing. Yet something strange remains, something earned from the text's passage through Italian. The sentences are shorter than those in Lahiri's earlier work, everything is more controlled.... The reader feels spooked, unsettled.'

It is widely acknowledged that after Milan Kundera began writing in French in the 1990s, his works lost some of their power.

It is glib to say that translation is impossible, just as it is true to say that without translation, there would be no literature. Without translation, we would be denied access to the works of Márquez, Cortazar, Llosa, Proust, Dostoevsky, Paz, Pushkin, Chekhov, Kundera, Eco, Allende, Kawabata, Neruda, Pamuk. Translation is long, lonely, even dangerous work (the Japanese translator of *Satanic Verses* was slain).

We know who wrote *One Hundred Years of Solitude, Hopscotch, The Name of the Rose, The Unbearable Lightness of Being* and a hundred other classics. But do we know who translated these works so we could enjoy them in a language we understand? Do we care?

'Without translation,' wrote Italo Calvino, 'I would be limited to the borders of my own country. The translator is my most important ally. He introduces me to the world.'

The novelist Carlos Fuentes called Edith Grossman's translation of *Don Quixote* 'a major literary achievement'. Grossman says 'authors must see themselves as transmitters rather than creators of texts'. Borges told his translator not to write what he said but what he meant to say.

Márquez called his translator Gregory Rabassa, 'The best Latin American writer in the English language', and went so far as to say that Rabassa's version of *One Hundred Years of Solitude* was superior to his own. He preferred, he said, to read his books in English as translated by Grossman and Rabassa. Rabassa said he was merely 'exposing the English that was hiding behind Márquez's Spanish.'

As the critic Edmund White has pointed out, Nabokov thought that Dostoevsky read better in English and the French version of

Faulkner's *The Sound and the Fury* was superior to the original.

In Kerala, they joke that Márquez is the best writer in Malayalam; that is the language many have read his books in. It is easier to get Malayalam translations of books in Spanish and Portuguese than it is to get of books in Punjabi or Gujarati. I am sure the reverse is also true. The field is large in India, but untapped.

In her charming book on translation, *This Little Art*, Kate Briggs says, 'We need translations. The world, the English-speaking world, needs translations. Clearly and urgently it does; we do.' I like the passion there, even if the ambition is limited. We need more than just English translations.

Translators often tend to write about their work in highly technical terms, as if it were a scientific project and every time you put two languages together in a test tube and shook it, you always got the same final translation. Translation is a service, often shining a light on the hidden aspects of a novel.

'Fidelity is our highest aim,' says Grossman, 'but a translation is not made with tracing paper. It is an act of critical interpretation. Languages trail immense histories behind them, and no two languages, with all their accretions of tradition and culture, ever dovetail perfectly.'

It is this understanding that gives her book *Why Translation Matters* a special feel. Rabassa's *If This Be Treason* discusses translation and his own role in it with a lightness of touch that reflects the fun he had translating Cortazar, Llosa and others.

In *Mouse or Rat?*, Umberto Eco speaks of translation as negotiation, arguing that negotiation is not just between words but between cultures. The Italian 'ratto' is rat while 'topo', he says, can be either rat or mouse, and a shriek followed by a cry of 'Un topo' is acceptable in an Italian translation of Shakespeare.

But in a translation of Albert Camus's *La Peste*, the rat presages the plague, and therefore only 'ratto' will do.

All great texts contain their potential translation between the lines, wrote Walter Benjamin. All translations are a compromise between two mutually exclusive exigencies—fidelity to the literality of the words and fidelity to the literary intention of the author.

Translation is an art, and like all art can be imprecise. Some writers take it upon themselves to help a translator, while others like Márquez see it as a different discipline altogether and leave everything to the translator.

Can there be an untranslateable work? I once imagined *Finnegans Wake* would be untranslatable. After all, the joke was: which language are you translating from? But since then, there have been Chinese, Japanese, Polish, French and even a 'plain English' translation. Herve Michel, who translated it into French, considered the book the sacred scripture of the modern era and gave it his 'interpretative spin'. The 'plain English' translation by a University of Chicago scholar, James Badwater, ran to 175,000 pages. It takes an estimated forty-two years to read.

As Grossman said, 'Where literature exists, translation exists. Joined at the hip, they are absolutely inseparable, and, in the long run, what happens to one happens to the other. Despite all the difficulties the two have faced, sometimes separately, usually together, they need and nurture each other, and their long-term relationship, often problematic but always illuminating, will surely continue for as long as they both shall live.'

Born for an age like this

It is as easy to venerate George Orwell for all the wrong reasons as it is to condemn him for misunderstood ones. This might be a strange reaction to a man whose prose was so clear as to be transparent (the windowpane analogy he used applied best to himself). Yet, if so many groups, from right-wing fanatics to left-wing extremists, claim kinship with Orwell, convinced he was speaking for them, then surely there must be something confusing about his writing, something inconsistent, something not clearly understood?

In fact, it is not that his writings are misinterpreted (although there is a fair bit of that), but as Christopher Hitchens has said, 'People want what they think he's got, it's just that they don't realise what it would take to get it. They want the idea of integrity, honesty and authenticity. They want to brush up against him. They want to be in the same photo-op as him, to use a modern idiom.'

This is the power of the man. Many writers have undertaken the task of reconciling Orwell's contradictions. This is doomed to failure for two reasons. The obvious one, of course, is that Orwell was a man of contradictions, these were a part of who he was, and to eliminate them would be to reduce his Orwellianism, if an ugly usage is permitted. Also, the tempting simplicity of his prose was bound to mean all things to all people.

Now that the Orwell image is more or less set in stone—as a man of integrity who went to war to fight for his principles and on another occasion starved while gathering material for a book, and as an uncompromising commentator who 'grew colder the closer you got to him' and a prophet who saw that the choice was between freedom and tyranny and not between political systems—it is possible to think of him as a writer who occasionally got things wrong.

Orwell began one of his poems thus: '*A happy vicar I might have been/ Two hundred years ago/ to preach upon eternal doom/ And watch my walnuts grow.*

'*But,*' he points out, '*born alas in an evil time,/ I missed that pleasant haven.*'

The poem ends with: '*I wasn't born for an age like this;/ Was Smith, was Jones, were you?*'

He was conscious of not only recording his times, but delineating where the evil might lead if unchecked. His *1984* was not a prediction, but a *reductio ad absurdum* of his times, the story of a system stretched beyond its usefulness.

The important thing to remember about Orwell is that he was a political writer who elevated the calling by participatory journalism (long before that phrase became fashionable). He was, too, that rare animal, a columnist and essayist who wrote uncomplicated prose because he had the gift of breaking up complex thoughts into simpler components. He fought intellectualism and abstract ideas and was an Everyman whose searchlight carved a wide arc from dirty postcards to Salvador Dali to the English language.

When it was revealed at the turn of the century, some fifty

years after his death, that Orwell had played Big Brother, giving the Foreign Office a list of names of fellow travellers, there was shock all around. This liberal, power-hating, group-bashing democratic socialist had, in the words of his detractors on the Left, 'given the other side ammunition'. He fell in the eyes of many, although the list was made as a guide to his friend Celia Kirwan, suggesting whom to avoid when asking people to write for the Information Research Department where she worked.

It wasn't anything like the McCarthy-era lists in the US. Michael Redgrave, who was among the thirty-eight in the list, went on to star in the film adaptation of *1984*. The journalist Peter Smollett, also in the list, got an OBE. No one suffered, not even in retrospect.

What is interesting about the list, however, is that in it Orwell proclaims his blind spots to the world: his anti-Semitism (not rabid, but 'intellectual', for want of a better word), his homophobia and his apparent misogyny.

Orwell's writings take up twenty volumes, and even the most casual reader will find many contradictions there. But in one short list, Orwell gives a glimpse into a world he seldom wrote or spoke about. He said he 'named names' not because of any private vendetta, but because totalitarianism posed a greater threat to liberty than providing information on those with a history of supporting the Soviet Union. The lie had to be acknowledged.

Funnily enough, Orwell began as a lie, changing his name from Eric Blair before the publication of his first book, *Down and Out in Paris and London.* River Orwell, from which he took his name, flows through Suffolk in England.

Many things he wrote (including the essay on his school, 'Such, Such Were the Joys') were true in essence rather than in fact, and anyone taking his essays and novels literally is bound to get tangled up in semantics. He saw writing as truth of a higher order. In an essay on Dickens, he wrote about that writer's habit of telling small lies in order to emphasise the big truth. It was a technique Orwell borrowed.

But even if he hadn't written *Animal Farm* and *1984*, Orwell was guaranteed a place among the truth-sayers, fit to rank with Jonathan Swift. He was both political and a writer, so the description 'political writer' sat well on him. In Cyril Connolly's memorable line, 'He could not blow his nose without moralising on conditions in the handkerchief industry.' Connolly also gives another clue to Orwell's personality when he writes, 'He felt enormously at home in the Blitz, among the bombs, the bravery, the rubble, the shortages, the homeless, the signs of rising revolutionary temper.'

Was Orwell's prose too straightforward for his own good? Did its simplicity cause people to see him as simplistic? Did the Nobel committee ignore him because he was political and popular or because he trod on the toes of both the Right and the Left? Perhaps—and this is the most likely explanation—he died too early, aged forty-six, a year after *1984* was published.

Was he a great writer? Hitchens was clear on this. 'Orwell isn't a very great writer,' he says. 'He's a very honest and courageous writer and he does a lot of work and he does have a certain gift of phrase, there's no doubt about that. But he's not in the first rank of writers. And that's a good thing because it shows what average, ordinary people can do if they care to, and it abolishes some of the alibis and excuses for people who aren't brave.'

But the phrase 'very great writer' seems like a cop-out. Hitchens, a fan (the title of the book he wrote was *Why Orwell Matters*), was making the same mistake the rest were: raising the bar so high only because it concerned a man who was doing the same in his writings. Orwell was not just a significant writer—there can be few arguments here—but a great writer too.

In his 1946 essay, 'Why I Write', Orwell says, 'Looking back through my work, I see that it is invariably where I lacked a political purpose that I wrote lifeless books and was betrayed into purple passages, sentences without meaning, decorative adjectives and humbug generally.'

Orwell set out to make the unfamiliar familiar and vice versa, and you can't ask more from a writer. He had the gift of facing unpleasant facts, which is a quality rarer than we think. His greatness as a writer lay in his ability to clarify complex ideas through the sieve of his prose. His integrity was of an order that placed ideas above people, principles above relationships.

The biggest assaults on Orwell's reputation have come from the Left. E.P. Thompson, Edward Said, Salman Rushdie have portrayed Orwell as a reactionary and a surreptitious conservative. Isaac Deutscher, the Marxist writer, claims that *1984* provided the masses with a 'bogey-cum-scapegoat', allowing them to 'flee from their own responsibility for mankind's destiny.'

The contradictions in Orwell are yet to fall into a pattern. He hasn't been neatly tied up, all mysteries resolved, nothing new to be discovered. Which is why he continues to be relevant.

The number of copies sold of *1984*, according to *The New York Times*, went up by 9,500 per cent when Donald Trump took office as president of the US. Orwell saw the novel as a warning rather than a prophecy, but prophecies come true when warnings aren't heeded. 'Who controls the present,' he wrote, 'controls the past.' Orwell swung back into the news again, seventy years after his death, as the man who—in the words of Hitchens—'faced the despotisms of his day with little more than a battered typewriter and a stubborn personality.'

Orwell didn't change history, but he helped us understand it better. 'One defeats a fanatic,' he wrote in a letter to a friend, 'precisely by not being a fanatic oneself, but on the contrary, by using one's intelligence.' Orwell is invoked around the world wherever civil rights are endangered or human decency is stifled by a fanatical adherence to its opposite.

The word 'Orwellian' is used to mean tyranny and fear of conformism, but as Hitchens points out, a piece of writing described as 'Orwellian' recognises that human resistance to the terrors is unquenchable.

Some writers startle by fission, by breaking things up; Orwell went the other way, surprising by fusion, by bringing things together.

'In a time of deceit,' he once wrote, 'telling the truth is a revolutionary act.' On another occasion: 'People sleep peaceably in their beds at night only because rough men stand ready to do violence on their behalf.'

How did he know about us?

That's the question populations fighting tyranny have asked for decades.

During a time when 'nationalism' and 'patriotism' are being used interchangeably, it is useful to remember Orwell's distinction. 'By patriotism,' he wrote, 'I mean devotion to a particular place and a particular way of life which one believes to be the best in the world but has no wish to force upon other people. Patriotism by its nature is defensive, both militarily and culturally.'

Nationalism, he said, involves 'identifying oneself with a single nation or other unit, placing it beyond good and evil and recognising no other duty than that of advancing its interests. It is inseparable from the desire for power.'

That might be a commentary on the political narrative of the first couple of decades of the twenty-first century.

The reach and impact of Orwell's fiction apart, in many ways, he lives in his essays. What makes them so fresh, writes George Woodcock in a study (*The Crystal Spirit*), 'is the informality, the sense of linear development which gives one the feeling of being inside the author's mind as he is developing his thoughts. In the essays on individual writers, the sense of participation is deepened by the fact that Orwell can never resist thinking of another writer as a person and trying to see him in his mind's eye (and) we get from his criticism a kind of imaginative satisfaction analogous to that induced by certain elusive types of fiction.'

There is, too, the satisfaction that Orwell reveals as much about himself as his subject, says Woodcock.

Orwell's consistent topicality might be an accident of history, but he entered the language as an adjective by right. In telling us about our world, he carved out a world that was unique to his writing. He was an angry man who did something constructive with his anger.

He is 'the only writer of genius among the litterateurs of social revolt between the two Wars,' wrote Arthur Koestler, saying he was the link between Swift and Kafka.

'To speak for a generation without being typical of it is one of the marks by which we can tell the exceptional writers of any time,' wrote Woodcock, for whom Orwell was the physical embodiment of Don Quixote, which was 'appropriate, for in many ways, Orwell can only be understood as a quixotic man.'

Orwell will live for a few more generations and be invoked every time man's inhumanity to man is manifest.

Science and self-interest

When his wife heard that Venki Ramakrishnan had won the Nobel Prize, she said, 'I thought you had to be really smart to win one of those.' Behind every successful man, says Venki, stands a surprised woman. It is one of the few family anecdotes in *Gene Machine*, the scientist's book on the race to decipher the ribosome.

This, the story of how science progresses, through a maze of egos, ambitions, accidents, failures and incremental successes, is on a par with *The Double Helix* by James Watson, the story of the discovery of the structure of the DNA.

Watson has more than a walk-on part in the story of the ribosome—he too had worked on the problem. Later, he said when he realised how complex it was, he assumed we would never know the structure.

Scientists who write with lucidity and demystify concepts are a gift to both science and literature. *Gene Machine* is about one man's journey towards a pathbreaking discovery as well as a peep into the way the system works. Venki, who had a doctorate in physics, switches fields to biology, entering it with only vague notions of what a gene is, or the role of the ribosome. An article in *Scientific American* makes him realise his training as a physicist would be useful. 'Almost a decade after I had switched, it looked like my second career was going down the tubes just like my first one.'

Throughout, however, Venki tackles the big questions. The difficult attracts the truly creative and original minds capable of profound insights, while those satisfied with less are the also-rans of science.

In *The Double Helix*, Watson said, 'Science seldom proceeds in the straightforward logical manner imagined by outsiders. Instead, its steps forward are often very human events in which personalities and cultural traditions play major roles.' Venki's book is further evidence. 'The truth is,' he says, 'scientists will collaborate or compete depending on what is in their self-interest.'

As the race heats up, so too does the politics, and disasters in the lab, and Venki the outsider moves towards the inner circle by the force of his work. Competition can be good for science, he says.

It has long seemed illogical that the greatest Indian-born scientist of the day is not widely feted in his own country. One reason might be his response when asked if he had been offered a directorship of an institution in India. No, he said, adding he wouldn't accept it anyway. Nationality, he explained, was an accident of birth. Bad PR! The Hindutva brigade apparently were already upset that in 2002 Venki had supported a scholarship for poor Muslim girls in the aftermath of the Gujarat riots. 'I did it,' he explains, 'partly because the education of girls lifts society as a whole everywhere.'

The Chidambaram-born, Baroda-graduate citizen of both the US and the UK and president of the Royal Society has written a thriller that just happens to be factual.

Nobel for a song

When the Nigerian Wole Soyinka was awarded the Nobel Prize in Literature in 1986, V.S. Naipaul commented that the Nobel Prize Committee was 'pissing on literature ... from a great height.' In three decades since, the committee has worked its way to even greater heights to perform the same act. My generation grew up on Bob Dylan; most of us can quote him with greater ease than we can Shakespeare or the Bible. Heroes of our youth winning the best that mankind has to offer ought to somehow validate us. Yet, it is more embarrassing than uplifting.

It is easy to see this as a highbrow versus lowbrow argument. The labels nourish each other, bringing the other into sharper focus (although not always with greater understanding) by providing the counterpoint. Occasionally, highbrow kicks its shoes off, lets its hair down, reaches below and pulls up lowbrow. This is a concession from the exclusive to the egalitarian; from quality to equality.

In art, kitsch was thus elevated. In movies, the work of Alfred Hitchcock was given a similar boost by the critics of *Cahiers du cinema*.

Dylan may be the finest songwriter of this or any other

generation, with sheer longevity and volume of work placing him above Woody Guthrie or Leonard Cohen (actually, even as I write this, I am not so sure). But literature? The Swedish Academy has played it safe by implying that though Dylan's lyrics may be poetry, it is the whole caboodle—the music, the social commentary, the public performance that mattered.

'And he's a very interesting traditionalist, in a highly original way,' it said. 'Not just the written tradition, but also the oral one; not just high literature, but also low literature.' Don't miss the defensive tone.

The committee could not give the award to Homer, so they gave it to Dylan instead. This puts the singer in the same literary class as W.B. Yeats, George Bernard Shaw, Ernest Hemingway and William Faulkner, and above Leo Tolstoy, Anton Chekhov, Jorge Luis Borges, James Joyce and Joseph Conrad, who were not thought good enough.

The response in the literary world has been interesting. Older writers like Salman Rushdie, Joyce Carol Oates and Toni Morrison have welcomed it. Hari Kunzru's reaction is typical of the young: 'This feels like the lamest Nobel win since they gave it to Obama for not being Bush,' he tweeted.

This is the battle between cool and uncool. It is uncool to suggest that a musical icon is no literary giant, however attractive his lyrics and however haunting his music. It is cool to admit that sure, Dylan could not have written Thomas Pynchon's *The Crying of Lot 49* or anything by Philip Roth or Haruki Murakami, and ask, 'But then, could any of these writers have written "Tambourine Man" or "Subterranean Homesick Blues"?'

In one corner, therefore, are the yeasayers, those who believe the time had come to honour Dylan (who has been on the fringes of Nobel discussions for some time now) and in the other are the naysayers, who think that the committee has opened the floodgates to everybody who has ever put pen to paper, including writers of detective fiction and advertisement jingles, and art critics.

This can be cause for both encouragement and despair. The individual can hope—the system has been tweaked to make it less elitist. Justin Bieber can start dreaming.

There are always two ways of justifying the Nobel Prize, and not just in literature. 'If someone like x could win it, then surely y is no worse,' goes one, and you can fill in the names of *x* and *y* (Sully Prudhomme and Pearl Buck?). The other is the 'affected millions of people' argument. The committee, for so long allergic to the popular writer (Graham Greene didn't win because he was seen as too popular, too well known), has now swung to the other extreme and picked someone who is not only popular and well known, but may not be a writer even. 'If Dylan's a poet,' wrote Norman Mailer years ago, 'then I am a basketball player.'

Dylanologists beg to differ. The best known, Christopher Ricks, former professor of English at Cambridge University and then professor of humanities at Boston University, has compared Dylan to the great poets. In *Dylan's Visions of Sin*, Ricks has drawn parallels between Dylan's *Lay, Lady, Lay* and John Donne's poem, *To His Mistress Going to Bed*. Dylan's *Not Dark Yet* has been compared to Keats's *Ode to a Nightingale*.

Which is all good fun, of course. Ricks and Greil Marcus, another academic, have been beating Dylan's drum, as have a host of lesser known critics and writers. Some have made a virtue of Dylan's appropriation of others' works, saying there is a long tradition of borrowing in art, literature and music. Life and art, Dylan himself once said, are a matter of interpretation, not fact.

His best line about his own work was in response to someone

who asked him what his songs were about. 'Some are about three minutes and some are about five minutes,' he replied, suggesting, as he often did, that he personally didn't take this 'voice of a generation' business too seriously.

If it were left to him, he'd probably sit down to write another poem/song along the lines of 'It's Alright, Ma (I'm only laughing—all the way to the bank and the pantheon of literary heroes).'

Roth and Rushdie, Oates and Murakami, Don DeLillo and Ngugi wa Thiong'o are probably working furiously on their first rock albums now.

A reader's curiosity

It is possible that Alberto Manguel has read more books than anybody else on earth. He can lecture in English and French, reads Italian and has translated works into Spanish. He lives in Canada, having spent his childhood in Israel (where his father was Argentina's ambassador) and in Argentina. The first language he spoke was German ('with a Czech accent, thanks to the maid,' he says). He has been described variously as an essayist, critic, translator, novelist, anthologist, but Manguel refers to himself as a 'reader'. His *A History of Reading* is already a classic.

His latest book, *Curiosity*, begins with the line, 'I am curious about curiosity.' Then follows the dazzling interplay of words and thoughts, of connections and severances, of history and reinterpretations. And above all, a journey with Dante.

'Books are very patient,' he told a rapt audience at the London Review Bookshop. He was referring to the fact that he came to Dante rather late in life. 'Books wait for you,' he said encouragingly. Still, even if the youngest audience member there read a book every day for the rest of his life in three or four different languages, it is unlikely he would have read as much as Manguel already has.

It is the kind of thought that might discourage some. Luckily,

Manguel has inspired more people to read books than most. There is his passion, for one. And his gift for connecting dots and delving into history and culture that bring books alive. A casual glance at the index of *Curiosity*, under the letter 'B', gives us Beckett, Berlin (Isaiah), Bhagavad Gita, Burroughs (Edgar Rice), Pope Boniface VIII, Borges. Manguel can bring them all together, perhaps adding Plato and Tarzan for seasoning—all in one paragraph. And do it naturally, without strain.

In that list, Jorge Luis Borges is special. When Manguel was sixteen and working in a bookshop, Borges walked in and asked if the youngster would be willing to read to the blind writer. It was the most fortuitous meeting in literature. Borges became Manguel's guide and philosopher, taking him through the highways and bylanes of literature, giving him a sense of what can only be called Borgesian.

Besides a love for the mischievous, the association perhaps convinced Manguel that it is sometimes more important to ask the question than to provide resolutions. *Curiosity* is a ride through books and what make them. It continues a lifelong journey into writing and its equal partner, reading. Dante's *Divine Comedy*, Manguel told his audience in London, is possibly the greatest work in literature, greater than anything Cervantes or Shakespeare ever wrote. Sitting beside him, John Sutherland, the English academic and writer who was 'in conversation' as they say at book launches, refused to rise to the bait.

Sutherland brought to the discussion a delightful combination of seriousness and laughter. 'Manguel vaults over the traditional fences of genre, literary history, and discipline with breathtaking virtuosity,' he said of *Curiosity*. 'He is the Montaigne of our day. If they put another rover on Mars they should call it "Manguel".'

Curiosity might just as easily be the title of Manguel's

autobiography. The quality of curiosity is never strained. Not in Manguel's case, not in the case of his hero, Dante. Thanks to modern methods of communication, Manguel passes on his curiosity to his readers, through the written word, through the spoken word and through his words in other people's writings. It is a journey that we take along with him, grateful for his signposts and even more for his singular lack of condescension. From a man who owns some 30,000 books (he has them in a house in France) and has read so much, this is amazing kindness.

'The library in the daytime is an organised place,' he told me in India once, 'but at night you can imagine the books talking to one another, making love and producing new books. It is a different world.' It is a world Manguel has explored in *The Library at Night*, a joyous coming together of his love for books, of order and disorder and what ifs.

'Stories are our memory, libraries are the storerooms of that memory, and reading is the craft by means of which we can recreate that memory by reciting it and glossing it, by translating it back into our own experience, by allowing ourselves to build upon that which previous generations have seen fit to preserve,' he wrote.

If the poet can see a world in a grain of sand, a reader can see his own life cohere in his book collection. Manguel has more Plato than Aristotle, more Zola than Maupassant and no John Grisham at all, although there are hundreds of detective novels.

Once, around Christmas, Manguel sat down to write a letter, but, as he says, words kept escaping him, disappearing into thin air. He had had a stroke. 'To prove to myself I had not lost the capacity for remembering words, only that of expressing them out aloud, I began to recite in my head bits of literature I knew by heart. Poe, Dante, Hugo.

'It left me with a question. What are these thoughts that have not yet achieved their verbal state of maturity?'

This is the essential Manguel—one who moves from the personal to the specific to the universal. He is a philosopher of the written word. And books are 'home' for this travelling purveyor of stories and ideas. 'As a child it can be disconcerting shifting from city to city, country to country,' he once said. 'But when I opened my books, and saw the prints and the illustrations, I felt comforted. I knew I was home.'

Today, the world is his home—he brings that cliché alive—and the written word anywhere is his raw material. Cervantes and Dante, Borges and Hume, Auden and Fuentes, murder mysteries, erotic literature, are all filtered through the experiences of this remarkable man. A man of infinite curiosity.

I have been fascinated by Manguel ever since his *A History of Reading* and his collections of essays, *Into the Looking Glass Wood*. Meeting him has always been a delight. On the first occasion, he wanted to know all about cricket, and ended up signing a book to me thus: 'To Suresh, who knows all in life isn't cricket.' There is both the precision and the ambiguity of a poet in that line.

Enemies of promise

My first job was with *Deccan Herald* in Bengaluru. I was just out of university and came under the spell of its assistant editor P.K. Srinivasan, a polymath with a remarkable felicity for words. He ought to have written a dozen books by then. 'PK' held court regularly, either in the office or at a watering hole nearby. When I asked in all innocence why he hadn't written a book, he said, 'I dissipated it all in talking.'

Later, I came across this line in Cyril Connolly's *Enemies of Promise*: 'A good talker can talk away the substance of twenty books in as many evenings.' The late PK was one of two people I regret didn't write books, the other being my old school chum Anil Kuruvilla, of whom I have written elsewhere. They had wonderfully inclusive minds, the ability to join dots to make unexpected pictures and the immersion in language that brought everything alive.

George Steiner tells us in *My Unwritten Books* that 'publication cheapens and falsifies belief irremediably.' It is only one of the reasons he didn't publish any of the seven books he discusses—the seven deadly sins, from sex to inadequacy, that prevented him from writing those books. He has, of course, written twenty other books.

In 1938, Connolly set out to inquire into 'the problem of how to write a book which lasts ten years.' The edition I have was reprinted in 1979, so clearly *Enemies of Promise* is its own answer.

The first of three parts is a critical look at the literature of his time, and the third is an autobiography. It is the middle part that concerns us here—where he discusses the weeds that literature can get lost in.

Connolly famously declared that it was the 'true function' of a writer to try to produce a masterpiece and that 'no other task is of any consequence'.

And what are the obstacles en route to achieving this for a promising writer? Connolly borrows his metaphors from the eighteenth-century poet George Crabbe's *The Village:*

There thistles stretch their prickly arms afar,
And to the ragged infant threaten war;
There poppies, nodding, mock the hope of toil,
There the blue bugloss paints the sterile soil;
Hardy and high, above the slender sheaf,
The slimy mallow waves her silky leaf;
O'er the young shoot the charlock throws a shade,
And the wild tare clings round the sickly blade;
With mingled tints the rocky coasts abound,
And a sad splendor vainly shines around.

Thistles stands for politics, the *nodding poppies* for day-dreams, conversation, drink and other narcotics, *blue bugloss* is journalism, *slimy mallow* represents worldly success, *charlock* is sex and its obsessions, *clasping tares* the ties of duty and domesticity. *Mangled tints* are the varieties of talents which appear, *sad splendor* is vanished promise. These are the parasites of literature. 'They are blights,' says Connolly, 'from which no writer is immune.'

Connolly was criticised for his lifestyle and the kind of lunch he describes having while his country was preparing for war (omelette, vichy, peaches on a table underneath a tree with a gramophone playing in the next room), but that need not detain us here. Eight decades after the list was first published, how well does it apply to our less rigid times, when literary Venn diagrams overlap variously?

It is tempting (to take the above in the order in which they are written) to believe that *thistles* do not affect writers any more, but we have no way of knowing how many promising writers in dictatorships simply chose a safer profession. Or just how many young minds were attracted to the rough and tumble of the political game and lost their initial vision. On the other hand, some of the finest contemporary writers have evolved in opposition to the politics of their land. Orhan Pamuk and Elif Shifak in Turkey, Mohammed Hanif, Nadeem Aslam and a host of writers from Pakistan, and the later Arundhati Roy in India are only some of these writers.

'Canvassing, making speeches, and pamphleteering are not the best medium for sensitive writers,' says Connolly. But writers take such activities in their stride today, changing garbs with all the ease of superheroes in telephone booths. They are able to separate their writing from their activism (Margaret Atwood is a sterling example) or incorporate their worldview into their books without compromising on literary quality (Amitav Ghosh).

Iris Murdoch, the philosopher-novelist, once told an interviewer, 'I feel an absolute horror of putting theories into a book. As a novelist, I would rather know about sailing ships and hospitals than about philosophy.' But if all art is propaganda, as Orwell maintained, then the choice is really between being obvious and being subtle.

The escapism promised by the *poppies* caused Connolly to comment that there is but one crime—'to escape from our talent, to abort the growth of that which, ripening and maturing, must be the justification of the demands we make on society.' Alcohol and drugs apart, there is religion too, which corrupts the promising. 'Whom the gods wish to destroy,' says Connolly, 'they first call promising.'

The *poppies* remain as much of a threat. The Irish poet and novelist Brendan Behan seemed to speak for many writers when he described himself as a 'drinker with a writing problem'. Kingsley Amis didn't mind if he were to be known as one of 'the great drunks of our time.'

Laziness, and a failure to fully exploit one's talents are often by-products. 'Sloth in writers is always a symptom of an acute inner conflict,' says Connolly, 'especially that laziness which renders them incapable of doing the thing which they are most looking forward to.' But, as he points out, slothful writers Johnson and Coleridge have more to their credit than Macaulay, Scott or Trollope. These names can be replaced by others in every generation.

Connolly himself is a good example. 'Myself a lazy, irresolute person,' he writes, 'overvain and overmodest, unsure in my judgements and unable to finish what I have begun, I have profited from journalism ... '

Just how insidious is journalism and the temptation of the here and now as opposed to future, perhaps posthumous renown?

Hemingway began as a journalist, as did Márquez, but they would have become great writers, it is safe to say, even if they had started out as bank robbers or car mechanics. Still, reviewing, criticism, column-writing, while relatively profitable, take away from the time and effort needed to focus on serious novel writing. Reviewing poetry, says Connolly, is the worst profession for a poet while 'broadcasting, advertising, journalism or lecturing all pluck feathers from the blue bird of inspiration and cast them on the wind.' Little wonder then that Connolly calls it the deadliest of the weeds on Crabbe's Heath.

'Of all the enemies of literature,' says Connolly, 'success is the most insidious.' 'Success,' says Trollope, 'is a poison that should only be taken late in life and then only in small doses.' Failure too is a poison, as Connolly concedes, but then adds, 'Where a choice is offered, prefer the alkaline.' No writer is likely to agree. Even for masochists, failure cannot be more attractive than success, however you define these, especially in monetary terms.

Hemingway has written about how America did not have great writers because good writers make money off early success, raise their standard of living, then write more to keep afloat when they have nothing to say (he calls such work 'slop'), justify writing thus and give us more slop.

When I first entered journalism, my ambition was to write the great Indian novel by the age of thirty. It would mean I would be established for life, wouldn't have to work in journalism or anywhere for as long as I lived, secure, financially sound and with the freedom of time and space to write at my pace.

And since I loved cricket and both reading and writing about it, that seemed to be a natural fit, a way to mark time while I wrote my masterpiece.

Two things happened, however. I enjoyed my job hugely, the writing, the travel, the instant recognition. And I began to do well professionally, becoming the sports editor of the highest-selling national newspaper by the age of thirty or so, and soon an editor at the same newspaper.

Job satisfaction and success—Connolly speaks about the latter but misses out on the pernicious nature of the former. This, of course, assumes I had a great novel bubbling within and only the exigencies of earning the daily bread kept me from writing it! As one grows older, that is initially comforting, then amusing and finally irritating.

'In recent times, the balance of literary success late in life is in favour of the childless writer. Children dissipate the longing for immortality which is the compensation of the childless writer's work ... domestic happiness is one of those escapes from talent ...' writes Connolly, and I am not sure he is on the right track. Samuel Johnson once said that a man who is not married is only half a man; Connolly thinks a man who is married is only half a writer. 'There is no more sombre enemy of good art than the pram in the hall.'

But that hasn't interfered with the productivity of writers such as Nabokov (he was married to Vera for over fifty years), Joan Didion, Zadie Smith or, earlier, Robert Browning (or his wife, Elizabeth Barrett Browning).

The *charlock's shade*, or sex and its excesses, are probably not as dangerous since syphilis was conquered or Aids brought under a measure of control, although Bruce Chatwin, Michel Foucault and James Merrill succumbed to the latter in the last century.

Since Connolly's time, however, new enemies have emerged. Social media, for one, which is a wonderful refuge of the mediocre writer looking for 'clicks' and finding publicity (or notoriety) with greater ease than at any other time. There is, too, its marketing power, which often sees the populist, the current, the easily-digested rise to the top.

The easy access to self-publishing has given us too many

books fighting for too little attention. It has led to a compromise where half-baked writers publish too early and are satisfied with that effort. The compulsion to write the masterpiece is overtaken by the satisfaction of seeing one's efforts in print or online.

Connolly has taken us through the basement of the literary life—where uncared for weeds threaten to overrun talent. His exploration has little time for the attic, however, where memories are stored and which serves as the subconscious from which all novels emerge. *Friends of Promise* is a book waiting to be written.

Metaphors in illness

'Perhaps it's good for one to suffer,' the English novelist Aldous Huxley wrote. 'Can an artist do anything if he's happy?'

This is the romantic notion of the writer suffering for his art, and its appeal has only increased over the centuries. The artist in his garret, the writer struggling with his words in the interval between coughing up blood are enduring clichés. Poverty was seen as a necessary element too, as depicted in the nineteenth-century German artist Carl Spitzweg's *The Poor Poet.*

Here, a poet lies on a mattress (because he can't afford a bed), with an umbrella to protect him from the water dripping through the roof. On his knees are pages from a manuscript, and with his right hand he is either counting the metre of his poem or killing a flea. It is winter, very cold (there is snow outside), and the poet has to remain in bed to keep warm. The alternative is to keep warm by burning his works. You can probably imagine the tuberculosis.

Suffering for his art.

The concept is so powerful that you could be forgiven for believing that suffering is a necessary condition for creating great works. Many concurred with Chris Patten, leader of Britain's

Conservative Party, when he said: 'Those of us who had a perfectly healthy childhood should be able to sue for deprivation of literary royalties.'

The response to such assumed romanticism is best articulated by the novelist A.L. Kennedy. 'I can say very firmly,' she wrote, 'that in my experience, suffering is largely of no bloody use to anyone, and definitely not a prerequisite for creation. If an artist has managed to take something appalling and make it into art, that's because the artist is an artist, not because something appalling is naturally art.'

Kennedy suffered recurrent bouts of labyrinthitis, an inner ear problem that caused giddiness, nausea and loss of balance, but that was not the reason she was a successful writer.

Would Dostoevsky have been a lesser writer without his epilepsy, Virginia Woolf less than ordinary without her depression?

Woolf, in her essay, *On Being Ill*, remarked that literature had so little to say about illness. 'Considering how common illness is, how tremendous the spiritual change that it brings, how astonishing, when the lights of health go down, the undiscovered countries that are then disclosed, what wastes and deserts of the soul a slight attack of influenza brings to light ... it becomes strange indeed that illness has not taken its place with love, battle, and jealousy among the prime themes of literature ...

'Novels, one would have thought, would have been devoted to influenza; epic poems to typhoid; odes to pneumonia, lyrics to toothache. But no ...' That was written over a century ago, and since then we have had medical men and women writing about illness from the experiences of their patients, and a whole genre of medico-literature has sprung up.

When you recall how many maladies some of our writers have been subject to in their lifetimes, you can only marvel that they wrote at all. Thomas De Quincey had neuralgia and digestive issues, even poor eyesight; Guy de Maupassant had syphilis, Flannery O'Connor lupus, and there might be a sub-genre of those with tuberculosis: John Keats, Katherine Mansfield, George Orwell.

Those with a variety of mental illnesses include Sylvia Plath, Virginia Woolf, Robert Lowell, David Foster Wallace. Most of these are twentieth-century writers, and diagnostics had improved vastly since the days of William Shakespeare.

Yet they wrote on and on, not because they were ill but in spite of it.

Shakespeare—now there's a subject for medical analysis. So little is known of the greatest literary figure in the English language that the field of Shakespeare studies is fertile ground for conjecture as well as literary and biographical dot-joining. The only medical fact known is that his handwriting deteriorated in his final years (corroboration: his six surviving signatures).

From this, and from the author's intimate knowledge of syphilis (he called it 'pox') as evidenced by his plays (forty-three lines in *Measure for Measure*, fifty-one in *Troilus and Cressida*), a contemporary surgeon, Dr John Ross, has concluded that Shakespeare was syphilitic. Or perhaps he had essential tremor, but Ross presents stronger arguments for syphilis.

As D.H. Lawrence wrote, 'I am convinced that some of Shakespeare's love and despair in his tragedies, arose from the shock of his consciousness of syphilis.'

A diagnosis more than three centuries after the patient's death calls for both expertise and imagination, and Dr Ross, a physician at Boston's Brigham and Women's Hospital and an assistant professor at Harvard Medical School, possesses both.

There is a delightful story—probably apocryphal, and

therefore true in essence—told about Dr Joseph Bell, the real-life inspiration for Sherlock Holmes, standing before a painting in an art gallery. It is of a patient in bed with a nurse standing nearby.

'So what do you think?' his companion asks, seeking the great diagnostician's opinion on the work of art.

'Malaria,' replies Dr Bell confidently.

Dr John Ross is not a modern-day Dr Joseph Bell. For one, he has more to go on than his predecessor did—wider medical knowledge, better record-keeping and lots of biographies of his subjects to consult. After opening his consultation rooms to the likes of Milton and Joyce, Hawthorne and Yeats, Melville and the Bronte sisters, he gave us *Orwell's Cough: Diagnosing the Medical Maladies and Last Gasps of the Great Writers.*

Orwell's cough is probably the best known of the maladies discussed. How did these seriously ill people find the time and passion to write their masterpieces? Ross has a counter-suggestion in one case. He argues that *Paradise Lost* might not have been written at all if Milton had not been blind. For one thing, he says, the experience of illness and defeat provided him with a maturity and emotional depth he had previously lacked. And for another, he might otherwise have been dead.

This is a fascinating line of reasoning. Milton was probably myopic from his youth, leading to retinal detachment. Later, he suffered from gout and severe abdominal pain—which possibly meant he had lead poisoning owing to his medication, mostly herbal. After he became blind, he stopped the lead-inspired medication, and was thus saved from fatal poisoning. Although it was assumed when Milton died that gout had claimed him, Dr Ross thinks a more plausible cause is cardiac arrhythmia.

No one has written a book on the joy of illness, but Brian Dillon, in his marvellous *Tormented Hope*, mirrors this argument.

One of his subjects, Charles Darwin, was a semi-invalid for much of his life. 'It meant,' writes Dillon, 'that he could retreat from the world, the better to pursue his scientific inquiries.'

After Susan Sontag recovered from breast cancer in the 1970s, she told *The New York Times:* 'It's fantastic knowing you're going to die; it really makes having priorities and trying to follow them very real to you ... I would like to keep some of that feeling of crisis.'

In *Illness as Metaphor*, she said, 'Everyone who is born holds dual citizenship in the kingdom of the well and in the kingdom of the sick.'

Arrhythmia is a condition the Irish poet William Butler Yeats too had. This, among his other maladies: Malta fever (brucellosis), keratoconus (a degenerative condition of the cornea), prosopagnosia (inability to recognise faces), Asperger's syndrome, hypertension, dropsy, kidney problems. His Spanish doctor once diagnosed he was: 'an antique cardio-renal sclerotic of advanced years,' which his regular physician said sounded like a lord of Upper Egypt.

And yet he wrote some of the finest poetry of the last century and won the Nobel in his fifties.

The question remains: How? Where did the strength come from?

Jonathan Swift, satirist, was plagued by dizziness most of his life after what he claimed was an orgy of apple-eating. He probably had Meniere's disease and tinnitus (he described it as 'a hundred oceans rolling in my ears') and gradually slipped into dementia. He left his fortune for the founding of a facility for the mentally ill in Dublin, the St Patrick's Hospital.

Herman Melville, the creator of the great American Novel, *Moby-Dick*, was bipolar, suffered from photophobia (pain on exposure to light), which meant he stepped out mostly at night and his eyes, in his words, were 'as tender as young sparrows'. He was an alcoholic, and in his fifties was incapacitated by bilateral hand arthritis, and later rheumatoid arthritis, and died of heart failure arising from a leaky valve.

One can only imagine what an average day in the life of these sufferers was like. Perhaps illness was a necessary condition for literary genius to flower. As Ross says, 'Literary genius more often arises from disappointment and chagrin than comfort and complacency; the rich and content have no need of imagination.'

That sounds convenient. Disappointment and chagrin might be sufficient conditions, but they are not necessary ones.

The list of the arrhythmic, demented, alcoholic, unseeing, syphilitic, epileptic, manic-depressive writers who make up our literary pantheon is as inspiring as the works they wrote.

Alberto Manguel was speaking for both writer and reader when he wrote, 'Life happened because I turned the pages.'

Encountering yourself

'When I watch concerts on TV,' wrote Jenny Erpenbeck, 'I often wish the camera didn't always show the oboist at the moment when the oboe enters, but instead showed someone like the 4th French horn player, waiting his turn to play again.'

Erpenbeck is the master of focusing on the fourth French horn player when the oboist is the one playing—her characters are slightly off-centre. The focus is on the fringes, the fringes of history, the fringes of consciousness, the fringes of knowledge, the fringes of time, the fringes of the expected.

Uniquely, she tells the big story through what happens in the fringes, combining beauty and brutality with casual power. The revelations are surprising; Erpenbeck delays them, almost challenging us to out-think her. Possibilities abound. Any thread could lead to a garment of a different feel and texture.

The gaps between potential narratives are filled with novelistic dark matter, uninhabited yet making their universe heavier than the words on the page suggest. Erpenbeck says it better than anybody else: '[I] use language above all to give shape to the gaps between the words, to give rhythm to the silence between words … ' Silence cannot be merely the absence of sound. It is more poetic than that.

Pauses are important to this writer with a background in both theatre and music. Language is music, she has said. It might explain the cadences of her prose and the harmony of her processes.

Erpenbeck packs more into her slim volumes of fiction than most writers manage to get into huge novels. There is a precision in the writing, an exactitude that both describes what is and suggests what could be. Such sure-footedness can come only with a thorough knowledge of the terrain she takes us on.

Exile, whether forced or voluntary, is often seen as the driving force of the twentieth-century writer—from James Joyce and Vladimir Nabokov to Naipaul and Amit Chaudhuri. The country remains, but the writer leaves or is forced to leave. In Erpenbeck's case, it was her country, East Germany, that disappeared while she remained. She woke up one day to find her country no longer existed.

Erpenbeck explains in her memoir *Not a Novel*: 'I spent the evening with friends, just a few blocks from the spot where world history was being made, and then: I slept. I literally slept through that moment of world history, and while I was asleep, the pot wasn't just being stirred, it was being knocked over and smashed to bits. The next morning I learnt: We didn't even need pots any more.' And later, 'From that moment on, my childhood belonged in a museum.'

Yet, as she insists, you can have a wonderful childhood in a 'rogue' country too. It is important to remember this. As she writes, 'There is nothing better for a child than to grow up at the ends of the earth. There's not much traffic there, so the asphalt is free for roller-skating, and parents don't have to worry about any bad guys roaming around. What business would a bad guy have on a dead-end street?'

Erpenbeck was born in Pankow, East Berlin, in 1967. Her mother, Doris, was a translator of Arabic who worked with the Egyptian Nobel laureate Naguib Mahfouz. Her maternal grandmother was a seamstress who was taken to Siberia as a prisoner of war. Jenny's father, John, is a physicist and philosopher of science. Her paternal grandmother, Hedda Zinner, was an actress and writer, and a communist who fled to the Soviet Union in the 1930s. Hedda's husband, Fritz, was a publisher, editor, writer and actor.

Writing, Erpenbeck says, is a game in which she encounters herself. It was not an automatic choice despite being the family business. She resisted initially, doing a stint as a bookbinder, then backstage at a theatre and moving on to direct musical theatre before becoming an opera director as the century she chronicles so well was ending. By then her first novella, *The Story of the Old Child*, was published. She began to write a biweekly column, which was later collected and published in English as *Things That Are Disappearing*.

Clearly, the pull was strong. The desk she sits at is her grandfather's desk which then became her mother's desk. She keeps her paper clips in the same drawer in which her mother kept hers, she informs us with that attention to detail that characterises her writing.

Many of Erpenbeck's characters—like the author herself—stand at an angle to history; individual will is subsumed by the larger events over which there is no control. *Visitation,* her first novel, is about a lake house and the stories of its various occupants over seven decades. It paints a picture of twentieth-century Germany, as the occupants flee every time there is political unrest. Everything adds up, every story is part of the big story. The reverse, too, is true.

Already, the main themes of Erpenbeck's work are all present here in miniature. Loss, identity, loss of identity, memory, time (the passage of, lack of control over), displacement, empathy, impermanence, transition.

An architect builds a house thinking to himself, 'A house is your third skin, after the skin made of flesh and clothing.' He and his wife are aware—and here's the authorial exactitude—that the stairs creak at the second, seventh and penultimate step. Soon after the war, the couple is forced to leave and the house is taken over by the East German government.

Stories of the later occupants are told alongside those of the gardener, the one constant in all this change. He too decays as the house does; his professional work is described in great detail. He is the silent witness as people and events put him just outside the circle of involvement. It is the sort of distance Erpenbeck herself keeps from her characters. As she writes in another context in another novel, *The Book of Words*, silence is health. The silent survive.

Time is crucial too. Although the architect was master of three dimensions, 'the fourth dimension has caught up with him: time, which is now expelling him from house and home.'

Erpenbeck's techniques are already present too. Characters are mostly nameless, dialogues nearly non-existent. We read about the architect and what happened to him, but we have to get into the stories of future occupants of the house to understand his temperament and motivations. This is true of many others too. The future holds a torch to the past.

There is, too, the technique of repeated sentences, which serves to help the reader fully understand their initial import. The repetition brings a sense of foreboding too, and a realisation that sentences can mean different things when contexts change.

End of Days begins with the sentence 'The Lord gave and the Lord took away ...' which is quite a startling comment on Erpenbeck's technique in this book of choices and possibilities. She gives us a lead character, kills her and then resurrects her.

This story of one woman, like a cubist painting, shows more than one profile simultaneously. It begins with the death of a child, but then sees her growing as an adult; in each avatar, the author asks the question, 'What if she had survived, what if she had made another choice, what if this had not happened?' and then proceeds to tell us what might have happened. Our expectations are subverted at each turn.

The journey through the twentieth century is accompanied by a character who dies and lives alternately and survives the many horrors of the period knowing 'some death or other will eventually be her death'.

At one point a character asks, 'How much better it would be ... if the world were ruled by chance not a God', and Erpenbeck is telling us that the world is indeed ruled by chance.

In the beginning, the grieving mother of the dead child thinks that perhaps 'their child ... needed only a short while to complete something begun in an earlier life'. By the end of the book, the message is both depressing and uplifting, depending on your temperament. Depressing if the message for you is that it doesn't matter how many lives you lead, your task is never completed. Uplifting if it is: everything is here and now. Nothing remains to be done. Everything is as it should be.

Erpenbeck writes with what her brilliant translator, the American professor Susan Bernofsky, calls 'perspectival sleight of hand'.

As always, the author herself keeps a distance from her theme. If the writing is any more restrained, there is the danger of it appearing banal; zealous, and it trips over into preaching, even sentimentality.

It is a risk Erpenbeck avoids (quite easily by now, a decade after her first novel) in *Go, Went, Gone*, the story of an encounter between a German professor and asylum seekers from Africa. All the elements of a potential cliché are here, with redemption awaiting at the end, but Erpenbeck's novel avoids them with alacrity and purpose. The studied balance gives both the narrative and the narration a rare strength. The moral question of our time has no easy answers, but there are humane responses that must necessarily go beyond what bureaucrats and politicians dream up.

The book was published three months after Erpenbeck put the final full stop on her manuscript because the theme was topical. Asylum seekers were the news in Europe.

Richard, a widower, is a recently retired professor of classical philology. He has lived a life where things happen to him; now he goes out to make things happen by first learning about the refugees, then inviting some of them to his home and all of them into his heart. He gives them classical names. Thus, Apollo is the man from Niger, Tristan is from Ghana. Rashid from Nigeria was on a boat to Italy that carried eight hundred people. It capsized, killing five hundred and fifty.

The stories are told in prose that is occasionally matter-of-fact. The impact of this understated style is powerful.

Perhaps Richard empathises with his new friends as a former East German living in a former West German region, making him a second-class citizen in his mind. Perhaps there is some other motivation we can only guess at. Richard's ignorance is hardly bliss. 'Richard has read Foucault and Baudrillard, and also Hegel and Nietzsche, but he doesn't know what you can eat when you have no money to buy food.'

What price education if it cannot help you survive? But that sounds too overt a conclusion to point to in this writer of great subtlety.

The writing may be unemotional, but the characters are not. Richard's initial interest might have been driven by curiosity for people and their places of origin he knew little about, but gradually a friendship develops with a Nigerian, Osarobo, whom he teaches to play the piano. At one point, when facing possible deportation from Berlin, one of the refugees explodes with anger.

Their presence is a mirror to his own life, though. Just as Richard and his friends are unclear about Burkina Faso, Osarobo hasn't heard of Hitler.

At one point, Richard muses upon the prosperity of his own country, one in which his former countrymen also share, even if undeservingly. 'But if this prosperity couldn't be attributed to their own personal merit, then by the same token the refugees weren't to blame for their reduced circumstances. Things might have turned out the other way around.' There but for the grace of god ...

In a moving obituary of Bashir Zakarayau in *Not a Novel*—Bashir is one of the people she thanks in *Go, Went, Gone*—Erpenbeck writes: 'He survived the unrest in Nigeria, where his father was burnt to death. He survived the war in Libya, where black Africans were hunted openly on the street. When the boat he was forced onto by Gaddafi's people capsized, his five-year-old daughter and three-year-old son drowned ...'

In his essay, *Reflections on Exile*, Edward Said wrote, 'Exile is strangely compelling to think about but terrible to experience. It is the unhealable rift forced between a human being and a native place, between the self and its true home; its essential sadness can never be surmounted. And while it is true that literature and history contain heroic, romantic, glorious, even triumphant episodes in an exile's life, these are no more than efforts meant to overcome the crippling sorrows of estrangement. The achievements of exile are permanently undermined by the loss of something forever.'

Inevitably, as one reads about forced exile in *Go, Went, Gone*, about man's inhumanity to man as well as man's resilience, Simone Weil's words come to mind. 'To be rooted is perhaps the most important and least recognised need of the human soul.'

As *The New Yorker* critic James Wood wrote, 'When Erpenbeck wins the Nobel Prize in a few years, I suspect that this novel will be cited.'

Woods's confession

When Donald Woods died, I felt I had lost a friend. I had met him briefly during the cricket World Cup in Australia in 1992. By then he had done it all: befriended the Black leader Steve Biko and written a book about him that kept the fight against apartheid in South Africa in the forefront of the world's consciousness; escaped from his country dressed as a priest after he had been banned for his writings; made a speech at the UN Security Council; written a successful autobiography; seen Kevin Kline play him in Lord Attenborough's movie *Cry Freedom* based on his books (Denzel Washington played Biko); seen apartheid defeated and the first representative government take charge in South Africa.

Woods was born in Transkei and studied law in Cape Town before becoming a journalist. He witnessed a debate in parliament and was convinced of the 'great obscene lie of apartheid'. He had grown up speaking both English and Xhosa and by thirty-one became the editor of the *Daily Dispatch*, South Africa's anti-apartheid newspaper.

It was after a meeting with Biko—later to be tortured and killed by the police at the age of thirty—that Woods's philosophy crystallised. He wrote: 'I emerged from that meeting with a fuller perception of not only Black Consciousness but of blackness in South Africa and all its implications ... the longer I knew him the more my admiration grew. It was through Steve Biko that I gained a clearer understanding not only of the realities of black politics in South Africa, but of the Third World viewpoint generally.'

When I met him in the press box at the Sydney Cricket Ground, Woods said he was fulfilling a lifelong ambition—to watch cricket for a whole year. He had done a few things I hadn't, and now he was doing something I had been doing for years, I joked. 'I played school cricket back home and who knows, had I kept at it I might have played for South Africa,' he said, echoing the favourite fantasy of cricket writers.

Later, I discovered he had been a good opening batsman who became a golfer. And he had once held the Grand Master Viktor Korchnoi to a draw.

Asking for Trouble, his autobiography, begins with the question: 'Why am I a White South African escaping in disguise in fear of political police? The answer will fill a book—and this is that book.'

'In the White world,' he wrote in his book, 'you talked of who had dined with whom; in the black world, of who had been arrested or searched that week.' Woods had to escape, and it was so dramatic that there are four incidents that Attenborough did not include in the film because they stretched cinematic credibility and appear hyped or melodramatic.

Woods had flown into Australia for the World Cup from the US; he was keen to watch Sachin Tendulkar bat. 'Your country produces the most artistic of players,' he told me. He was keen to talk cricket—not too keen to speak about his own role in a struggle where the colour of his skin ensured he would not be the victim. 'We escaped to Lesotho like the Von Trapp family,' he said, much struck by the humour of it all. The hills were alive with more than the sound of music then.

Woods's final book—*Rainbow Nation Revisited*—was on the new South Africa. He also, crucially for a man who regularly put his cause above his family, confessed that it was not worth doing that. Back in the 1950s, he had decided to marry Wendy Bruce when he discovered she wasn't all that bored during an England-South Africa Test match. They had five children. No cause is greater than the family—it was an epitaph he would have loved.

There was one story Donald Woods loved to tell in later years. Of how Nelson Mandela called him up in London to thank him for his support for the Black movement. Woods loved to say how he stood at attention for the duration of the call.

Dante helps

When Mary Ann Evans (who as George Eliot wrote *Silas Marner*) married a younger man at fifty-three, they spent their honeymoon in Italy, reading Dante together. At one point, while reading of the love of a couple in Canto Five of *The Inferno*, she turned to her husband to say she hoped their union would be a physical one and not merely a spiritual one. Upon hearing this, John Cross (for that was the young man's name) jumped from the balcony. Luckily, both he and his marriage survived. Dante's influence on men (and women) in the seven centuries since his death has been enormous.

In Harriet Rubin's *Dante in Love*, we meet them, the artists, poets, novelists and songwriters who took inspiration from *The Divine Comedy*, which Thomas Carlyle called 'the unfathomable heart song'.

Dante in Love is not merely a succinct, intelligent guide to the Italian poet, but an example of a genre of writing that combines literary criticism with self-help. These are strange bedfellows, but the number of books that turn to a classic to find messages in it for the modern, troubled mind is increasing.

The superior books of this kind are marked by enthusiasm, energy and an easy familiarity with the subject. Scholarship is worn lightly. Rubin's book is a wonderful example of this for the manner in which it follows a great poet in exile and shows how inevitable it was that he would write the great poem. T.S. Eliot said, 'Dante and Shakespeare divide the modern world between them; there is no third.'

An older cousin of *Dante in Love* is probably Alain de Botton's *How Proust Can Change Your Life*. Proust described his customary state as 'suspended between caffeine, aspirin, asthma, angina pectoris and altogether between life and death every six days out of seven.'

That might not seem a state of mind guaranteed to inspire those in need of inspiration from other people's lives. Yet, de Botton manages to see in Proust's life lessons on how to suffer successfully, how to be a good friend, how to be happy in love and so on. Proust wrote only one book, *Remembrance of Things Past* (modern translations call it *In Search of Lost Time*), but if you read it closely, suggests de Botton, that's enough.

It is a sentiment shared by Phyllis Rose in *The Year of Reading Proust*, published in the same year (1997). It is the lighter book, focusing more on the author's determined efforts to read Proust and the parallels in her own life that seemed to be so precisely predicted by the writer, with a solution round every corner. There is enough in it for the life-lessons-seeking reader.

Dante shows you how to turn loss into salvation, says Rubin. 'By current self-help standards, it is unusual for high art like the *Divine Comedy* to be utilised to heal the reader, but not in the Middle Ages where texts were not simply transmitters of information. They were depths that one entered. One disappeared into words.'

Dante represents the point at which literary criticism becomes living medicine. But it is medicine of a higher quality and attacks a variety of ailments.

Kindness to characters

It was an old college mate, Prof. Bobby Banerjee, in London, who introduced me to two favourite authors, both Pakistan-born. Nadeem Aslam and Kamila Shamsie. Each is unique, admitting of no literary lineage stylistically. Despite their distinctly different personalities, they have in common a compassion and humanity that come through in their writings.

Shamsie is a fourth-generation writer (she became a British citizen in 2013); her grand-aunts wrote too. She has often said that so many family members wrote that it didn't seem a matter of distinction. Her great-grandmother Inam Habibullah wrote a memoir of her travels in Europe, her grandmother Jahanara about life in the princely state of Rampur. Her mother Muneeza is a well-known critic and author.

Kamila is a cricket-lover (our first conversation was about the game) and lives near the Lord's cricket ground. In 2016, she was invited as guest speaker at the annual Wisden dinner at Lord's where the almanack is launched.

The best of the generation in the subcontinent following Salman Rushdie, Vikram Seth, Amitav Ghosh and, to extend the time frame, Arundhati Roy, has emerged not from India, but from neighbouring Pakistan.

Why do Pakistani writers—Mohsin Hamid, Mohammed Hanif, Nadeem Aslam, Kamila Shamsie, Daniyal Mueenuddin—tackle the big issues while their counterparts who live and write in India seem content with versions of chick lit—slick lit, myth lit, flick lit and so on? I asked this question of an Indian writer partly in mock horror and partly to provoke.

Perhaps, I continued glibly, the post-liberalisation writers in India have become a trifle smug, a trifle too satisfied, and those are not the qualifications for digging deep into the human condition. Pakistan is a mess as a country and as an idea, and writers react best to suffering.

It was a cruel characterisation, to be sure. For one, the two countries are at different stages of their development, and for another, my friend said, Indian publishers are largely a conservative lot, rather like Bollywood producers who are happy to focus their energies on the tried and tested. And for a third, writers like Jeet Thayil (especially in his poetry) and Meena Kandaswamy have broached subjects beyond the tried and tested.

'Pakistani writing,' Shamsie once said, 'is like the new young fast bowler on the scene but Indian writing is like the spinner who's been going for years and whose greatness is assumed.' True, but the new spinners still have to live up to a legacy.

I was being overcritical—after all, deciding what a novelist should and should not write is nobody's business but the writer's. But something Shamsie had once told the poet and novelist Tishani Doshi in an interview has remained with me: 'In places where writers are not going to face death for what they write, they seem to think it's fine to not address what's pressing, to not address injustice. But there is a responsibility when you have the ability, to write about what's going on in the world, when you see certain stories aren't being told. You're a writer and you have the voice and the platform and the intelligence, but you choose not to do it because you don't want to get your hands dirty with the political. Then I think you're really failing.'

She wasn't speaking of Indian writers, or any set of writers in particular, but the point is made. Repression need not be the only catalyst for self-expression.

Writers from Pakistan have no problems getting their hands dirty with the political. 'All writing is political,' according to Nadeem Aslam, who sees himself as a 'political writer'. That is not a way of limiting his talent. If anything, I think it elevates it.

The late Kashmiri poet Agha Shahid Ali, who taught at Amherst, the school Shamsie went to in the US, said that a good writer never sacrifices the aesthetics of a line in order to make a political point. It has to work at the level of poetry first, he said. That applies equally to the novelist's prose. Political novels have to work at the level of the novel first; how the message is received depends on the skill of the writer and the sophistication of the reader.

This two-way street has run smoothly for the writers mentioned. Shamsie's *Burnt Shadows* is set against the background of two disasters of the twentieth century—the dropping of the atom bomb on Nagasaki that ended the Second World War, and the 11 September attacks on the World Trade Center. In between, the events take place in Pakistan. Indians have not had to live through anything comparable, although the recent political upheavals might give rise to a new type of writing. Megha Majumdar's *A Burning,* which made it to *The New York Times* bestseller list, might be representative.

The epigraph to Daniyal Mueenuddin's *In Other Rooms, Other Wonders* is the Punjabi proverb: 'Three things for which we kill—

land, women and gold.' But there is a fourth: religion, as both countries have shown.

When I once spoke to Shamsie about a 'Pakistan school' of writing, she gently put me down with 'Come on! We are just a few people here and there, hardly a school.' Yet, for some years now—and certainly since Mohsin Hamid's *The Reluctant Fundamentalist* (2007), Pakistani writers have written with a greater freedom and maturity than any other group, although Daniyal is not too excited about being known as a 'Pakistani' writer. He'd rather be called a writer, pure and simple.

Shamsie's *Home Fire* is easily one of the finest novels of recent years, tackling contemporary issues of identity and what it means to be Muslim in Britain. It is, in the end, a love story but a love story that fails to reach its natural conclusion thanks to the political immovables it is embedded in. There is, of course, no reason to believe that a happy ending is the natural one; a narrative flowing in the other direction can be equally inevitable and often, more 'right'.

Shamsie is the kindest of writers, kind to her characters, allowing them a narrative shorn of literary coercion. There is a naturalness, even inevitability, to their growth when viewed from the other end of the tale, which is always the sign of a born storyteller. Of the two Muslim families in London whose trajectories meet in the story, one is that of the new Home Secretary, Karamat Lone, the model immigrant with his Irish-American wife and two children. The other is represented by the Pasha siblings, Isma, Aneeka and Parvaiz, who carry the burden of their late father, a jihadist.

The novel begins with an interrogation at a US airport, as Isma prepares to resume her life there.

'Do you consider yourself British?' the interrogator asks.

'I am British,' is the reply.

'But do you consider yourself British?'

And with that the tone is set, the future hinted at. You are more than your passport (or less than it), authorities everywhere seem to believe. The stamp can say one thing, but we know your genes say something else. Even the biggest democracies in the world operate in the gap between what is and what they think it should be.

The interrogation continues for two hours. 'He wanted to know her thoughts on Shias, homosexuals, the Queen, democracy, the Great British Bake Off, the invasion of Iraq, Israel, suicide bombers, dating websites.' The younger sister, Aneeka, has a name and a 'how-to' prepared for GWM—Googling While Muslim.

At no point are things simple. At any point the story could have taken a different route. It required great control to keep everything in balance, and Shamsie accomplishes this without a wasted word or an extra one, building the tension with increasing tempo and limpid prose. The nod to Sophocles's *Antigone*, the Greek play, where a young girl is forced to choose between obeying the law of the land and religious law, gives the whole story a feel of history repeating itself in different centuries, in different countries, among different sets of human beings, but with the same lack of humanity. Faith and family, faith and country, family and country, and the role of romantic love in all this is explored with a combination of engagement and distance.

Balance is the key to keeping the characters poised between the stereotype of the group and the uniqueness of the individual. The question of why young people or professionals decide to join an outfit like the Islamic State (ISIS) is generally answered in the West by invoking hatred, anger, want, frustration, boredom, the promise of future greatness. What drives Parvaiz—and many like him—is a whole different set of motives, which Shamsie explores.

Parvaiz supports the Arsenal Football Club. His recruiter is a Real Madrid man, and both are fans of Mesut Ozil, the German footballer. Shamsie's detailing of the alienation of such a man and the need he has for a sense of belonging is both nuanced and a trifle worrying. There are no simple answers because the questions asked are not the right ones.

Confronted with the notion that she is using the Home Secretary's son to get to see her brother, who is following their father's path, Aneeka asks, 'Why shouldn't I admit it? What would you stop at to help the people you love most?'

It is a question being asked increasingly around the world. E.M. Forster's prayer is newly relevant: 'If I had to choose between betraying my country and betraying my friend, I hope I should have the guts to betray my country.' For 'friend' read 'relative'.

Even quoting that line could get you into trouble in some societies.

On second thoughts, maybe 'school' is a misnomer, and Kamila was right to set the record straight. But distinctive it certainly is, and energetic, and passionate. The writers have won major international awards or been shortlisted for them. And Kamila Shamsie, not yet fifty, is, as cricketers say, in peak mid-season form.

Beauty and terror

For some time now I have felt that the finest contemporary writer in the English language is the Pakistan-born Nadeem Aslam. The English novel is not unused to being better handled by those born outside Britain, Joseph Conrad, Vladimir Nabokov, Michael Ondatje, being some examples.

When I first met Nadeem in London, I had just read *The Wasted Vigil* and been smitten by the beauty of the writing. An uncomfortable beauty, because I had not yet worked out in my mind how a story of such cruelty and casual brutality could be narrated in language that was so poetic. I had been stunned by this startling juxtaposition. Now I was stunned by the writer himself.

This was a man who knew, who had seen and who understood. And who had both accepted and rebelled. That might be a strange thing to say about a writer who is politically sharp, whose family, a left-wing atheist father and a devout Muslim mother, had to leave Pakistan in exile, and whose books are about not accepting. Perhaps it was his serenity; perhaps it was his gentle speech and childlike demeanour. Those around him recognised two things early—that he was the outstanding writer of our time, and that he needed to be looked after. He inspired maternal instincts, and not just in women.

Yet, for all the depth and range of his books, the seriousness of the themes and the heartbreaks involved in them, Nadeem himself is a man with a sense of mischief, who loves to laugh and is fully aware of both what is being said and left unsaid around him. That combination of intensity and relaxation is reflected in his writings.

When he came to England aged fourteen, his family fleeing General Zia-ul-Haq's authoritarian regime, Nadeem barely knew English. He taught himself the language by reading everything. He told an interviewer, 'I copied the whole of *Lolita* by hand because I wanted to learn. I copied the whole of *Moby Dick* because I wanted to see how the commas fell.' Islam and Marxism, he said, were the two strands of his DNA, the former inherited from his mother and the latter from his father and uncles.

While speaking to him in London, in India and then at a PEN Writers do in New York, the contradictions in my mind resolved themselves. In some ways, Nadeem is the quintessential writer from Pakistan—reacting to the mess in the country of his birth with the tools provided by the country he lives in. My work has both beauty and terror, he explained. I want to show the ugliness without extinguishing the reader's ability to love.

Nadeem is a man of well-chosen words, spoken with the kind of care with which he writes. In this he is like another favourite of mine, Pico Iyer. Few writers speak as well. Partly this is because Nadeem is the opposite of being visually challenged; he is visually enhanced, seeing more than others. He often paints his characters and situations physically, as an aid to the writing. The colours and textures of his novels, their imagery and the minutely observed details are all of a piece with this harmony.

Speaking to an interviewer, Nadeem brought his obsessions together with : 'Donald Trump wishing to build a wall reminds me of a beautiful painting Frida Kahlo made in the 1930s, standing in a pink dress on the border between Mexico and the USA. I look at that painting, and think: "If they wish to build a wall we can't stop them; but we'll be the Frida Kahlo standing on that wall, defiant, in the most beautiful clothes we can find." Their summer lasts a solid year, Emily Dickinson said of poets. That's what art is, that's what I want my novels to be.' Any addition to that or analysis of it would be the equivalent of gilding the lily.

Even before many people had read Nadeem, his uniqueness was well known. Of how he spent long periods, days, weeks, months, in seclusion; of how he taped his eyes every hour of every day of the week for a while to get into the head of his character in *The Blind Man's Garden*; of how he taped back his fingers to do the same for a character who had had his fingers sliced off. No one lives as intimately with his characters as Nadeem does; no one writes as intimately about them.

In an essay for *Granta*, Nadeem wrote that literature is a 'public act' and a 'powerful instrument against injustice'.

Yet, he says, this does not mean that his work is composed of slogans. 'I am a novelist. And happiest when I write something that satisfies me aesthetically but which also repays some of the debt I feel I owe to the world.'

On another occasion he said, 'I come from Pakistan and live in England as a brown man. I don't have the luxury to be non-political, either in life or in my work.'

If his books were superior political novels from someone physically and emotionally affected by the depths to which man can sink but finding fragility within strength, they would still be remarkable. But they are more, much more. Nadeem handles surrealism with the ease of a subcontinental writer who accepts books nailed to the ceiling (*The Wasted Vigil*) as not just plausible, but necessary. There is empathy for human weakness; few modern writers have this.

I use a language that has twenty-six alphabets, he once told me, but the words these make are informed by the thirty-eight letters of the Urdu alphabet too. My initials in Urdu, he said, look like a pen next to an inkwell. I didn't have the wit then to ask him to show me. It was said casually, in the middle of a conversation about Hollywood's heist movies, as we were trying to remember the name of the movie in which two different sets of robbers hold up a bank on the same day.

Nadeem's father was a poet who gave up the calling when marriage and family duties took over. 'Wamaq Saleem', who is referred to in Nadeem's first two novels as a great Urdu poet, was his pen name. 'In the Pakistan of my novels, my father is the poet he could never be in his life because of financial reasons,' he told Kamila Shamsie in an interview.

It took Nadeem eleven years to write his second novel, *Maps for Lost Lovers*, a story of cultural tension and the breakdown of a family. That's when the legend around him began to grow. The intense solitude, the obsessive rewriting (he reportedly saved only one sentence from a seventy-page section written in long hand), the story that he heard of the 11 September attacks of 2001 only in 2004 because he had cut himself off from the world so thoroughly.

That second book was important for a man who had determined to be a writer, no matter what. And as often with such decisions, he made sure he had no plan B. He dropped out of university before graduating, saying he didn't want a safety net. Later, he said that in the eleven years it took him to write his novel, if he had a fallback position, he might have been tempted to fall back and the book would not have been written.

And then came *The Wasted Vigil*. The title is from a delicate water colour by Abdur Rahman Chugtai. It is of a woman waiting partly in hope but suggesting hopelessness all the same. Or it could be read as its exact opposite: hoping against hope, perhaps. It is a metaphor for our times and for Nadeem's novel.

The disconnect between the brutality of the theme and the extravagance of the prose can be disconcerting. Nadeem's Afghanistan is savage and unforgiving, and he describes the tortures and the violence of the Taliban in pitiless detail; it is not so much the amputations and the blow-torch-in-the-eye that startle so much as the easy acceptance of these as part of everyday life by ordinary people with the extraordinary strength that gives the novel its power.

While writing this book, Nadeem isolated himself from all human activity, draped his windows with black curtains and stayed in at all times. His family brought him food while he was sleeping (the book is dedicated to his brother and sister-in-law, who did this). Aslam's black curtains are set to become as famous in the literary world as Marcel Proust's cork-lined room from which that author seldom emerged while writing his magnum opus.

The Wasted Vigil is the story of a disparate bunch of people. Lara, a Russian woman, comes to Afghanistan looking for her brother, a defector from the Russian army. She arrives at the house of the Englishman Marcus Caldwell. Also arriving are an American, David Town, who was a CIA agent, and Casa, a radicalised young man. Told in flashback are the horror stories of the people near and dear to them.

In delineating the connections between his characters—Lara's brother had raped Marcus's daughter, who was once the lover of the American, for example—and letting their stories bleed into one another while keeping a tight grip on both the action and the emotion, Nadeem shows a remarkable awareness of how the particular flows into the general and vice versa. Especially since the main characters are Russian, American, Afghan and all that such origins mean today in a mutilated country which has forgotten what peace means. The symbolism is inescapable, and so is the misery of loss. The fundamentalists do not always win—thriving in this mixture is Dunia, who runs a school while defying them. The various factions in the Afghan turmoil are not just well represented, but given flesh and blood and breath.

'Pull a thread here and you'll find it's attached to the rest of the world,' says Marcus as the novel winds down, having taken in the hardships of the innocent and the confusion of the oppressors as well as the moral ambiguity of those responsible for both.

This is a complex tale, and Nadeem tells it with empathy. No one is beyond redemption; simple motives lead to complicated actions. Midway through the novel, this simple creed is articulated: 'Men walking by averted their eyes and quickened their pace if a woman was being lashed in the street—if they tried to prevent it they would be set upon. It was best to see as little as possible. Afghanistan became a land whose geology was fear instead of rock, where you breathed terror, not air.'

The heroes are not those who take up arms against the oppressors, but those who attempt to preserve a sense of normalcy by hiding their books or works of art or a tape recorder—which, if found, would be destroyed along with those who owned them. The past encroaches on the present, and in the same way, the bravery and toughness of the present will flow into the future. That is the hope. Like the country itself, *The Wasted Vigil* is a book of extremes. The writing needed to reflect that.

Later, while teaching at George Washington University in 2009, Nadeem would pass the White House, and think of 'how words on grey paper in the 1980s became fists, electric wires and instruments of torture which broke members of my family and friends'.

When I learnt that Nadeem was speaking in New York while I was there on holiday, I sent him a message saying I would be there 'to heckle him'. Nadeem wrote back that he was 'looking forward to being booed by those I love.'

Here, he spoke of his debt to the Polish writer Bruno Schulz. 'I vote every time I write a sentence,' he told the audience, after reading from the title short story from Schulz's 1934 collection, *The Street of Crocodiles*. It is almost as if a colour of the spectrum would be missing, he said, had Schulz not been alive and writing.

It endorsed another important quality of Nadeem's: gratitude. Gratitude for those who went before, gratitude for friends, gratitude for where he is now, gratitude that some clichés—like the one about hard work paying off—come true in one's lifetime. A remarkable writer and a remarkable man.

Monet's lament

At some of the most decisive moments in science, scientists have turned to poetry to describe their feelings. Robert Oppenheimer, the father of the atom bomb, quoted from the Bhagavad Gita as the famous mushroom cloud rose into the heavens. Roald Hoffman, Nobel Prize winner in chemistry, wrote poetry. Yet, it is a modern conceit that poetry and science belong to mutually exclusive clubs and any attempt to smuggle the one into the other would cause major upheavals.

Mathematicians use words like 'elegant' and 'beautiful' to describe their work, and they agree with the poet Keats that truth is beauty and beauty truth. After all, both scientists and poets are concerned with life, death, love, lust, sea, time, infinity, the ultimate question, the final answer and so on. It is not difficult to imagine a kinship.

'Your coffee grows cold on the kitchen table,/ Which means the universe is dying,' begins the poem *Entropy* by Neil Rollinson, and ends '... I think of the sun/ consuming its fuel, the afternoon that is past,/ and your dress that only this morning/ was warm to my touch.'

Here is science, despair, hope and love all in one package. *Entropy* is one of the poems in *A Quark for Mister Mark*, an anthology of 101 poems about science edited by Maurice Riordan and Jon Turney. This is not the first such anthology—an earlier one was edited by John Stubbs and Phillips Salman and contained some of the same poems. The editors of the later book made a rule: only English language poets to be included, and then broke that rule by including Primo Levi and Miroslav Holub, the Czech immunologist.

That the editors have enjoyed their job is clear from their inclusion of such delights as Albert Goldbarth's poem on being married and yet apart; it plays with the imagery of space-time as a fabric with holes in it: 'sleepy at last, she/ wraps herself in her blanket and,/ if some of it, somewhere in it, isn't blanket/ she wraps herself in that too.'

In *Monet Refuses the Operation*, the artist says, 'Doctor, you say there are no haloes/ around the streetlights in Paris/ and what I see is an aberration/ I tell you it has taken me all my life/ to arrive at the vision of gas lamps as angels.' And quite appropriately, he proceeds to put the doctor in his place for his too-literal approach to life and the living, and expresses pity that he lives in such a closed world.

Not all the poems are about the higher emotions. Some, like *The Urine Specimen*, find poetry in providing a urine sample to your doctor 'who in it will read your future,/ wringing his hands. You lift the chalice and toast/ the long life of your friend there in the mirror,/ who wanly smiles, but does not drink to you.'

What makes it all special is that the editors do not make a big deal about science or the arts or the exclusivity or the common ground. The essence of their approach is summed up in the introduction where they say: 'People have been noticing science more lately. This isn't surprising. There's a lot of it about. The sheer amount of science produced in the last hundred years, and the way it has affected our everyday life, has no precedent. And poets, who ought to be good at noticing things, have noticed too.'

The classical response by the poet to the advances of science is articulated by W.H. Auden in his *After Reading a Child's Guide to Modern Physics*. 'This passion of our kind/ For the process of finding out/ Is a fact one can hardly doubt/ But I would rejoice in it more/ If I knew more clearly what we wanted the knowledge for/ Felt certain still that the mind/ Is free to know or not.'

Time's arrow moves only in one direction and cannot reverse itself. So Auden's lament has its limitations. But already the great physicist Stephen Hawking has suggested that time travel is possible under certain conditions. So, there's a theme for an epic—or not, as Auden might have said. At some future date, maybe Auden himself can change some of his opinions if he gets to know where science has taken us—and that we have a fair idea of what we want to do with that knowledge.

Reduced to stats

Jane Austen used forty-five clichés per 100,000 words, Virginia Woolf sixty-two and Khaled Hosseini seventy-one. At the other end of the scale, James Patterson used 160, Tom Wolfe 142 and Salman Rushdie 131. Nabokov used the word 'mauve' at least once in all of his eight books. On an average, the bestseller Nora Roberts's name used up thirty-seven per cent of the space on her book covers. Danielle Steele began her novels (she wrote ninety-two) with a mention of the weather forty-six per cent of the time.

How do we know all this? And does knowing all this make us either better writers or better readers? The statistics have been worked out by American writer Ben Blatt, who has analysed 1,500 books, including bestsellers, classics and popular novels as well as reams of 'amateur' writing to give us the figures. His book *Nabokov's Favourite Word is Mauve: The Literary Quirks and Oddities of Our Most Loved Authors* provides loads of good old-fashioned fun.

I say 'old-fashioned' because it is a sophisticated version of the 'analysis' we used to carry out on our school textbooks during the most boring classes. One day, we would tote up the number of times the word 'the' appeared on a page or the word most likely to follow 'Now listen here ...' when the teacher spoke. Some of us looked for the placement of letters which might spell out our names.

Blatt had gone beyond all that, and using a friendly computer, arrived at more fascinating conclusions. His book brings together the three R's in a way no one else has, analysing our reading and writing through 'rithmetic. He takes particular delight in checking if writers followed their own instructions on writing well.

Elmore Leonard wrote: 'You are allowed no more than two or three exclamation marks per 100,000 words.' He used fewer than most, but even he used forty-nine (Tom Wolfe, not surprisingly, used 929).

Some conclusions—like Nabokov's use of mauve—are susceptible to psychological explanations. Nabokov was a synesthete, which means he sometimes saw words as colours. Synesthesia is a condition where one sensation is felt as a completely different one. Thus sound 'appears' as a colour or smell 'feels' like a shape and so on.

'I present a fine case of coloured hearing,' Nabokov wrote in his autobiography, *Speak, Memory.* 'The long *a* of the English alphabet has for me the tint of weathered wood, but a French *a* evokes polished ebony.'

Blatt's analysis shows that Thomas Pynchon and J.D. Salinger were indeed two different people and not the same writer as rumour once had it. He suggests ways—based on maths, frequency of word usage—to distinguish between male and female writers based on text.

What he doesn't tell us is if Shakespeare's plays were written by the man from Stratford-on-Avon or Francis Bacon or anybody else (years ago, someone showed, using a similar technique, that they were written by Agatha Christie). But that's a minor crib in a book of fun and surprising conclusions.

Rejecting Naipaul

Some years ago, when London's *The Sunday Times* sent out the first chapter of a novel without the author's name, it was clearly looking for a good story, but even the newspaper must have been surprised at the response.

Quite the remarkable thing about the twenty or so publishers turning down V.S. Naipaul's Booker-winning novel *In A Free State* is that none of them recognised it. There's something sad and funny here. What are editors doing at publishing houses if they are unable to identify the work of a man considered the finest writer in the English language, a Nobel Prize winner and one with a distinctive touch in both form and content?

For aspiring writers, it must have been confirmation of long-held theories about the lack of education and professionalism in the publishing industry. As Naipaul himself said, 'To see something is well written and appetisingly written takes a lot of talent, and there is not a great deal of that around. With all the other forms of entertainment today, there are very few people around who would understand what a good paragraph is.'

There may be other lessons to be drawn from this. Perhaps tastes have changed in the years since *In a Free State* appeared and publishers are no longer looking for another Naipaul.

Perhaps, thanks to the work of Naipaul among others (Trinidad has produced two Nobel laureates, the poet Derek Walcott being the other), the West Indies islands are not as exotic as they once were nor is cultural alienation a new literary theme. Perhaps ... perhaps ...

I have tried to be kind, but the conclusion seems inescapable: publishers go by the personality more often than they go by the work. It is easier for a successful writer to publish a mediocre book than it is for a new writer to publish anything brilliant if he does not come with the right package.

It was to demonstrate this very thing that Doris Lessing, already a published author of twenty-five successful books, wrote two novels as 'Jane Somers' and submitted them to publishers. In the preface to *The Diaries of Jane Somers* (1984), which contains both books in one volume, she wrote of her reasons for doing so: 'I wanted to be reviewed on merit, as a new writer without a "name". I wanted to cheer up young writers who often have such a hard time of it, by illustrating that certain attitudes are mechanical.' The third reason, she wrote, was 'frankly malicious.'

The reactions from publishers were interesting. Jonathan Cape turned it down. Granada said it was too depressing to publish. Michael Joseph, her first publisher, said it reminded him of Doris Lessing. Bob Gottlieb of Knopf recognised it at once and asked Lessing, 'Who do you think you are kidding?' Her French publishers asked if Lessing had helped Jane Somers.

Lessing was sure that the reviewers would guess immediately. Not one did.

The New York Times Book Review said it was 'an extremely courageous attempt, and Jane Somers is a courageous writer.' The *Los Angeles Times* found it cryptic and 'a little like a beautiful sweater made by a woman with arthritis. Through unravellings and dropped stitches, you can make out a lovely pattern, but can't quite figure out what it is.'

'Some of the so-called experts on my work,' wrote Lessing, 'didn't recognise it was me. And many of the readers' reports to the publishers were very patronizing and very nasty.'

When the second Jane Somers book came out, wrote Lessing in the preface, 'Predictably, people who had liked the first book were disappointed by the second. And vice versa. Never mind about the problems of publishers: the main problem of some writers is that most reviewers want you to go on writing the same book.'

It is easy to get cynical about the whole thing, acknowledge the role played by luck and public relations merely to get a publisher interested in a work, and agree with a German writer who said that one of the signs of Napoleon's greatness was that he once had a publisher shot. The Lessing case is different from *The Sunday Times* one mainly because the latter submitted an already published book recognised by most (but obviously not by the twenty publishers) as a modern classic.

On the other hand, if Naipaul is rejected, what of the many Thomases, Richards and Harolds who don't have a Nobel Prize to show for their efforts? Rumours of publishers turning down *Hamlet*, I am told, are unfounded.

Double and triple whammy

At the basic level, journalism is about information: *the cat sat on the mat*. Then comes interpretation—*the cat sat on the mat because the floor was wet.* At the third stage, there is a self-conscious attempt at 'style': *The feline was clearly a rug addict.*

Finally, there is journalism as literature—factual, interpretative, stylish and intensely personal all at once. The first, without the other three is boring; the second by itself can be dangerous; style without substance is pathetic; and stage four without the others is self-indulgent. Few have found the right proportion.

In today's shrunken world, the interpreter brings to us events sieved through personal experience. Bruce Chatwin wrote about countries untouched by revolution, V.S. Naipaul followed upheavals. These were superior writers I looked up to in my early days in the profession.

Newspaper offices were different places then, I was on the cusp of change from the old typewriter-and-telex system to the modern computer-driven one. Every reporter walked into the office carrying a notebook and nursing a hangover. In later years, both these essentials had disappeared. This was perhaps the biggest change in journalism. Sure, journalists drink, and sure some get drunk, but newsrooms have taken on an antiseptic feel.

I hadn't been working for long in my first job when this appeared on the notice board: 'It is noticed that some reporters coming to work after lunch have alcohol on their breaths. This probably doesn't affect your work, but could you please refrain from getting drunk while on duty?' Well, not exactly those words, but I was struck by the note's restraint and its distinction between drinking and getting drunk.

The Press Club (alcohol at subsidised rates) was nearby and it was possible we were living the cliché, or were simply either having a good time or trying to forget a bad one. In an essay on Fleet Street, which once housed most of the British newspapers, the journalist Alan Watkins wrote: 'The entire ship, anchored beside the Thames between the Law Courts and St Paul's, floated on a sea of alcohol. Perhaps the explanation lay in the longstanding connection between writing for newspapers and drinking in pubs ...'

Evelyn Waugh was probably speaking up for the tribe when he wrote in his diary: Tuesday, a drunken day; lunched at *Beefsteak....* Drinking in *White's* most of the afternoon. Then to *Beefsteak* where I got drunk.... Then to *St James's* for another bottle of champagne.'

I seldom hear anyone speak of Waugh these days. This is either a comment on the company I keep or a reminder that the author of one of the finest novels of the last century, *Scoop*, is no longer in fashion. Waugh was born in the same year as George Orwell and Malcolm Muggeridge, both of whom had their centenary celebrated in 2003, but he appears the most dated of the lot. The affectations—size, snobbery, ear trumpet—distract from his prose. In any case, you needed to be familiar with a particular English type to fully appreciate Waugh.

Stephen Fry, who directed a film version of Waugh's *Vile Bodies* said: 'Towards the end of his life, Evelyn was more or less a howling shit. He took the pessimistic view whenever possible. He had a very low view of humanity.' Now humanity is getting its own back on him.

Scoop is the story of William Boot, who is accidentally sent off to cover a war in Ishmaelia (a thinly disguised Ethiopia), when it was John Boot who had been recommended by the proprietor's friend. William arrives in Ishmaelia with a ton of luggage, and finding no war at hand, does what his competitors are doing and sends home stirring dispatches about the action. He becomes a hero. His newspaper throws a banquet, where yet another wrong Boot, Uncle Theodore, is honoured for his excellent reporting from Ishmaelia.

What is scary about *Scoop*—and I found this out much after I had read the book—is that most of the incidents mentioned actually took place.

Philip Knightley in *The First Casualty*, writing about the Italo-Ethiopian war on which the book is based (Waugh was sent as a correspondent for the *Daily Mail*) wrote: 'Nothing that the correspondents imagined about covering the war could match the hilarious reality. When *Scoop* was published in 1938, it was hailed as a "brilliant parody" of Waugh's experiences in Ethiopia. What only the war correspondents present at the time knew was that *Scoop* was actually a piece of straight reportage, thinly disguised as a novel to protect the author from libel actions.'

The real-life *Daily Express* reporter *did* receive cables from his office about how the *Daily Telegraph* man was filing exciting stories of spearmen and tigers and the Emperor Haile Selassie's palace square looking like London's Picadilly Circus. The beaten man then discovered that his rival had been lifting passages from an old book, *In the Country of the Blue Nile*, and proceeded to do the same himself. His office now sent him congratulatory cables.

Waugh himself missed the one authentic scoop of the war, when the government signed over large portions of the country to American oil interests in an attempt to check Mussolini's advance. When the Italian invasion was imminent, Waugh sent a long cable to his office—in Latin, to keep it from the prying eyes of his competitors. This might have been a scoop, but by the time the sub-editor in London figured out what it meant, the attack had begun and the scoop had melted.

Someone who covered the war with Waugh, and indeed was his roommate for a while, W.F. Deedes, wrote *At War with Waugh: The Real Story of Scoop*. Over the years, Deedes alternately suggested and denied that he was the original William Boot. Like Boot, Deedes, later editor of the *Daily Telegraph,* prepared for the trip by shopping on Oxford Street. 'We bought everything,' he wrote, 'riding breeches for summer and winter, and all kinds of summer hats and khaki shorts. Unfortunately, we didn't know that Ethiopia was in the mountains, so I had to wear the same suit the whole time I was there. I never did get to wearing those riding breeches.'

Young journalists must read *Scoop* and Michael Frayn's *Towards the End of the Morning*, a gentler, less aggressive look at the profession, written three decades later. Parody can hit at the truth faster than autobiographies.

In Frayn's book, television is already beginning to make inroads. There is an elegiac air of the last days of Fleet Street. The old need to adapt to survive; so few of them are equipped to do so.

I doubt if we will get another 'insider' novel on newspapers again. Even the most satirical one will owe more to history than human frailty. The future *Scoop* and *Towards the End of the Morning* will be about sitting at home and creating 'news' out of thin air and sending it out on social media.

Or possibly about a blogger or some other species that hasn't been discovered yet.

Excerpts from a pandemic diary

Friends die in pandemics. Loved ones suffer. The illogic of death is brought home. As is the randomness of life. None of us will ever be the same again, we have seen too much, felt too much. If the virus doesn't get you, politicians will. It doesn't matter where you live—the US, UK or India—you are susceptible to both.

We tell ourselves that once things get back to normal, we will be better people, do better things. Not complain so much, not expect too much. We owe it to the dead, we tell ourselves. We owe it to the living. But we know in our hearts it will not work out that way.

The god-fearing become god-hating and vice versa. We become the opposite of who we were. The knowledge that they are not in control can affect people in strange ways. The epicurean becomes spartan, the quiet becomes loud, the acceptor becomes the questioner. Those who advocate moderation turn to extremism in thought and action. If there is no god, why bother? On the other hand, if there is no god, then we had better bother.

We can justify, explain, rationalise. Or decide that nothing can be justified, explained or rationalised. In general, it is as likely that something good will happen as something bad will, and what we wish for, or sacrifice towards, has nothing to do with either outcome.

We will carry the painful memory of the deadly havoc. That is a line from Boccaccio, writing about the plague in the fourteenth century. His *Decameron* enjoyed a resurgence in the early days of the pandemic.

As one writer put it, 'For Boccaccio and his contemporaries, plague became the ultimate test of the fine line between knowledge and ignorance, truth and deception, as much as it also defined the limits of greed and compassion.' Ditto the COVID-19 pandemic. The more things change, etc.

You lose friends in other ways too. The one who refuses to believe the virus is real or dangerous. The one who refuses to wear a mask. The one who thinks vaccination is for the birds. Friendship shouldn't depend on thinking alike. But stupidity is a turn-off.

Another realisation: you can survive with fewer friends with whom you are in touch more regularly. It doesn't matter where they are. Zoom and Facetime bring friends home more often than Uber does.

Will our grandchildren ask us how we survived the pandemic? I would love to say I read the classics and caught up on reading in general. But I had reader's block through most of it, unable to focus on a book, unable to read fiction through. My favourite reading was books on books, long essays, the occasional biography. It is weird, this reader's block.

Having the occasional writer's block is acceptable, even understandable. We are human, it happens. But a reader's block is a new discovery. Death and stupidity are a powerful combination, frustrating for what could have been done but wasn't.

Every day was a version of the movie *Groundhog Day*. Wednesday was like Thursday which was an exact copy of Friday which could have been Saturday, a day startlingly like Sunday, a twin of Monday which unfolded like Tuesday. It was troubling, but better than the alternative because the choice was between staying in one place and sinking into a bottomless pit.

1

The seventeenth-century French mathematician and philosopher Blaise Pascal said that all the troubles of humanity came about because of the difficulty men had in simply being happy to sit alone in their rooms. More than half the world is currently sitting alone in their rooms—and many are thinking of happiness past and happiness future, but remain uncertain about happiness present.

More men and women are being forced to work from home (WFH). 'Social distancing, but digital closeness' is the new mantra. 'Only connect,' E.M. Forster told us, and we haven't really had the time to gather our fragments together. Now is the time, since we are disconnected from everything else.

I am one of the lucky ones, and grateful for that. When other professionals complain about their daily commute, I get a glazed look in my eyes—or so they tell me. That's because my daily commute is a few seconds: from my bedroom to the study. This has been my WFH routine for years. It's amazing how many meetings are unnecessary.

Handwashing is fine, but my problem is face-touching (the virus inspires double-barrelled, over-hyphenated expressions). According to one study, we touch our faces twenty-three times an hour. One way out is to wash our hands with cow's urine rather than soap.

But then, those who enjoy it (the video of the cow urine party went coronaviral recently) will probably end up touching their face more often.

2

Happy Birthday to You. We are told singing this twice while washing hands puts in the requisite twenty seconds to fight the coronavirus.

Stayin' Alive by the Bee Gees works too, even if it does go on for four seconds longer. It is best known for being the rhythm for CPR (cardiopulmonary resuscitation). The pace is exactly right. As, of course, is the title. I think it's useful to keep that song in mind as both handwashing and CPR might play key roles in the days to come.

Another One Bites the Dust has been recommended for CPR too, but there's something about that title ...

For those who find singing a strain on their voices and nerves, there is poetry. John Donne's *No Man Is an Island* and Shelley's *Ozymandias* fit the bill. Importantly, they remind us of the times we live in, our interdependency, and what happens to egomaniacs.

3

The poet Rilke wrote, 'I live my life in widening circles.' My plan is the reverse. I shall live my life in narrowing circles. Concentric circles. If I stand in the centre, I need to ensure that for six feet no one shares my space.

4

In the war between mankind and the coronavirus, I am on the side of mankind.

I am not sure if all of mankind feels that way. My neighbours, for example, insist on walking around without masks. How can they say in all honesty that they are fighting on the right side? After all, there is no confusion here about which camp has right on its side.

And what of those who fill the bars, rush to beaches or celebrate weddings with more people to the square foot than is safe? We know which side they are on, whether they accept it or not. We go to war unprotected.

Wearing a mask is not a gesture of selfishness, quite the reverse. Altruism is forced upon us because we are all in it together. If you don't take your diabetes medicine, it doesn't affect me; if I don't take my cough syrup, it doesn't affect you. But if either of us doesn't wear a mask, it could affect us both. Many people I know haven't figured this out yet.

Not wearing a mask is not macho; washing hands or maintaining social distancing is not a sign of weakness. Our continued existence depends on these simple acts, not on clapping from balconies, lighting lamps or dropping flower petals from aircraft, as recommended by the prime minister.

Somewhere between the panic of the man who ingests disinfectants and the smugness of the one who thinks this is all a huge conspiracy, is the ideal soldier. One who doesn't believe that the best way to act during a pandemic is to do the opposite of what doctors recommend. In fact, some have had religious conversions, arguing that like god, the virus cannot be seen with the naked eye, and therefore god must exist. Logic is a casualty.

So, too, are statistics. We are bombarded with graphs and numbers, some of which make sense, but coincidentally arrive at conclusions we want to hear. You might as well publish the batting averages of the Indian cricket team and conclude: 'Therefore the virus is under control.'

The virus will be conquered by 15 May 2020, one official said in April, and we were shown graphs and figures, and there was talk about curves being flattened. Bureaucrats slip into jargon with all the enthusiasm of small boys who, having discovered the four-letter word, use it on every occasion.

A mask tells us more than a face, said Oscar Wilde, and he was right. It tells us that the wearer is fighting on our side, that we are on the same team.

Take off your mask and reveal yourself is old wisdom; the new one is, put on your mask and reveal yourself. In this war, the mask exposes the truth.

5

I read a wonderful line from Thoreau: 'I am a genius at staying at home.' Today my wife and I celebrate—if that's the word—one hundred days of solitude, even if 'solitude' doesn't strictly apply.

What I object to is not the self-isolation so much as the attempts at self-actualisation. I am perfectly happy sitting in a corner doing my work, ignoring the world, but then I am told this is the greatest opportunity we will have to realise our true selves. Well, not to put too fine a point upon it, this is my true self.

Others can *carpe* all the *diems* they want, others can change the world. In my youth I did set out to change the world, but on second thoughts decided to leave it as it is. This is my true self.

Why should I learn a new way to make an omelette, Zoom

or Skype people around the world, put out inspiring videos on reading or gardening? If you have a garden and a library, you have everything you need. True, but no need to bore others with the details.

If I was useless before the pandemic, why should I be less useless when the lockdown is fully lifted? I tell my friends: Stop trying to make a better man of me. This is the completed project.

My true self cannot be bothered about making everything count, every day, every hour, every minute. I read a new expression the other day: quarantine-shaming. It is apparently a way of shaming people into doing meaningful things during the isolation.

The most meaningful thing I have done in the past 100 days is have a haircut at home. I hugged and kissed the barber, for it was my wife who did the job. As Márquez said in *One Hundred Years of Solitude*, there is always something left to love.

6

No one I know is handling isolation better than my mother, who prefers to live alone. There is a lesson in everything she does. One that reveals itself subtly, from lived example. She hasn't stepped out of her house, but is far more cheerful and life-affirming than most. She visited temples every day, now she doesn't; she has a group of friends nearby she met everyday, now she doesn't; she loves long walks, she has had to give that up. Through all this (and we haven't met meanwhile), I never once heard her complain or grumble. She just turned eighty-one.

She knows the value of routine, understands that not every alternative is the better one. We are the lucky ones, she reminds us. Children and grandchildren are with loved ones, what more can anyone ask for? To be happy and not know it is tragedy. She calls up the postman and the vegetable vendor and the newspaperman to check on them and ensure they have someone to talk to.

She was seventy when she sent her first email, and delights in googling information. She keeps in touch with a host of friends and relatives on Facebook. She has taken to sketching, something she last did when she was in school. She has also begun to nurture vegetables in grow bags and pots around the house. She writes out by hand the Ramayana. It's an exercise for the mind, body and spirit, she says.

She never takes anything for granted—my father had been in fine health when he passed away nearly a decade ago. There is acceptance in her every move, gratitude whatever she does. To be grateful for life is a great quality. She is not just cheerful herself, but the cause of cheer in others.

My parents were married for over fifty years. She continues to live in the house they shared because she feels my father's presence there, comforting, protecting, shielding her from harshness as he had done before.

Had she been born a generation or two later, she might have been a top sportswoman. She played a mean game of badminton even in her fifties. She might have been a cricketer. She has a natural ball sense, occasionally startling young children with her ability as a juggler! She is a gifted singer, and dancer too. Talents that might have led to fame and fortune, but ones she merely saw as being for enjoyment—her own, and that of loved ones.

7

Of all the public statements regarding a cure for COVID-19—from cow urine therapy to drinking rum with pepper and two eggs—the Karnataka Health Minister's is the most scary. 'Only god can save us,' he says. Now, unless by 'god' he means 'science' (thus providing the first recorded instance of faith bringing in science through the backdoor, when usually the traffic is in the other direction), we ought to be scared. Very, very scared, as the posters of Stephen King movies tell us.

Whether the lockdowns have helped or not, the aftermath of their lifting hasn't been good. And the time lag (about two weeks) between cause and effect leads many into believing that the virus has slunk away. We tend to bet on our biases.

India just crossed the one-million mark. Masks can no longer be a personal choice. The question has divided otherwise intelligent people, though.

Some people don't wear a mask because it interferes with what they consider their good looks, others because it is inconvenient, especially if they wear glasses. A third group has a problem with masculinity, figuring that to be seen wearing a mask somehow diminishes their image. Then there is the rebel who will not wear one because others are telling him to.

The former UP Chief Minister Laloo Prasad Yadav explained the rationale behind his having nine children thus: The government of the day was saying that family planning was important, 'Ek ya do bas' ('Have only one child or two') was the slogan. But since he was in the opposition, he had to oppose the government's policies and thus had more than four times the prescribed number. Not wearing a mask might arise from a similar mentality.

8

I am beginning to think that no one exists on earth apart from me. I have no way of telling whether those on television are real people or merely anchor-shaped images who speak like real people.

Sometimes I wonder if even I exist, and then I remember what a robot named Rene Descartes once slipped into my computer's memory: 'I think, therefore I am.' But to be honest, I don't know if I think or merely think I think. Life has become more complicated since the lockdown. We examine everything, we introspect, we ask ourselves if sandwiches should be cut in triangles or squares.

I (at least, I think it is 'I') ask myself if the concept of 'other people' is something I invented to console myself that the world exists and therefore I must too. Hell is other people, wrote Sartre. The coronavirus has reversed that philosophy. Now heaven is other people.

9

Herd mentalities are sweet, but what of those unheard? President Trump's almost-Keats moment didn't go far, but his Freudian slip tells us something about the manner in which the three countries worst affected by COVID-19—US, India and Brazil—are handling it. As the numbers rise, authorities are saying in effect, 'Deal with it.'

The herd, meanwhile, is convinced that the virus has been wiped out, and it is time to pack the beaches, fill the pubs and crowd temples to pray for ancestors (whom they might be joining sooner than expected). COVID-19 fatigue is palpable;

administrators, professionals, citizens all seem to be afflicted after several months of restrictions.

The Union Health Minister told Parliament that thanks to the original lockdown, twenty-nine lakh Indians did not get affected by the virus and 78,000 did not die. This is commendable statistical work from a government which cannot tell us how many migrant workers died while walking the hundreds of kilometres home, or the number of doctors who perished doing their jobs.

The Indian Medical Association says 382 doctors died of the coronavirus. The health minister could have told us, in this new fashion, that '383 doctors did not die.' The ability to convey certitude through the negative is a politician's gift.

As is the ability to cherry-pick statistics to present the least worrying picture. Five million cases? Don't worry, that's only 0.38 per ent of the population. Eighty thousand dead? Well, that's 0.006 per cent. Deaths per million? Sixty-one. Then there's doubling rate, recovery rate and so on. Yet here we are, with nearly one lakh cases daily, and that does not include the asymptomatic or those untested. These are flesh-and-blood people we are talking about, not merely dots on a graph.

Only our television channels are dealing with all this with the seriousness they deserve—by focusing on the actor Kangana Ranaut's shenanigans. When politicians don't give straight answers, there's always Bollywood. It is disappointing, however, that we haven't been told what the Chinese Premier Xi Jinping thinks of another actor, Rhea Chakraborty.

When President Trump said, 'I don't think science knows, actually,' he was pointing to the kind of science denialism prevalent in India too. So-called godmen attempt to sell unproven 'medicines', while those in power have discovered it is useful in both politics and religion to hark back to a 'scientific' past when India invented flying machines and produced test-tube babies.

Getting this herd to wear masks and maintain social distancing is a bigly—to borrow a word from Trump—job. There's little point in losing ourselves in, as Trump said, 'the oranges of the investigation'. No, I don't know either.

10

If you thought it is the journey that matters, not the destination, Singapore Airlines has a non-flight to nowhere. Neither the journey nor the destination matters. 'Passengers' come aboard the aircraft (Airbus A380), have a meal and then go home. This is pandemic creativity.

It is possible that for an additional amount, the airline loses your luggage—just to give you that authentic flying experience.

On Qantas and some other airlines, you can actually fly. But to nowhere in particular. You can buy a ticket for a flight starting in Sydney and landing at the same place. So what, you ask? So this: you don't get off anywhere in between. Tickets were sold out in ten minutes. Further proof that there is one born every minute. That special flight takes off next week (ticket prices vary from US$ 566 to US$ 2,734). Obviously, as its popularity shows, that is cheap for a seven-hour flight that brings you back where you started.

11

It is beginning to dawn on us that making plans for the future is fraught with tension and uncertainty. Earlier this year, for example, I had planned to visit the UK, but here we are, the UK is still where it is—and so am I. Neither has moved much.

There's only one thing to be done. Stop planning for the future and plan for the past, where we know that we will never be disappointed. Last week I planned to be at the cricket stadium in Mumbai to watch India win the 2011 cricket World Cup.

Planning for April 2011 today might be looked down upon. But, on the other hand, I will not be disappointed. There will be no flight cancellations, I will not have to quarantine myself for a week or two, and there is no suspense about the result. I might even write a book about it—which party poopers will say I have already done.

Some of the best moments in our lives, wrote the poet, occur when they come unexpected. Probably true. But this has taken a lot out of me, and I am happier to schedule for the past rather than the future, which is really another country.

When in doubt, go backwards.

12

We know it will be over soon, all this excessive handwashing and people-avoiding and restaurant-eschewing and party-ignoring and vaccine-hoping. And those of us who have stayed home for the duration have one worry. Will we have to relearn social graces all over again, like patients relearn how to walk after a surgery?

Would the long periods of isolation drive out of us the element that distinguishes us from the lower animals: the ability to say 'Good morning' or inquire after the children of friends?

There's a scene in *Gone with the Wind* where Rhett Butler and Scarlet O'Hara go for a walk. Butler keeps raising his hat to passing ladies and wishing total strangers 'Good day' till it irritates his companion who asks, 'Why are you doing this?' The answer sums up what I am trying to say here: 'Because we live in a society.'

Good manners is a learnt activity that can atrophy through lack of use. We need to keep saying 'Good morning' and 'How are you' to our chairs and tables just to keep in touch. Practice will keep us from looking vulgar and boorish.

13

This is probably the worst time in history to be twenty-eight, male, fit and healthy. You will have to go to the back of the queue when the COVID-19 vaccines are being handed out. Blessed are the middle-aged and the elderly for they shall inherit, especially if they have more than one morbidity.

Over a million and a half people have died already, but with the news of the imminent vaccine, many have begun to do something for the first time in months: smile. A friend called to say how he had 'spent all this time lying in bed—just to save the world,' pointing out how much his father had criticised him for doing that in his schooldays. Another said he was looking forward to next year because this one 'went viral'.

The vaccine will soon be here. But that doesn't mean we can throw caution to the winds. Caution doesn't travel as easily through air as the virus does.

In India, who will receive the vaccines first? I suspect the best chance to go to the head of the queue is to be a sixty-five-year-old with diabetes and a heart condition.

14

I am feeling Keatsian today. My heart aches, and a drowsy numbness pains my sense. The latter from the first jab of the COVID-19 vaccine.

We were told the rules early: You had to be over sixty or over forty-five and the proud possessor of a morbidity.

'I have two morbidities, but I need only one; can I interest you in the other?' a friend of a friend who thought I was forty-five and needed help called with the offer. Another had a different proposition. 'Can I give you my diabetes and hypertension?' he asked, claiming he qualified on age but was married to someone who—unfortunately, under the circumstances—was some years yet from the mark and didn't have a morbidity to speak of.

'What is the first thing you will do when this is all over and you won't have to wear a mask anymore?' someone asked.

I suspect I would have grown so used to the mask that I shall miss it and go back to wearing it again. Like Linus's security blanket in the comic strip, I might need to keep on my security mask.

15

India's three great obsessions acted as superspreaders for COVID-19: politics, cricket and religion. The matches in Ahmedabad against England, religious festivals and election rallies. There is something disingenuous about our leaders exhorting us to wear masks and avoid gatherings when they are addressing large crowds of people, most of whom wear no masks.

The Kumbh Mela saw 300 pilgrims testing positive for COVID-19 at the start. Over a million people gathered every day and five million on special days. The imagination boggles.

We are so busy patting ourselves on the back for successes real and imaginary that we ignore proper data collection and interpretation. We take credit for developing the Oxford-Astra Zeneca vaccine simply because it is being produced at the Serum Institute in Pune.

When we say that the country has over a lakh cases daily, that is with minimal testing. To get caught off guard the first time was unfortunate, but to be unprepared a second time is unforgiveable. The plate-banging and flower-dropping a year back seem more puerile now. The coronavirus isn't impressed by slogans.

For not learning from our mistakes, we continue to repeat them. First we were—like most countries—in the COVID-19 mess, but we added to the disaster by creating one of our own in the terrible, unplanned lockdown which provoked the migrant crisis and untold misery. We came across as an unsympathetic, uncompassionate people.

This is not unique to us, of course. At an election rally in the US, Trump said that COVID-19 affects only the elderly, so it wasn't anything to worry about. The implication that his government didn't care about the elderly was mirrored by our attitude towards migrant workers.

And now we have the vaccine mess. The mistake with the handling of the virus continues with the handling of the vaccine—over-centralisation. Delegation is seen as a dilution of power.

16

It is impossible to think of COVID-19 without thinking of the prime minister too. For one, there is his image on the 'final certificate' issued by the Health Ministry after the second vaccination. It shows him in his bearded avatar, lips slightly parted, hair neatly groomed and with an expression behind his rimless glasses that suggests a favourite uncle about to tell you he is cutting you out of his will.

Do we hang it on our walls like a major award? Or hide it away in the bottom drawer like an embarrassing school report card? Unlike the choice of vaccines, we don't get a choice of politicians on our ominous-sounding 'final certificate'. And anyway, I can't think of a politician's face I'd like to have on it. If it were absolutely necessary to have a picture, why not R2D2, that loveable robot from Star Wars? Or the image of our pet cat or dog which we could upload ourselves?

As far back as October–November, experts had predicted the second wave. Yet, rather than prepare for it, we chose to pretend COVID-19 had left our shores and congratulated ourselves. Ministers tripped over themselves to tell us how they had conquered the virus. The premature triumphalism was frightening. We knew, but we didn't care.

The visuals on television, of desperate families, of undignified cremations, of shortages of beds, shortages of medicines, shortages of vaccines, shortages of qualified personnel, shortages of oxygen, of sharks making the most of other people's misery sear our souls. They diminish our humanity. Anxiety and depression have become constant companions. We are helpless, frustrated.

Where is the prime minister in all this? The country loved him for his oratory, for his fifty-six-inch chest, for his decisiveness. But his oratory has been reduced to patting himself on the back for drawing crowds, his chest is heaving with the burden of things not done. And decision delayed is decision denied.

He is not solely responsible for the crisis. But the buck stops with him. He once took credit for the drop in oil prices and later, a good monsoon. To mix a metaphor, what was sauce in the good times ...

17

The home minister tells us that we have successfully fought the COVID-19 pandemic. Where have we heard this before? Ah yes. His boss had said something similar at the World Economic Forum at the end of January. Since then we've had close to twenty million cases.

The chief minister of Uttarakhand assures us that the coronavirus is a living being too, and has the right to life like the rest of us. Luckily for the rest of us, he hasn't taken the matter to court. He has criticised the Delhi government for vaccinating 'too quickly' and suggests that one way of making the vaccines last is to slow down the process.

He is right. With a little planning we can make the pandemic last till 2030, spreading out the small amount of vaccines we currently have.

The phrase 'vaccine hesitancy' means different things in different countries. In most places, it is the reluctance of people to get themselves vaccinated because they don't believe it will help or they think it is a trick by Bill Gates to get into their blood stream, thus microchipping away their individuality.

In India, vaccine hesitancy refers to the government's hesitancy in ordering vaccines in time from the manufacturers.

The poet Lord Tennyson wrote about how one good custom could corrupt the world. Our poets ruling from Delhi are probably hoping now that the reverse is equally true: that one bad custom can restore our world.

In Karnataka, a politician leads a procession pushing a cart containing a burning fire of cow-dung cakes, camphor, etc. because, he tells us, it would cure COVID-19. We have the cure, dear MLA, it just needs to reach the people. Perhaps he can push some vaccines on a cart and ensure they reach our citizens in remote areas.

Why are we so intent on attracting ridicule?

18

Post-virus, let's hope some of the good practices remain. Like better hygiene and social distancing, especially in queues.

We are terrible in queues. Stand in one at a bank, at the airport check-in or waiting to board a flight and you will feel the breath of the person behind you in your ear. Sometimes a chin on your shoulder too, as an attempt is made to check out your newspaper or book. Personal space is an alien concept for many.

19

Now that hope is around the corner with the efficacy rates of various vaccines reading like the cut-off marks of our students looking for college admissions (94 per cent, 95 per cent), let us throw our minds back. What adjustments were we forced to make in the old normal?

Here's a glimpse: 'The writer learns how not to write. The actor not to act. The painter how never to see her studio, and so on. The artists without children are delighted by all the free time, for a time, until time itself begins to take on an accusatory look, a judgemental cast, because the fact is it is hard to fill all this time sufficiently, given the sufferings of others ...

'The single human, in the city apartment thinks: *I have never known such loneliness*. The married human, in the country place with partner and children, dreams of isolation within isolation ...

'The widower enters a second widowhood. The pensioner an

early twilight. Everybody learns the irrelevance of these matters next to "real suffering".'

These lines are from Zadie Smith's *Intimations*, a slim volume of six essays, a significant contribution to lockdown literature. 'The misery,' she writes, 'is very precisely designed, and different for each person ...'

Will those of us who look back when it is all over suffer survivor's guilt?

20

I woke up today thinking I hadn't met a stranger in nearly a year and a half. I have missed friends too, but you can always catch up with friends. With strangers, that is impossible. The stranger you see today is not the stranger you see tomorrow.

The last friend I met was at a private dinner. We were a small group in the year 1 BC (Before COVID-19), unaware that our freedoms would be hacked away. I can't remember who the last stranger I met was.

With friends, it is different. 'Do come over,' I invited an old schoolmate for dinner, leaving the date to be filled in later. And then we spoke of books and movies, cabbages and kings. I asked him, 'By the way, have you been vaccinated yet?'

'I don't believe in vaccines,' he said in the kind of tone he presumably uses when declaring he believes in ghosts or unicorns. It was a phone call, but I could sense the atmosphere thicken with foreboding. There goes another friend, I said to myself. You can come, I told him, but you will have to bring your own food and have it outside in the garden, away from the house (you can't say that to a stranger).

How many more unvaccinated friends am I likely to lose?

There are no strangers, wrote the poet W.B. Yeats, only friends you haven't yet met. But I am beginning to think there are no strangers, only friends you haven't offended yet.

In our more rational moments we fauci (a common word meaning 'act sensibly', from the American immunologist Anthony Fauci), and we tell our friends and relatives to fauci too.

21

I had a message from a funeral advisor last week. Is this a representative on earth of the appropriate authority above? Why is he advising me funerally? Is there a hint in it?

Annoyed, I deleted the message without reading it, but when you get an email like that, the possible underlying message always remains with you.

Maybe the FA has worked out that there is money in the morbidity business and he might as well gain the first-mover advantage.

COVID-19 is the contemporary man's *memento mori.* In ancient Rome, when a triumphant general headed a procession, he had a slave behind to remind him that he was only human. *Memento mori* is a reminder of what happens in the end to all humans.

I didn't get a message from a birth advisor when I was born, or a maturity advisor or a marriage advisor. So this message was probably special. Too bad I won't know what it was. I don't see myself heading a triumphant procession any time soon, but *memento mori* is never wasted.

Acknowledgements

My thanks to Karthika V.K., in whose fertile brain the idea for this book first germinated. Her creativity as a publisher is matched only by her patience, but this was one time when she didn't have to send gentle reminders about approaching deadlines. My thanks to her for editing these essays and being my GPS. Thanks to Saurabh Garge for the excellent cover design.

Some of the essays here have appeared in different forms in publications I have written for, and my thanks to N. Ram, Malini Seshadhri, the late Vinod Mehta, Binoo John, Parsa Venkateswara Rao Jr, K.N. Shanth Kumar, Monobina Gupta, T.M. Veeraraghav, Satish Padmanabhan, Suresh Nambath, S. Bageshree, Ayon Sengupta.

Special thanks to Ramachandra Guha, Fr. Julian Fernandez, the late Sarvotham Shanbhag, Bobby Banerjee and Goldie Osuri, Anita Nair, Ashish and Munira Sen, Tushar and Rachel.

Most importantly, thanks to my wife Dimpy without whom, nothing. Her sculpture, *In Thought*, also on the cover of this book, has been a companion through many hours of work.

Not being a great sports fan, Dimpy hasn't read my books on cricket. 'Why don't you write something I might read?' she has often asked. Hope this book is that book.